Short-Term Object Relations Couples Therapy

Short-Term Object Relations Couples Therapy

The Five-Step Model

James M. Donovan, Ph.D.

Brunner-Routledge

New York and Hove

Published in 2003 by
Brunner-Routledge
29 West 35th Street
New York, NY 10001
www.brunner-routledge.com

Published in Great Britain by
Brunner-Routledge
27 Church Road
Hove, East Sussex
BN3 2FA
www.brunner-routledge.co.uk

10 9 8 7 6 5 4 3 2 1

Library of Congress Cataloging-in-Publication Data
    Donovan, James M. (James Montgomery), 1943–
      Short-term object relations couples therapy : the five-step model / James
M. Donovan.
          p. ; cm.
    Includes bibliographical references and index.
      ISBN 1-58391-368-8 (hbk. : alk. paper)
    1. Marital psychotherapy. 2. Object relations (Psychoanalysis)
      [DNLM: 1. Couples Therapy—methods. 2. Marital Therapy—methods.
    3. Object Attachment. 4. Psychotherapy, Brief—methods. WM 430.5.M3 D687s
    2003] I. Title.

    RC488.5.D66 2003
    616.89′156—dc21
                                                                    2003002719

For Connie, Liz, Abbie, and Brian
You've taught me so much about long-term
family life

Contents

Foreword

by Michael P. Nichols

Although there are by now dozens of excellent books on the practice of family therapy, I can think of only three or four first-rate books about couples therapy. Without a doubt, Jim Donovan's *Short-Term Object Relations Couples Therapy* belongs on that list.

Couples therapists function, for the most part, as expensive crutches. Unhappy couples bring their fights to therapists who give them what they don't get at home—a sympathetic ear and a little understanding. They calm down, they feel better—then they go home. There, sooner or later, another version of the same fight erupts again, with all its attendant hurt and pain. Weekly, or in some cases episodically, the warring partners return to therapy for another dose of solace and sympathy. Of course, couples therapists themselves don't see it that way. They see their coaching, clarification, and cognitive restructuring as transformative rather than palliative. Would that it were so.

What makes real change in couples so hard, and so rare? If I said "human nature," you'd know what I mean. The truth is, people don't change much, in or out of therapy. But let's be a little more specific. Couples tend to get stuck in two dimensions—interactional and intrapsychic. The interactional dimension refers to the interlocking patterns of communication and behavior in which two people, both trying to do the best they can, unfortunately often end up perpetuating repetitive cycles of hurt and misunderstanding. What makes these patterns so maddeningly intransigent is that both partners' unproductive responses are triggered by the other's provocations—and both parties tend to remain fixed on the other one's contributions. This is the familiar refrain of "he never" and "she always." Therapies that fail to help partners achieve sufficient self-reflective awareness to recognize their own reactivity and change their counterproductive responses are unlikely to achieve anything more than temporary ceasefires in the couples wars.

But let's ask again the question that distinguishes psychotherapists from

advice-givers and psychiatrists: why?[1] *Why* do couples get stuck in the repetitive patterns of interaction that drive them into therapy? The answer is
that—despite the best efforts of narrative and solution-focused therapists
to deny it—couples often fight because of conflicts in what they want from
each other.

Would it be all right if I gave a personal example to illustrate this
point? I've been married for 35 years to a woman with more good qualities
than I could possibly list in a brief paragraph. But, let me be honest, she has
one very conspicuous failing. She doesn't always do exactly what I want.
And, again let's be frank, this can be annoying. What's more, I suspect this
same problem may exist in other couples as well.

Some conflicts that couples bring to therapy are easy to understand
and not too hard to resolve. (One trick to resolving conflicts is to see the
familiar pattern of demand-and-withdraw as part of an incomplete negotiation in which the payoff for complying to requests hasn't been specified.
This perspective allows one partner to make requests without feeling like a
nag and the other partner to feel like a participant in a negotiation rather
than a brow-beaten mate asked to give in to his partner.) She wants to go
out more often, but he wants to stay home? Maybe they can agree to go out
once a week, if he gets to take some initiative in where they go.

Unfortunately, some couples' conflicts seem to resist all efforts at negotiation and compromise. (Oh, you've noticed?) These, of course, are the
discords that touch on unconscious issues. When she can't seem to stop
flying off the handle when he complains about something or he can't seem
to accept that she likes to spend a little time with her friends, you can bet
that there's more going on than meets the eye.

The first virtue of *Short-Term Object Relations Couples Therapy* is
that it deals, as the vast majority of books on couples therapy do not, with
the unconscious longings and unrealistic expectations that drive couples
into repetitive cycles of conflict. Nowhere in print will you find a better
guide to conceptualizing the complex nature of the inner demons that cause
couples to hurt and disappoint each other as they so often, and so tragically, do. Donovan has distilled some of the most useful concepts from
object relations theory into a well-worked-out guide to understanding the
roots of couples' conflicts.

The essence of object relations theory is, of course, simple: We relate
to people in the present on the basis of expectations formed in past experience. The residue of these critical early relationships leaves *internal objects*—mental images of self and others built up from experience and
expectation. Those internal images form the core of the personality—an

---

[1]Instead of just trying to get rid of unwanted behavior—anxiety, depression,
anger—psychotherapists try to figure out *why* a person is anxious or depressed or
angry. Believe it or not, there are reasons why people behave as they do.

open system developing and maintaining its identity through intimate relationships, present and past. That seems clear enough, doesn't it? But what exactly are those "internal objects," and how does the working clinician uncover them in the midst of a clamorous therapy session?

Unfortunately, for all the elaborate lingo employed by people who claim to practice object relations therapy, their "interpretations" often boil down to psychoanalytic clichés: "You're still angry at your mother." "Your father wasn't always there for you, was he?" In Donovan's hands, however, object relations theory doesn't impose a set of pat ideas; rather it tells therapists where to look, so that they can discover the real and specific family experiences at the root of the excessive affects that underlie present-day couples' conflicts. Good analytic work is a process of discovery. Theory helps guide that discovery, and therefore must be given its due. However, the insights that make a difference must always come out of very specific memories of personal experience. A careful reading of the case examples in this book will show you what an unbiased process of discovery looks like.

As any student can tell you, psychoanalytic therapy works through insight. But the idea that insight cures is misleading. Insight is necessary, but not sufficient, for effective analytic treatment. In object relations therapy, members of a couple can expand their insight by learning that their problems with each other are due in part to unfinished business from their own families. To be of any real use, however, whatever insights are achieved must be put into action—that is, translated into new and more productive ways of interacting. And here therapists have a choice. They can either wait for this translation to take root—in a slow and steady process of *working through*—or they can move things along by actively encouraging intimate partners to start behaving differently with each other. The latter approach is, in fact, the norm in clinical practice. But it is problematic.

If you read carefully in the case studies of experiential (e.g., emotionally focused couples therapy) and psychoanalytic therapists who first explore the past and then make (or imply) suggestions in the present, you'll see that many of these explorations are all too brief. Very little uncovering is necessary to come up with clichéd interpretations—"You fight with each other because your attachment needs are threatened." If that's all that's accomplished in the exploratory phase of the work, the more active efforts that follow are no real improvement over the usual approaches that let the sleeping dogs of unconscious memory lie.

This is a critical point and in case I haven't made it clearly, I'm going to reiterate it: To get at the truth of the past, you have to keep digging. You have to resist the urge to seal things over with reassurance, advice, or admonition. Let me give you an example from a different context. Many therapists who work with the victims of sexual abuse can't resist offering their clients the assurance that what happened wasn't their fault. Unfortunately, this well-intentioned reassurance means that the victim never gets a chance to realize and voice her own psychological truth, which may be that what happened *was* in part her fault. She secretly wanted to get as close as possible to her stepfather. Although she felt dirty and victimized by what happened, it may also have felt good in some ways. Reassurance that doesn't allow for the possibility of such deep feelings of shame isn't very reassuring. And the self-recrimination that lies buried at the root of these painful experiences never really gets dealt with. The same pattern is true in any attempt to uncover the past roots of current-day conflict: The process of uncovering must not be short-circuited by the wish to make things all better.

Donovan avoids the trap of premature closure in two ways. First of all, his explorations are just that. He helps couples look into their pasts but does not rush to judgment about what they will find there. But please do not take my word for that. Do not take the word of any writer who tells you that his or her approach is based on a process of exploring the client's past. Read the case material! Consider for yourself whether the explorations are a genuine process of discovery or whether they are fishing expeditions for a set of the author's pet theories. Insight must be discovered, not imposed.

The second thing Donovan does to prevent his active encouragement from undermining the process of self-discovery is to make clever use of counterprojective comments. Thus, for example, before suggesting to a man bullied in the past by his family and bullied now by his wife that perhaps he could begin to speak up more, Donovan explicitly acknowledges that the man has been pushed around a great deal and that should he feel pushed around by the therapist it would be reasonable to get angry. In this example, as with this entire book, I find the meat of good clinical work hard to summarize. It's easy enough to talk about the importance of uncovering the unconscious roots of current problems and even to describe a variety of clever concepts for doing so. But the real value of the work comes in the details of practice. I've been lucky enough to see some great therapists at work. No reading of Murray Bowen can convey the warmth and humor he brought to his clinical encounters. Nothing in Salvador Minuchin's books or videotaped demonstrations captures the subtlety of his efforts to get through to people. And Sid Rueben, one of the most brilliant psychoanalytic therapists who ever dared work with hospitalized schizophrenics, never published a thing. The point is, to put it in technical terms: The proof is in the pudding.

In *Short-Term Object Relations Couples Therapy*, Jim Donovan has produced one of the most useful guides to couples therapy ever written. His explication of object relations theory and formulas for putting it into practice are challenging but profoundly rewarding. But the real payoff here is in the clinical material. Put yourself in the hands of this seasoned therapist and pay careful attention to the details of the sustained engagement that makes for really effective couples work.

Preface

Who would choose to become a couple therapist and then sit down to write a book about it?

The unconscious seeds underlying vocational choice often appear to have been planted long ago. I strongly suspect that many mental health practitioners, particularly couple therapists—myself included—as children worked to resolve real or imagined family conflict. When these clinicians began to develop their careers, they inevitably felt drawn to perform the role as professional adults for which they apprenticed much earlier in life.

So, psychological motives abound to support an interest in couple therapy. With the divorce rate still hovering on either side of 50%, we can also demonstrate without much effort an acute public need for these services. Ironically, though, couple therapy remains an underutilized modality. Forty percent of mental health referrals focus on a marital problem (Budman & Gurman, 1988, chap. 6), but if family or couple treatment comprise 15% of all the psychotherapy offered, it would surprise many of us.

We can speculate about why couple therapy seems insufficiently available. I won't pursue that controversy here, although I do at several points in the body of the book. Whatever the causes, the field lacks adequate theoretical and technical definition. We have few widely agreed-upon principles of approach based on well-articulated metapsychologies that clearly conceptualize couple attachment and subsequent couple conflict (Johnson, 1999). We can never know whether we underuse the modality because we cannot lean on a solid theory for its application or the inverse. Either way, I've found that young therapists, with initial interest in marital treatment, may become discouraged, and perhaps frightened, at the prospect of pursuing it further, lacking the guidance to learn the field sufficiently thoroughly. Often they gravitate to more mainstream areas, in which they may feel less alone and exposed. I wrote this book to provide some of the theoretical and technical structure we're missing. I take as my intended audience clinicians, more experienced or less, who wish to pursue couple work, but who remain confused about how to move to the next step in their learning.

I can readily identify with this quandary. Thirty-five years ago in graduate school, at the University of Michigan, I remember struggling to grasp psychodynamic psychotherapy. I searched for any text to help me clarify my understanding of this daunting subject. At last, my supervisor told me that Ralph Greenson's *The Technique and Practice of Psychoanalysis* (1967) had just entered publication. When the mailman delivered my copy, I remember almost grabbing it out of his hands. I wasn't disappointed. Greenson explained psychoanalytic psychotherapy so specifically and linked theory so expertly to guide particular interventions that I almost felt his presence in the room, patiently answering my series of questions. I recall reading the book until 2:00 A.M. that first night and waking up early the next morning to finish it that day. I know my book won't become a classic, but if it keeps some young clinician up late for the same reasons, I'll be happy.

I've tried to construct a volume about couple therapy that I wish I could have read 30 years ago, when I started in this field. About half my practice has evolved into couple work. I treat couples solo, and once or twice a year I co-lead, with a postdoctoral fellow, a 15-session, closed-ended group. I have a small private practice, but most of the couple treatment I've offered has taken place within an HMO setting at Harvard Vanguard Medical Associates in Boston and in Wellesley, Massachusetts. Typical for managed care, most couple therapy episodes there last 20 sessions or less per calendar year.

As a clinician, therefore, I was raised on practicality. I did not begin my couple work with a theory, because, frankly, when I discovered this interest in 1970, there weren't many theories from which to choose. I started quite by the seat of my pants, trying to study the spontaneous drift of the first few sessions with each couple. Most introduced their recurrent fight as their immediate focus of pain. They then associated to connections between that fight and themes from their family of origin. Finally, they seemed concerned with the character problems that each of the pair might display. These, too, seemed to linked with parental figures. Perhaps the wife pointed out that her husband seemed stubborn like his father. Or the husband complained that both his wife and his mother struck him as hypochondrical. Perhaps 10 years ago, I realized that object relations theory explained the interconnection between these three areas in helpful ways. Each of the pair appeared to reencounter an old object, or an old conflict, in the new marriage. So I tried to adapt object relations theory to brief couple interventions, the endeavor that ultimately became the subject of this book.

In chapter 2, I summarize the object relations approach and its past applications to marital work. I include some case illustrations in that discussion, but this is the most theoretical section of the volume. It represents the necessary introduction to the subsequent chapters, which I've organized around a series of clinical vignettes. You may find yourself needing to read chapter 2 twice, because it's a complex attempt to integrate the points of view of several previous authors. The next few chapters will reward your effort, though, because they illustrate how this theory brings a fresh understanding to the complicated couple cases we encounter in our offices each day.

For me, reading psychotherapy texts can feel intimidating and demoralizing. Often the authors seem to have known all along how the treatment would unfold. They explain exactly which steps they devised to shepherd the matter to its inevitable, and invariably successful, conclusion. The writers can appear omnipotently wise, and any reader who didn't guess the right interventions embarrassingly inept. Unfortunately, the experience of providing psychotherapy rarely progresses this way for me. I'm often confused about how to choose the optimal move at any given moment. Sometimes I test an approach only to abandon it, if the results seem unsatisfactory, and try another strategy. Often the case seems to take shape only through this trial-and-error fumbling. I include several vignettes in which I think I never do find a clear path to help the couple. Frequently, I am as startled by the dénouement as the clients are. Sometimes the couple that initially seems the least promising gains a great deal from the therapy, and an apparently more advantaged pair gains much less. I've thought a lot about these quixotic outcomes, and I try to explicate some of them at different points in the narrative. You'll see that much ambiguity still remains for all of us to ponder, however.

Some words about style and tone—I do propose a theory in the book and a treatment model that proceeds from that theory. Each chapter, in turn, explores the sequence of phases that unfolds from the model. But psychotherapy stays a detective story for me. I don't know what will happen next. I'm not sure how the characters will behave or which new persons may enter the scene. I try to recreate the dramatic tension of the enterprise by transporting the reader inside the mind of the somewhat-overwhelmed therapist, at different places, and I attempt to explain that therapist's reasoning process and treatment planning as these evolve. I trust this will feel more immediate and helpful than presenting cases as any kind of fait accompli. By this style, I'm attempting to include the reader, step by step, as a participant in the complex search to understand each couple and to devise a method to help the partners genuinely and relatively quickly.

When I work as a therapist, I'm surprised so often myself that I wanted that tone to run through the book. As a patient and as a clinician, I've found that the capacity to remain open to the unexpected, to take the fresh look, represents a key feature of effective practice. I've noticed that one characteristic that differentiates truly skilled therapists from their less capable colleagues is their moment-to-moment wish to hear each sentence as if it were an entirely new, potentially rich clue into a meaning previously hidden. Ironically, in this regard, the most expert therapists behave as the least expert. They seem to assume nothing and enter into each hour with enthusiasm and wonder. I've attempted to present the book with some of this informal, curious flavor.

For the past 30 years, I've found the change process itself a continuing fascination. In the final two chapters, I chase after the core of the mechanisms of change. Staying the same can feel so familiar and so consoling, becoming different so risky. I've pondered why anyone would change, especially in interaction with another person. If we only understood more about this process in depth, couldn't we design our treatments more optimally? The last two chapters represent my attempt to grasp all the dimensions of couple therapy at once and then to sort through each strand to weigh its contribution to the mysterious lessons about change buried within successful cases. I hope I can touch readers' sense of adventure and draw them into participation in this project with me, page by page.

Many people have contributed to the book. I'm indebted to Shannon Vargo, my editor at Brunner-Routledge, for her patience. She understood that I could not necessarily complete a book about brief therapy in a brief time period. I want to thank my wife, Dr. Connie Donovan, and my friend Dr. Jim Sabin for their numerous perceptive comments on various chapters. In addition, Connie supportively endured my burying my head in manuscript pages, weekend after weekend. Finally, I could not have undertaken this project without the support of my remarkably skilled, unflappable, good-humored secretary, Lynda Pozerski.

The Harvard Pilgrim Health Care Foundation has supported me in this work and has underwritten our mental health training program for 20 years. I'm indebted to that dedicated group. I'm continually amazed and grateful for the enthusiasm of my students and for their capacity to remain enchanted by the field. In one way or another I tried out all these ideas on them, before I set them down in the book. They've helped me, more than I can ever repay, with their feedback and support. Finally, I've gained the most from my clients, as we've tried to learn from, and cooperate with, each other in our struggle to understand their recurrent difficulties.

Jim Donovan, PhD
Chestnut Hill, MA
January 2003

CHAPTER 1

Step 1: Study the Fight: Implementing the Five-Step Model

Couples have only one fight. The problem is they have it hundreds of times.

Over 40% of mental health referrals involve a marital problem (Budman & Gurman, 1988), yet, curiously, we often do not seem able, or willing, to treat those couples. Each outpatient department appears to have either one or no couple specialist. We have some books to read, a conference here or there to attend, but little outcome or process data to rely upon and few unified systems of couple therapy to follow. The administrative hurdles to arrange for the therapist and the pair to meet regularly, at the same time and place, can loom large. Medical insurance may require gerrymandering to support the treatment as well, but I think the real reasons that clinicians shy away from couple therapy lie elsewhere. Oedipal inhibitions about prying into someone else's marital and sexual relationship may well visit unconscious conflict upon the clinician, and many therapists also find it difficult to sort out and to maintain an alliance with two warring parties simultaneously.

Couple treatment can erupt into flames as well.

Broad-shouldered, pulsating, 50-year-old Jane leans into the face of her husband, gigantic Frank, age 52, a former heavyweight boxer, with biceps actually the size of my thigh. In a booming voice, Jane offers the following lay interpretation. "You're nothing but an alcoholic, Frank, a stinking alcoholic." As Frank's face purples, I am frightened that he will punch her at any second and can only stammer, "Jane, maybe another tone would be more helpful." The phone rings and my next-door colleague, overhearing the ruckus, asks if I'm okay. I'm not sure.

1

The outbursts in my office that I recall most vividly are like this one; nearly all were couple sessions, rarely group or individual meetings. Who would voluntarily seek out such experiences?

We do not know how frequently clinicians attempt couples therapy, but given the preponderance of marital problems, we can estimate that marital treatment remains a severely underutilized modality. Because clinicians and their training programs have underemphasized the field, for some of the reasons I've just pursued, we've found ourselves slow to construct a theoretical framework to support couple work. Clinicians can rest individual therapy on the psychodynamic, cognitive-behavioral, narrative, or solution-focused schools, all of which seem well thought out, thoroughly published, and frequently taught. Group therapy (Yalom, 1994) and family treatment (Nichols & Schwartz, 1998), though not as conceptually developed and historically refined as individual therapy, also can boast definitive, broadly accepted schools of approach, but couple work lags behind.

We can point to no generic model of couple dysfunction and its treatment to which a large number of practitioners more or less ascribe, and which has been widely studied and described. Equally distressing, we know that couple treatment, two-thirds of the time, lasts less than 20 sessions (Budman & Gurman, 1988), but we've only begun to articulate couple therapy models that directly address themselves to basic short-term treatment issues, such as finding the focus and planning the treatment (Dattilio, 1998a; Donovan, 1999).

The conceptual problem of couple treatment comes in delimiting the area of intervention. Each of the pair brings a complicated family history that clearly directly contributes to his or her central conflict, but the couple, just as plainly, suffers from present-day interactional difficulties. With each move, therapists may feel they've put the stress in the wrong place or on the wrong time period. Given these pressures, the treatment can easily wander, and if we're trying to work short term, we don't have much time. We need a model that can help us grasp both the present and the past simultaneously, or at least sequentially, in a manner that seems affectively genuine to all three participants. As we'll soon observe in this chapter, we have sections of that model now but, so far, no comprehensive format emphasizing both past and present.

No one book can, or should, attempt to fill this gap in one fell swoop, nor is that my purpose here. In this chapter I'll offer you an overview of the major current approaches to time-managed couple treatment and then, in the balance of the book, present my approach as one response to what's missing so far. I do not aim to complete the entire conceptual and clinical puzzle, but I do promise to insert a few pieces in what I think their proper place, so that we will gain a more complete picture of the kinds of couple therapy models the field requires.

For example, these should be applicable in less than 20 sessions per treatment episode and should be useful in most settings. Mine represents a self-professed, short-term approach, because I developed it during nearly 30 years of work in an HMO setting. It captures a focus and proceeds in five definable, teachable steps. The model's conceptual underpinning ties it to mainstream psychodynamic and object relations theory. The clinician does not need to learn a whole new metapsychological language and orientation to try it out. Furthermore, because the object relations approach attempts to explain present interaction in terms of past internalizations, this model may allow us to meld a focus emphasizing both time periods. But first, let's observe how other short-term therapists have confronted the substantial challenges of couple work.

THE SHORT-TERM COUPLE THERAPY SPECTRUM

Fortunately, in the last 3 or 4 years, Dattilio (1998a) and Donovan (1999) have published case books on brief couple treatment that, if we study them carefully, offer us a summary of the most recent and solid approaches. We can use the array of models offered by these two books as our primary resources to ascertain the current position of the couple treatment field and to define the directions we need to follow next.

As we read the Dattilio and Donovan anthologies, what do we notice first? We realize that all the authors seem preoccupied with one problem and that the array of chapters represents the different tacts taken by each writer toward that one issue. They all focus on *the fight,* the pair's recurrent conflict. Each couple appears to have only one fight but has it hundreds of times. Later I'll investigate the reasons behind this oddity, but, for now, let's go back to the different stances the authors take to the "fight"— my colloquialism, not theirs.

At its height, the fight can assume a multitude of forms, from cold distancing, to passive-aggressive lack of cooperation, to mutual sniping, to sneering disengagement, to screaming accusation, on to character assassination, and, finally, in some cases, to physical threats or overt violence. The content, though not the general form of the fight, differs from couple to couple. Almost like a Kabuki play, each member rigidly assumes the same role each time, as step by step, with the affect building, the pair locks in combat. The members listen to each other but selectively. They hear only what provokes, not what soothes or creates new meaning. The fight has two possible endings, both destructive. Either combatants will withdraw in an exchange of icy glares or demoralized resignation, or one or both will explode into shouts of frustration and recrimination.

As Gottman's (1994) pioneering direct observations of couples have taught us, when the fight repeatedly descends into overt disrespect and stone-walling, the partners find themselves sucked into dangerous waters that often propel them toward divorce. We can see that the fight represents the core of any couple conflict, but the standoff can take a "hot" form, replete with screaming and yelling, a cold pattern of distancing and alienation, or any mixture of both extremes. Paraphrasing T. S. Eliot, the fight can end with a bang, a whimper, or both.

The fight represents a cruelly ironic twist in human affairs but a near universal one. All couples I've encountered, in or out of the office, report some rendition of the fight. No matter how much effort and feeling the couple expends in attempting to avoid it or in having it out, resolution usually escapes the partners. They end where they began, just more frustrated and hopeless. The staggering number of marital problems among our referrals now seems less baffling. When the fight becomes intolerably painful for one or both of the pair, they often seek our services.

Well before any therapist attempted a couple session, the great writers seemed fully aware of the fight and struggled to portray and understand it. Dostoyevsky's *The Brothers Karamazov*, Faulkner's *The Sound and the Fury,* and Shakespeare's *King Lear* all took fights, of different configurations, as their principal subject matter. Later I will offer an object relations model of the fight and try to explain its central place in human affairs, but now I want to return to how other authors have chosen to approach it within their systems of treatment.

Couple therapists, from whatever school, must confront this same vexing, complicated problem with every pair they treat. The fight represents a rigid, stereotyped, upsetting, seemingly counterproductive exchange into which the couple readily slips or sometimes rushes pell mell. The fight appears daunting, if not downright frightening, to all three participants in the office, but it requires our primary focus.

As we study the fight, its defensive nature strikes us first. The partners repeat themselves, accuse, exaggerate, and misperceive the opposing argument, while stubbornly cleaving to their own. The schools of couple therapy define themselves by their characteristic response to this defensiveness: (1) the narrative and solution-focused camps attempt to circumvent the deadlock; (2) the systemic school stands above and repositions the parties in the conflict; (3) the behavioral and cognitive-behavioral practitioners directly coach the couple in alternatives to the fight; and (4) the dynamic group delves into the conflict to its affective roots. Using these positional metaphors of therapeutic intent, I can name the major players and summarize the contribution of each school. Of course, any couple therapist may borrow from more than one model at a given moment, which makes establishing that writer's place in the taxonomy a bit more challenging, but we can characterize each school by the extent to which it makes use of these four, almost topographical, basic approaches to the fight.

1. Narrative and Solution-Focused Models— Circumnavigate the Conflict

Steven Friedman and Eve Lipchick (1999), fine representatives of the solution-focused school, steer the boat around the typhoon by helping the couple to seek "exceptions" to the recurrent, destructive conflict. On what occasions did Sally and Howard not fight about his mother? How were they able to do this, when she appears so troubling a presence in their lives? The therapist can ask "The Miracle Question." What if they woke up one morning and Howard's mother were no longer a problem to them? If they can solve the issue of the mother-in-law, could they resolve other marital difficulties with the same methods? Just in this one, hypothetical, single case snippet, we can see how the solution-focused therapists try to skillfully move around the conflict. Emphasize the positive; identify solutions, not problems; find exceptions to the bad news; practice what works; and don't repeat what doesn't. Outcome, outcome, outcome! (solutions) Rate your success today on solving the mother-in-law conflict from 1 to 10.

Joseph Eron and Thomas Lund (1998, 1999) have founded a new hybrid school, the narrative-solution-focused approach. They use their model to move ingeniously around the fight in their new, noncouple, couple therapy. Eron and Lund, working with each member of the pair individually, sometimes with the partner present and often not, try to define a "preferred view of self." The clients can then perceive the unproductive aspects of their behavior in the fight and shift toward a stance more in concert with their positive self-image. For example, how does Jim (1999), a man who respects himself and others, and who has courageously faced and mastered his alcoholism, find himself snarling at his wife when she seeks more independence in their marriage?

This appeal to the client's positive ideal has many advantages. The approach clearly builds on the lifelong strengths and mature values of each client and experts, like Eron and Lund, can quickly turn these to treatment leverage. The positive outcome represents the "solution" in the designation "narrative-solutions therapy" and the search for the "preferred view of self" through the life history represents the "narrative" influence in the model. Later we'll see that this deceptively simple concept of the "preferred view of self" becomes a major contribution to our understanding of how people shed defensiveness.

2. Systemic Models—Stand Above the Fight

These approaches to couple treatment instruct the therapist to stand above the conflict and to attempt change by *repositioning the boundaries* between the participants. For this reason we call these schools *systemic*. Phillip Guerin's Bowenian format (Guerin, Fay, Fogarty, & Kautto, 1999) and Salvador Minuchin's and Michael Nichols's structural model (1998, 1999) stand as the major proponents of this tact.

Guerin and his coworkers study triadic relationships. They observe that when trouble brews within any dyad—husband–wife, parent–child, wife–mother-in-law—the twosome will likely attempt to solve the problem by involving a third party, creating a psychological triangle that unfortunately interdicts any real work on the original issue. Guerin finds that the couple or the family that comes to his office frequently presents him with these enmeshed triads to unravel.

For example, an eligible young man falls in love with an appropriate woman but develops terrifying panic attacks just after they become engaged. In the first interview Guerin discovers that this dutiful son has served as a confidante to his lonely mother, a lady apparently emotionally unsupported by her distant husband. Most therapists would treat the young man individually or maybe in conjunction with his fiancée, but Guerin wants to involve the whole system and asks the mother, the third member of the triangle, to join her son in the office. Guerin begins to separate the mother from the son so that he, more free, can move closer to his fiancée with less guilt. Guerin supports the mother to initiate more intimacy with her husband, lest she, abandoned, grasp her son more tightly.

Guerin clearly believes that all the relevant members of the system must join the treatment, or else change between any two will wash away, as they interact with numbers three and four. These attempts to reposition the members of the triangle represent the one-two-three of psychotherapy for Guerin, his signature technique, and, as we'll observe later in the book, a powerful intervention readily incorporated, in different forms, within many couple therapies.

Minuchin and Nichols (Minuchin & Nichols, 1998; Nichols & Minuchin, 1999) practice structural family therapy. They focus on the boundaries between partners or between multiple family members. Minuchin and Nichols usually discover that these boundaries have become too enmeshed or too rigid, a circumstance that leads to automatic stifling interactions. The participants fight when they thrash about in an unconscious attempt to renegotiate these boundaries. For instance, the exasperated father (Nichols & Minuchin, 1999) angrily demands that his 13-year-old stepson act more responsibility and cooperatively at home and at school. But the son can afford to ignore these directives because he's shielded by the relationship with his mother, who has retreated into closeness with her son as a refuge from her exacting husband. She clings to the boy and defends his inactivity, as she cannot defend herself toward her demanding mate. Mother and son passive-aggressively defeat the husband at every turn. The battle is joined, and the family repairs to the therapist's office. The wife feels lonely, the husband scapegoated, and the dependent boy too anxious to successfully enter adolescence—a fine state of affairs.

Minuchin and Nichols will work to solidify the boundary between mother and son and to soften the rigid wall between husband and wife. The son, more free of his mother's apron strings, can then recapture the path of his independent development, and the father can enjoy his wife again, and she him. It's all about renegotiating the boundaries.

3. The Behavioral, Collaborative, Cognitive-Behavioral, and Strategic Schools—Coach the Couple in Alternatives to the Fight

The late Neil Jacobson and his colleagues offer us the most comprehensive behavioral learning approach to couple treatment, integrative couple therapy (Lawrence, Eldridge, Christensen, & Jacobson, 1999). In this system the therapist coaches the partners as they acquire skills in emotional acceptance, behavioral exchange, and problem solving. The Jacobson-Christensen group explicitly defines and teaches various aspects of nondefensive communication. For example, the therapists encourage the couple to voice more tolerance, to express more vulnerability and less criticism, and to offer to trade unilaterally desired behaviors; for example, "I will go to a play with you" (he). "Okay. I'll cook one of your favorite meals" (she).

Jacobson discovered, however, that simply learning to exchange the desired behaviors does not work. Outcome research on the behavioral trading approach initially established positive findings, but these eroded over time. Influenced by the work of Dan Wile, whom we will meet in a minute, the Jacobson-Christensen group now first engages its couples in emotional acceptance exercises, before teaching the behavioral exchange and problem-solving methods. Preliminary results indicate the superiority of this second format. Emotional acceptance, therefore, appears a key in couple therapy. Without a prior atmosphere of empathic support, the most artful interventions, introduced by the most experienced therapist, will probably fall flat, and Jacobson and Christensen have the data to prove this point.

Dan Wile's (1981, 1999) *collaborative* approach to couple work represents a behavioral system because the therapist coaches his or her clients to incorporate a specific skill into their relationship—namely, to take turns expressing all their feelings to each other—but Wile does not introduce other learning tasks and does not see himself as a behavioral therapist. Wile's system is unique, in that it is not derived from another general school of therapy, such as the social learning, psychodynamic, or strategic methods. Wile would rightly blanch at the appellation *behaviorist,* but he is a coach par excellence.

Wile's work flows from one central observation. He emphasizes that anger, jealousy, competition, and guilt over all those feelings represent the inevitable by-products of any intimate relationship. The fight occurs when one or both members of the pair attempt to deny these feelings, to evade them, or to clandestinely act them out, instead of acknowledging them. Wile has found that the emotional atmosphere within a couple oscillates between the "adversarial," "alienated," and "collaborative" states. He offers extensive case transcripts aptly illustrating each of these conditions. A Wile dialogue might proceed as follows:

> *(He) I guess the party was okay. I feel sleepy now and don't feel like talking [alienated state]. Actually, I felt pretty jealous and inadequate, when you spent a damn hour talking to that handsome philosophy graduate student. Philosophy, ha! He'll never get a job [adversarial state]. (She) I'm sorry. I got jealous when they all asked about your new book. I guess jealousy can be a real bummer for both of us [collaborative state].*

Clearly, Wile takes as his sole objective to coach the partners back to a collaborative, mutual stance when they stray off into alienated or adversarial positions, as so frequently happens to all of us. To do this, Wile helps the partners build "a shared platform," a perspective from which they can view their relationship and they can use to help them confide and accept their feelings about their interaction. Because he realizes that most couples will have trouble learning to speak so frankly, he's developed his signature technique, "script writing," in which he voices the unsaid feelings of each partner and helps the partners exchange their real affects. Session by session, each member of the pair begins to take over from Wile, and they gradually learn to exchange openly with one another.

Wile's script-writing technique appears so odd at first. Aren't the clients supposed to do the talking in therapy? Yet he has discovered a method to encourage couples to speak out their real feelings nondefensively. Right here, Wile leads us to a central process of couple treatment, promoting more free exchange. We'll return to his method of script writing frequently.

Cognitive-behavioral practitioners, such as Frank Dattilio (1998b), use direct coaching about the client's thinking as their central method of intervention. Dattilio teaches his clients to examine their "schemas," their core dysfunctional assumptions about their partner, and to gradually correct the distortions in thinking embodied in those schemas. As the clients' thoughts become more realistic, their troubled feelings follow suit. Dattilio might focus like this on a wife's schema, "If Tom is to hear me, I must scream at him."

> *Francine, let's examine this assumption. How accurate is it? Does Tom really listen better when you scream? What evidence do you have for this? Does this behavior actually usually lead to an argument? Where did you learn screaming in the first place? How effective was it there? What do you think Tom really thinks about his problem of not listening? How would you find out?*

Dattilio embarks, then, with his clients on an exploration of the important cognitive assumptions, automatic thoughts, in their worldview and in their experience of intimate interactions, which are at least partially invalid and which lead to the recurrent difficulty in the couple.

Strategic therapists—for example, James Keim (1999)—represent coaches in pure state. Carol and Larry, in their mid-50s, fight because Larry has difficulty communicating with Carol and procrastinates in completing the household tasks she requests of him. Keim coaches the partners in win-win negotiating, and many of their problems lift. If Carol will give Larry 20 minutes to rest undisturbed when he returns home from work, he agrees to talk with her for 20 minutes. He offers to paint the house trim, if she will support his leaving later on a 3-hour fishing excursion. Both parties feel that their needs are met, and intimacy builds once again within the couple.

The therapists mentioned in this section often differ markedly from each other in theoretical allegiance or in style of intervention, but they share one general method. They teach the couples to avoid the fight by pursuing alternative, more constructive behaviors to mitigate conflict.

4. Psychodynamic Models—Delve Into the Affect

This group of therapists does not coach around the fight; the therapists help their clients to work it through affectively. Susan Johnson and Leslie Greenberg (Johnson, 1998, 1999) have offered us a rich dynamic-gestalt model of couple treatment, emotionally focused couple treatment. Greenberg and Johnson argue that the affects that accompany attachment lie at the center of couple functioning. Thus Greenberg and Johnson provide us with both a model of normal couple functioning and an accompanying system describing how that functioning goes awry and how to intervene to fix it.

The "softening" lies at the heart of the Johnson model. She feels that certain "hard" affects, such as critical anger, protect the self against vulnerable feelings—fear of abandonment, perhaps. The breakthrough in Johnson's therapy comes when, with the help of the therapist's interpretation, one partner can "soften" and acknowledge the affect beneath his or her attack or withdrawal. Johnson also does her share of gentle coaching toward more constructive interaction, but her model differs from previous ones when she wades directly into the affective maelstrom.

For example, Len and Clara, partners in their 60s (Johnson, 1999), present a standoff. Len appears distant and minimizing and Clara angry and critical. Clara has recently recovered from cancer but fears a relapse. Len, newly retired from a high-profile job, feels depressed and useless. Johnson helps Len admit that his distancing and occasional heavy drinking defend against his fear of losing Clara to separation through death or divorce. She supports Clara to realize that her anger covers profound feelings of helplessness about the threat of her disease and about the lack of meaningful support from her husband.

Johnson does not attempt her core intervention until the 8th, 9th, or 10th session, so she understands the couple well before she starts her major move. When she does interpret, she empathizes with the emotional position of each partner and then suggests to Clara, for instance, that she attacks out of fear. If Clara can then acknowledge her panicky feelings and their connection to her aggression, Johnson supports her and encourages Len to empathize as well. If Clara cannot admit this connection between vulnerability and attacking behavior, Johnson steps to the side, but, studying her case transcripts, we can see that she soon returns to her central interpretation, using slightly different examples. Johnson's persistence has a scientific rationale because her process research can demonstrate the relationship between "softening" events and positive treatment outcome. As we proceed, we'll observe, again and again, the crucial role played by the softening of the affective connections in the fight, about which Johnson teaches us.

Fred Sander (1998) uses a purely psychoanalytic, interpretive approach with his couples. A typical Sander interpretation unfolds as follows (1998). Louise longs for a third child, but her husband, Larry, refuses. This deadlock becomes bitter, and the couple comes to Doctor Sander. He discovers that Larry does not want to have a third child because he was an only child and unconsciously felt that his economically pressed parents had something to give him but nothing left over for themselves. This interpretation links the present couple dilemma, whether to have an additional child, with a past unconscious conviction produced in Larry's experience of his family of origin. Larry identifies with his struggling parents and feels that the present members of his family, particularly himself, will inevitably become cheated by the arrival of a new drain on resources. Sander helps Larry work on his withholdingness and Louise on her demandingness.

Sander—almost alone, among couple therapists—applies this traditional psychoanalytic methodology directly to the marital work. Sander, like myself, has experimented with treating many of his couples in small groups, and, in this venue as well, he uses psychoanalytic techniques almost exclusively, again a signature contribution. I've devoted chapter 5 to a discussion of short-term couple group.

David and Jill Scharff (1991) have adapted object relations theory to long-term couple therapy. For example, the Scharffs introduce a woman who lived an isolated, unprotected childhood, which included sexual abuse by her older brothers. This woman now cannot respond to her husband's advances. She suffers from a repressed inner image of a greedy, angry, deprived self. Sex with her husband threatens to bring this repressed self to life. The Scharffs will explore the repressed self-image with this client and will probably pursue the repressed object images of the rapacious brothers. They will then focus on the influence of these upon the object relationship between the couple.

Unlike other couple therapists, the Scarffs concentrate on transference and countertransference phenomena. Many of their insights about their couples derive from the manner in which the client's internalized object relations patterns spark reactions in the therapist. For example, when this previously mentioned wife tells her story, the therapist may feel the client's repressed anger and self-hatred in himself more intensely than the client does in herself—important clues to this woman's resistance to intimacy. The therapist then helps the client to work with her frightening, repressed self-image, which plays so central a role in the marital problem.

The Scharffs' approach carries particular importance because they represent the most comprehensive attempt since Dicks (1967) in the 1960s, to explore specific internalized object relation patterns, left over from the past, and to demonstrate the influence of these on the adults in the current marriage. This conceptual framework will prove incredibly helpful to us, because it more deeply explains the content of the fight and renders comprehensible its tenacity. If old, repressed self- and object images have become wound into that fight, no wonder its resolution is so hard won. The couple fights, only in part, over current matters. The Scharffs' psychological model of couple conflict has much in common with my own. In chapter 2, I will offer an object relations model of couple dysfunction and will study the Scharffs' and Dicks's work more completely at that time.

For now we must distinguish carefully the Scharffs' thinking about the *causes* of marital conflict from their *technical interventions* to treat that conflict. Their work sheds powerful light on the complexity of the fight, a light of which many couple therapists, working either shorter or longer term, can make use, but the Scharffs definitely describe a *long-term* intervention system—often meeting their couples twice weekly for 2 years or more. They also picture an emotionally attuned, but behaviorally passive, therapist, who may allow much material to emerge, and much time to pass, before offering interpretations linking the past to the present behavior. I share many theoretical assumptions with the Scharffs and have learned a great deal from reading their books. However, their model of intervention, in contrast to my own, decidedly does not fit a short-term format.

Visiting the previous work of others does not represent merely an academic or a competitive exercise. This overview helps us understand the key issues in the field and illustrates techniques that clinicians have devised to respond to those problems. As we'll see, not only can we borrow from these strategies, but we can now more fully appreciate the context within which I developed the five-step model and the specific clinical challenges to which it must answer.

What have we learned so far? All couple therapies focus on the fight, inevitably the presenting complaint. The therapist can then try to move around that fight, reposition the players, coach the pair through the conflict, or uncover the central affects beneath it. Hypothetically, the clinician doesn't have to choose one of these four approaches. He or she could make use of two or more at the same time.

But there appear complex preconditions for change. Jacobson and Christensen teach us that without increased mutual acceptance and decreased defensiveness, not much lasting progress seems possible. However, the Scharffs convincingly argue that the participants bring assumptions into the fight, about self and other, from the past, of which they, to say nothing of their partners, usually remain mostly unaware. We seem to require a model, both individual and interactional, that illuminates the unconscious of each, increases self and other understanding, and particularly supports a lifting of defenses. But all the while, that model needs to influence the pair toward current behavioral change. To add a note of urgency, our approach must be applicable in a short-term format, less than 20 sessions per treatment episode, in order not to exclude too many potential clients. All in all, quite the testing charge. Let's see how such a system might evolve as a clinician confronts an actual couple and attempts to grapple with the partners' complex, long-standing problem.

THE FIVE-STEP MODEL

Bill and Andrea: A Complicated Couple

Somber, bearded 52-year-old Bill, a computer consultant, follows anxious, visibly upset, 52-year-old Andrea, a social studies teacher, into my office. I've worked with this couple previously, and I can readily guess the details of the fight that the two will describe in a moment. Sure enough, Andrea, on the point of tears, blurts out that Bill is withdrawn, won't touch her, hardly speaks to her, and won't say what's wrong. When I turn to Bill, he explains in the flattest of tones, pushing his anger far away, that Andrea's not a "team" in their plans to renovate the house. He volunteers little more.

All of a sudden, we stand face-to-face with the dilemma of couple therapy. How to meld the need for a quick fix with that of a more lasting change? I can, and do, begin to coach Bill and Andrea, asking each to explain his or her position for 10 minutes without interruption from the other. As they continue, I model communication skills by empathizing with the affective position of each and by suggesting behavioral compromises and supportive interventions that each could make. In fact, both find difficulty in speaking out their feelings, so I now follow Dan Wile and do the talking for them, elaborating how each probably feels—my version of script writing.

In two sessions, at most, the icy standoff will thaw, and the partners will move closer to each other. But the three of us have traveled this road together before. In a few weeks or months Bill and Andrea will return, manning the same barricades. We require a method that will transport us behind the characteristic defensive stance of each member of the pair, so that we can work for a change in their fight that promises more permanence.

Standing outside the couple, I, and probably any experienced therapist, can readily grasp how the defenses of each contribute to the fight, but we need to understand the specific content of the defended against affects and the origin of the coping style of each of the pair, if we really hope to facilitate a shift in this locked-down system. We're only 10 minutes into the session, but already we need an approach that can link past with present and one that promises to help the three of us rapidly. I need to formulate a system that will allow us to understand and work effectively with the naturally occurring flow of information that unfolds as almost any couple confronts almost any recurrent conflict.

So now I begin my model.

Step 1: Study the Fight.

Because the thrust of my work will be to penetrate into the deeper psychological layers of the fight, I need to grasp each detail of it very clearly. I will devote most of the first two treatment sessions to that work. What events or changes in atmosphere signify the arrival of the fight? Exactly what feelings arise in each participant and at what point? What does each say, or do, to fan the flames? What is the affective situation for both at the fight's most intense point and later when it winds down?

Pausing momentarily, we can see that while I gather these details, if this were a new case, I could also undertake a brief psychiatric evaluation of each member and of the depth of disturbance in the couple's marriage. In other words, I could assess the rigidity of Bill's withdrawal and how over-wrought and desperate Andrea may become. Do I find major mental illness or substance abuse in either client? What about the potential for violence? How could I describe the best and the worst level of functioning for each member of the dyad and for the marriage? (Gustafson, 1984). In this case, after two meetings I can rule out serious psychopathology in either member.

In the meantime I'm starting to map the fight. I learn that either Bill or Andrea can begin the conflict. Bill may complain about Andrea's lack of commitment to a couple project, or Andrea may confront Bill about his immersion in his nonstop consulting work. The theme never changes. Each experiences the other as not available in a crucial fashion. Each then feels falsely accused and rationalizes his or her behavior. Frustration mounts on both sides. No resolution seems possible. The partners withdraw to pursue separate tasks on separate floors of their multilayered condominium, a home that they've owned for 20 years, but one that they can never satisfactorily finish remodeling, perhaps the metaphor for the unresolved conflicts be-tween them. Although no one raises his or her voice in the fight, the part-ners definitely reach an alienated state. As they drift away from each other, Bill may obliquely suggest divorce, by observing that perhaps this relation-ship will never meet his needs. Andrea then becomes terrified, but Bill will not reassure her. She's left alone with her panic.

This general pattern replays itself every 3 or 4 months. On the one hand, this couple presents a chronic and complex fight that is fit to test the skills of the most seasoned therapist. On the other, the pair, like nearly all couples I've seen, engages in only one fight, so we need worry about only one focus. Perhaps this is the saving grace of couple therapy.

Step 2: Investigate the Triangle of Focus.

In my experience, in both solo and group sessions, as couples wrestle with their fight, three topic areas naturally keep coming to the fore: (1) the machi-nations of the fight itself; (2) individual character issues, that is, Bill's pro-clivity to withdraw into bitter silence; and (3) family-of-origin history. Bill, for example, apparently rarely spoke a personal word to his parents and so has no practice in intimate communication. I call these three points of in-terest the triangle of focus. Note that this triangle encompasses both the past and the present time perspectives, because, from the start, the family

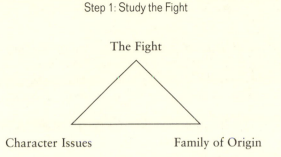

FIGURE 1.1. The Triangle of Focus

of origin works its way into the discussion. Also, the triangle of focus does not represent an artificially imposed structure to rearrange the material. It simply summarizes and organizes the data that spontaneously emerge in the first two or three meetings with almost any couple.

The action swirls from point to point, as the therapist and the couple draw parallels between any two of the three apexes of the triangle of focus. Now we begin to notice that one or both sets of parents may have had a fight in exactly the same form. (The fight connects to the family of origin.) Or that one or both members of the couple share a personality characteristic with a parent, that is, Bill and his father both seem remarkably stubborn. (Character issues connect to the family of origin.) So, exploration of the triangle of focus becomes an important preliminary phase of our model. Because the triangle of focus draws attention to the influence of the family of origin—in other words, of internalized persons from the past—object relations theory now enters the picture. I'll digress for a few minutes to introduce this important conceptual system.

Object Relations Theory

The triangle of focus emphasizes the shadow of the past playing over each participant. Bill and Andrea's behavior in the fight appears so rigid, so automatic, and of such long standing that we can quickly posit the strong influence of childhood and adolescent family issues. Should we require proof of this hypothesis, we can immediately inquire whether their characteristic troubled interaction dated from the very beginning of their relationship—in this case, in the late teenage years—and, predictably, it does. Now we know for sure that some of the themes in the fight were imported from the original families on both sides.

I have, then, to begin to rapidly delve into the early family relationships of each member of the couple. I'm looking as much for their associations to their families, and for my reaction to those associations, as I am for concrete information about their families, so I wait attentively for mention of a parent or a sibling. Next, I ask immediately for more feelings and memories. I want to grasp the early experiences that now directly contribute to the unconscious choices the partners make as they try and fail to get their needs met by each other, a failure that so often leads to the recurrent fight.

I learn that Bill, the middle child, apparently grew up in a stultifyingly uncommunicative family. His father, despite an Ivy League education, stolidly insisted on running the family dry goods store, which was slowly bankrupted by inexorable competition from the new giant chains. The father endlessly lectured Bill and his siblings about Yankee virtues and real-world success, of which he, of course, enjoyed less and less, day by day. If introverted, artistic Bill strayed from his father's ideas of proper behavior, this highly defended, angry man severely spanked his son with a ping pong paddle or a nearby board. Bill's mother seemed to have stood by silently. Bill's often-arrested, and later drug-addicted, older sister apparently carried the overt rebellion for the siblings. The message that Bill seemed to glean from his family read, "It's a harsh world. Men don't understand and don't want to understand. Women cannot or will not offer support. You're on your own." Already, we find ourselves deep in the triangle of focus and right back to the fight. No wonder Bill cannot experience any team around him, even a team of two with his wife, Andrea. He felt virtually no understanding from his family. He's no doubt furious about this, and maybe he's transferred that fury onto Andrea, projecting that she, too, chronically deserts him.

It often happens that when one partner begins musing about his family, the other offers parallel associations to hers. Through this process, I learn that the responsible Andrea is the oldest of three daughters. Her father, a small-town lawyer, rarely at home, upon his return seemed exhausted, irritable, and demanding toward his three girls—unfairly so, because each appeared well behaved and cooperative. Andrea, in particular, sought his favor through her studiousness and knowledge of politics and current events—not coincidentally, strong interests of his.

Andrea's mother, apparently a far more engaged woman than Bill's, worked hard to raise the girls on her own but did not permit anyone to feel anger over the idealized father's absence or over his cranky expectations. Evidently, she is strongly identified with her long-suffering, unfailingly cheerful mother, so hard-working, constructive Andrea in her marriage again feels herself unjustly criticized by a distant, demanding, idealized man whose approval she craves. She can't get angry, but, tipped into despair, she also cannot *listen* to her husband. Desperately, she hastens to justify her behavior, which prolongs the fight and makes progress toward resolution impossible. For Andrea, too, the family of origin connects to the fight and to an important character feature—here, guilty self-justification.

Once again, we've come face-to-face with the central problem of couple therapy. We must try to resolve a painful, present conflict between two distraught adults, but at the same time, we cannot ignore overwhelming evidence that the roots of the fight lie in the childhood worlds of each individual. To go forward from here, it seems that we require something like object relations theory to offer a bridge between these two universes, separated by time. I devote my second chapter to an exploration of object relations theory and what it can offer to a couple therapy, but I will now entice the reader by demonstrating, in briefest summary, the capability of this theory to understand Bill and Andrea's fight. I'll start by trying to bring to life Bill's inner objects.

Bill has struggled with every male work partner and employer he has had. In the latest installment of this trend, he has initiated a lawsuit against his present financial backers. He appears to have given up on men, but his mother also did not take his part. He seems always on a team of one. In object relations terms, he lives with a forever disappointing, abandoning object, which he now projects onto Andrea.

Next, the mechanism of projective identification comes into play. Andrea identifies with Bill's projection and, in fact, cannot participate on his team. She becomes so busy defending herself that they never do get to discuss the home renovations. Andrea, for her part, appears burdened with an inner object of a disapproving man and another of a woman who can't get angry—her mother. She projects the disapproving object onto Bill, who identifies with it and becomes all the more tight-lipped and critical. As a pair, they form a system in which the bad object (first he's the critical man; then she's the helpless, guilt-provoking, injured woman; then he's the critical man again) gets passed back and forth like a hot potato.

As the skirmish accelerates, both members regress into a war with their unreachable old objects, as well as with the present frustrating one, and the fight builds in intensity, circularity, and confusion. The energy within the mature ego of each partner gets siphoned off into both persons' immature egos, which politely, but implacably, flail away at each other. Bill expresses his disappointment at his silent, unsupporting mother, whose image he superimposes on Andrea. Andrea resents but begs forgiveness from her forever critical father, projected onto the disapproving Bill. We now begin to understand how well-educated, adult, civilized people get snared into the same battle, over and over. They're not just fighting each other. They're struggling with family ghosts as well, and they can't differentiate the old from the new.

In chapter 2, I will explicate object relations theory in much more depth and will demonstrate, more completely, its capability to unravel couple conflict. Now back to the five-stage model and Step 3, the triangle of conflict.

Step 3: Explore the Triangle of Conflict.

Returning to the triangle of focus for a moment before we move on, two poles of that triangle seem at least somewhat clear to us. We've described the fight at some length, and almost all couple therapists deal extensively with that phenomenon. Many also agree that family-of-origin issues, the past, impact on that fight. But when individual character matters join the focus, the discussion becomes complex indeed, because now we see that we're dealing not only with a troubled interaction, which probably has a complex, possibly multigeneration, history, but we must also confront the personality dynamics of each participant. Thankfully, the triangle of conflict helps us understand and work with the problematic character issues of each of the pair. At this point I'm interested in journeying *inside the psyche* of each of the dyad. Couple theorists do not help me very much here; they think about pairs, not individuals. But I can borrow from the theories of *short-term, individual* psychotherapy offered by David Malan (1976, 1979; Malan & Osimo, 1992) and Leigh McCullough-Vaillant (1994, 1997). They describe the triangle of conflict.

Each individual holds within specific *hidden feelings* (HF), which potentially promote psychological growth and closeness to others. However, we experience pain, guilt, and embarrassment over those feelings and powerful *anxiety* (A) that they can never reach fulfillment. When this anxiety mounts, we automatically *defend* against it with characteristic, self-defeating thoughts and behaviors (D).

The arrows within the triangle represent the flow of dynamic energy. The longing for the fulfillment of the hidden wish results in great anxiety and shame when these motives become stifled or threatened, thus the arrow from HF toward A. The person then quells that anxiety with repetitive defensive behavior, the A to D arrow. But the more defensive people be-

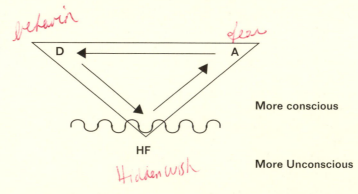

FIGURE 1.2. The Triangle of Conflict. (Adapted from Malan & Osimo, 1992)

come, the more they turn away from hopes for their HF, and the more unconscious that sector becomes. I depict this process with the D to HF arrow. Anxiety and defense represent partly unconscious mechanisms, of course, but the HF usually lies the most deeply buried, the more so when the A/D line becomes actively charged, so the wavy line represents a partial conscious/unconscious split in the individual psychodynamic economy.

With this conceptual instrument of the triangle of conflict, we can quickly diagram both Bill's and Andrea's psychological dilemma. Bill craves genuine understanding and approval (HF), but he suffers from a lifelong anxiety that others will devalue and dismiss him (A). When he fears rejection of this kind, he immediately withdraws and usually attacks (D). Indeed, many years previously Bill felt unrecognized (A) in his technical job with a large company and abruptly resigned (D) to pursue self-employed consulting. His hidden wish (HF) remains well hidden, but we guess that he yearns to express his creative self and receive genuine understanding for it, no matter how little he believes this feedback a possibility for him.

For her part, Andrea wishes to feel praised for her loyalty and constructive social and personal values (HF), but she's terrified of criticism (A), in the face of which she immediately rushes to excuse her behavior (D). "I've always been on your team. Don't you remember when . . . ?" The HF pole for both remains mostly out of their consciousness and the anxiety and defensive reactions somewhat more in the consciousness, thus again the wavy line illustrating the unconscious barrier.

Notice that for both Bill and Andrea, each point of the triangle of conflict relates to the internalized objects we began to hear about in Step 2, the triangle of focus. Bill learned his fear of dismissal at the hands of his distant parents and Andrea her fear of criticism from her exacting father.

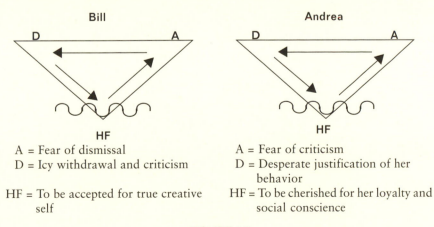

Bill

D   A

HF

A = Fear of dismissal
D = Icy withdrawal and criticism

HF = To be accepted for true creative self

Andrea

D   A

HF

A = Fear of criticism
D = Desperate justification of her behavior

HF = To be cherished for her loyalty and social conscience

FIGURE 1.3

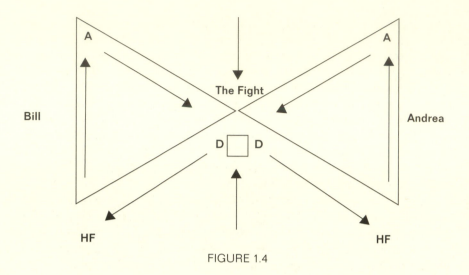

FIGURE 1.4

Our foray into the past, earlier, has helped us start to grasp the particulars of each triangle of conflict, which will, in turn, aid us immeasurably as we move on to Step 4, altering the triangle of conflict. We can now readily diagram the specifics of the conflicted psychological position of both partners by constructing their two triangles of conflict.

If we next place these two important triangles side by side and rotate each 90 degrees to illustrate an interlocking at the defensive pole, something exciting happens. We've developed a simple picture of Bill and Andrea's fight, one that could be applied to the battle between any two people.

In their fight, Bill, feeling dismissed and misunderstood (A), withdraws, and sullenly snipes at Andrea (D). She panics (A) and, in deeper and deeper sobs, pleads her innocence (D). Bill will not forgive, and Andrea cannot shed her guilt and frustration. The partners find themselves snared once again. Finally, they coldly withdraw to different parts of their townhouse, in the prototype of Wile's alienated state.

(Now I feel the need to interrupt myself. As I read over what I've put down, I realize that I've offered readers a good deal of information and a number of complex ideas in these first few pages describing the model. Perhaps we all need to catch our breath. Also, I need to clarify two or three matters.)

First, I've included much data here about Bill and Andrea, more than probably anyone could gather in the first two or three meetings with a new couple. Because I've treated them previously in a group format, I learned some of their background there. I've introduced them at this point to illustrate in detail the specific information we search for to build a full picture of the fight, but in three meetings an active therapist could amass much of this information, if his model aptly guided his search.

Second, the first three stages of the model overlap and alternate. We do not leave the triangle of focus and proceed to the triangle of conflict, never to return to the former. We gather the data for each triangle wherever we can, in unstructured fashion. I present my approach here as if we tallied the information under one heading, until we achieved comprehensive understanding of that area, before moving on. This conveys the process somewhat artificially. I present the model in this fashion in the interest of clarifying each phase as succinctly as possible.

Third, my students tell me that I expound to them at length on the triangle of focus and the triangle of conflict in our supervisory sessions, but when they collaborate with me in actually treating a couple—in our couple group, for instance (chapter 5)—they notice that I seem to engage in coaching and empathic reacting much more than in information gathering alone. Alliance building and attempting to calm the present conflict obviously represent important interventions in any couple treatment, so I proceed along two tracks simultaneously. The model guides my conceptual thinking, but, like most experienced couple therapists, I'm attempting to supportively interact with my clients as I'm trying to learn more facts to construct my picture of the psychological functioning of their inner lives. As we continue, I'll offer numerous verbatim excerpts of clinical interactions to allay any impression that I just tirelessly, impersonally query my clients for data to plug systematically into the model.

Step 4: Alter the Triangle of Conflict.

The diagram of the fight has more to tell us. As we study it, we can grasp that the crux of the treatment must reside in rearranging the triangles of conflict. In other words, the diagram shows us that we probably cannot change the fight until we help *each* member of the pair to shift at least some of the automatic relationship between anxiety, defense, and hidden wishes, which swirl around within both of them.

Psychoanalysts have defined reducing defensiveness over intimate issues as the primary goal of any dynamic therapy. "When the patient stops saying no, the analysis is over" (Elvin Semrad, in Rako & Mazer, 1980, p. 117). I pursue a similar but more limited goal for couple treatment. Rearranging the triangle of conflict stands as so important an aim in couple work that I devote all of chapters 4 and 6 to discussing this topic, but I will include a few introductory remarks here on shifts in the triangle of conflict.

In addition, I hope readers can keep this important triangle in mind and ponder how they would try to change it, for each partner, as they move through the next four chapters.

Finding the focus represents a key stage in all short-term therapy, regardless of theoretical persuasion (Donovan, 1999; Budman & Gurman, 1988). The focus for this form of couple therapy falls first on the fight and then, behind that, on the triangles of focus and of conflict that underlie the recurrent battle and, finally, on attempts to help each member of the couple to come to grips with his or her triangle of conflict. Examination of the fight will lead us straight into the two important triangles. By then, we will have organized most of the basic facts we require to begin the campaign to help the couple change. A little gentle coaching along the way toward more cooperative, less defensive relating won't hurt the cause, either.

Let's illustrate this change process by attempting to map Bill's triangle of conflict again and then make a first pass toward explaining how we might support him to alter that triangle. Bill sullenly withdraws from Andrea and carps at her, criticizing her loyalty and her commitment to the family project of home renovation. He refuses to consider any possibility that she has cooperated, or will cooperate, with him; that she appreciates his commitment to make the house beautiful for both of them; that she's "on the team" in any way. Clearly, he's furious. At first he maintains that he's just disappointed, but, gradually, I can bring his anger more into the open. This represents an important move in the treatment, although a frightening one for both Bill and Andrea. First, I get the client to acknowledge the affect—in this case, anger.

I've read Susan Johnson's work. I know that however primary an affect anger appears, it often arises for a reason. It can cover a vulnerability, a flash point of anxiety. I then need to comb through Bill's relationship history to formulate a guess about his central themes of vulnerability. When we time-travel back into Bill's childhood, alienation clearly seems the dominant feeling. Bill's parents didn't understand or support him, nor he they. He seems to have lived emotionally isolated, pursuing his own interests, so much so that he appears like a *Star Trek* voyager held hostage on a strange planet inhabited by his family. But when his world collided with his father's, savage punishment could result, and no one came to the rescue. Fundamental misunderstanding with intimates is not just lonely; it's also dangerous. Bill's defensive behavior (D) seems easy to describe. He is withdrawn and cynical about the intentions of others. But his deep anxiety, harder to define, appears a fear of annihilation, if his differences become discovered. No wonder his reactions to Andrea have become so rigid and unforgiving.

At this moment Bill stands somewhat aware of his defensive behavior and almost completely unaware of his core anxiety. With a technique akin to Wile's script writing, I try to speak out Bill's anxiety for him, to empathize sincerely with his need to withdraw but also to suggest that this coping stance does not work to his advantage. Here I begin to bring the third apex of the triangle of conflict into play—hidden feeling. I actively offer guesses about Bill's wishes, basing my forays on his associations to his family of origin, to himself, and to his marriage. This lonely man must desperately wish for understanding and cooperation from his wife (HF).

I need to support Bill to voice his hidden feeling and to acknowledge with him its validity and importance, so that I can help Bill enliven himself to his true psychological position and more fully acknowledge all the points on his triangle. Notice that if I can't contact Bill's HF in some way, it seems doubtful that he will feel understood and safe enough to consider lifting his A → D defensive shield of resistance (I'll dwell much more on this topic later). I can also probably move Andrea into a position where she, too, will genuinely understand and reinforce her husband. I hope this will help Bill become more open and will enable him to begin to explore his feelings of abandonment *with* Andrea, rather than to defensively attack her, in order to hide from those secret feelings. We can begin to see a path out of the thicket of the fight.

I can also lead the reader around the perimeter of Andrea's triangle of conflict and show how her inability to draw her husband out results from the machinations of her core anxiety, defensive behavior, and walled-off hidden wishes. Andrea's anxiety centers on her inner disapproving father. At work, her demanding boss withers Andrea with unfair criticism, and at home much the same dynamic prevails. She cannot stand up to the harsh inner object and its present-day real-life substitutes, and she has developed a corresponding self-representation of the guilty but resentful child, tearfully begging for approval—her familiar role in the fight. To alter her triangle of conflict, Andrea must, with our help, begin to face that terrifying inner father, the source of her anxiety (A) and her defensive protestations (D).

Leigh McCullough-Vaillant (1994) shows us that a therapist could initiate this process with Andrea in many ways. He or she could enter into a discussion of the client's maladaptive cognitions surrounding this father relationship, or the therapist could repeatedly point out the great cost of the defenses to the clients in their everyday interactions. I don't use either technique as much as a third approach. I'll try to engage Andrea in direct, gentle, but firm, confrontative examination of her feelings about her father. Now, in the eighth or ninth session, I can push Andrea hard to reexamine that relationship. What did he really ask of her? Was it fair? Beneath her idealization, is she also furious with him? How burdensome and costly are her consequent low self-confidence and deferential relationships? Can she dare more individuation and realistic anger? Can she begin to experience her hidden wish for self-esteem, independent of being prized for her loyalty by loved ones? In summary, what is her specific anxiety? How does she defend against it? And what does she really want? All three are poles of the triangle of conflict. Bill's attendance at, and participation in, this dialogue could pay enormous benefits, because I hope this will increase his empathy for her struggle and help him feel that his wife does not simply try to frustrate him.

Leigh McCullough-Vaillant (1994, 1997) and David Malan (1976, 1979; Malan & Osimo, 1992) obviously can teach us much about wrestling with the triangle of conflict. As I suggest here, they start by concentrating on the defense pole first and then work their way around the triangle of conflict to explore the anxiety that leads to the defense and finally to discover the hidden feeling that this anxiety protects or denies. The individual therapy clients, to whom McCullough and Malan introduce us, may display a number of HF, A, and D constellations, which require 30 or 40 sessions to unwind satisfactorily. However, we can observe that if Bill and Andrea could make progress on the one central issue that each brings to the fight—Bill's conviction that Andrea will overlook him, and Andrea's that Bill will unfairly criticize her—their relationship will improve substantially. Couple therapy includes circumscribed individual change goals. (I will explain more on this later.)

Step 5: Work Through the Fight. Develop Tools to Resolve It.

Step 4 directly leads into Step 5. As each of the pair struggles with his or her triangle of conflict, the other bears witness, so the psychology of each becomes open to the other. The fight occurs because the triangles of conflict remain unresolved, and each of the partners twists the other into playing a role in that triangle. When both achieve more insight and comfort with their triangles, they then begin to acknowledge the distortions that they bring to the fight. This new capacity allows the participants to start to negotiate their conflict, applying their new insights, rather than to fight it out. I call this working through the fight. Each can shoulder responsibility for his or her role in the battle and can reduce the blaming of the partner. Now we will hear statements such as, "I guess I do sound like my father. I'm being defensive. Tell me your point again." Clara, from Johnson's retired couple, described previously, admits she gets angry because she's terrified of the cancer returning, and she feels unable to control her fate and her husband's behavior toward her, during this crisis period.

As one member reduces his or her defensiveness, the other usually follows suit, and they can reverse the negative feedback loop of the fight. Rather than trading accusations, they attempt to offer each other support as they work toward a more cooperative outcome. They've gained greater independence of their triangles of conflict and can interact at a higher level of maturity. Change within this model implies shifts within each individual and then within the interaction.

As the partners work through the fight, they begin to develop individualized tools to resolve it. The ability to interact less defensively represents the most general and most important of these, but they also fashion other, more specific, ones. Some couples agree to postpone discussion of loaded topics until they find time and space to concentrate on them. Others devise code words to use when either senses trouble brewing. Others plan to talk prior to social or family events to review their mutual expectations, if these affairs have led to heated conflict in the past. Bill and Andrea must develop tools that allow them to anticipate the fight and to take some individual responsibility for their own roles. What they must support each other not doing is regressing into their characteristic defensive stances of he attacks, she justifies. When therapists observe couples devising tools on their own, tools that work most of the time, they sense that the partners have begun to assume responsibility for their relationship, and termination planning can begin. The threesome has discovered the only reliable road out of the morass of the fight that I know about.

Now seems like a good time to summarize the model succinctly, so that we can keep it firmly in our minds as we read further. The five-step model of couple treatment: (1) study the fight; (2) explore the triangle of focus; (3) investigate the triangle of conflict; (4) alter the triangle of conflict; and (5) work through the fight and devise tools to resolve it.

Let's see if the model works with another case—if anything, a more complex one than that of Bill and Andrea.

PAUL AND MARIA: A SECOND APPLICATION OF THE FIVE-STEP MODEL

Paul, a 40-year-old academic, from a semi-orthodox, religious background, marries Maria, also 40, also a scientist, but from Portugal. A physically diminutive pair, they fight like giants. From day one Maria feels unaccepted by Paul's parents and moralized to, and controlled by, Paul over tiny household issues, work schedules, and so on. Nearly every weekend, as she feels her precious free time pulled from her by Paul's apparent demands, she senses a straitjacket tightening, and she explodes. This life of perceived subjugation reminds her of a childhood dominated by her mentally ill father.

Step 1: Study the Fight.

Paul and Maria begin to fight when she feels stifled by his implicit demands. She protests to him, and he denies any responsibility for her discomfort. Both withdraw. The sequence takes place again, within 1 or 2 hours, but at higher decibels. Paul never voices any discomfort himself, save for the stress from Maria's complaints, and he never can think of any adjustments he might make. For him, the problem always lies in the limitations of external reality. There are only so many hours in a day, and so forth. Finally, Maria bursts into tears of anger, slams the bedroom door, and shouts threats of divorce underneath it. At this moment Paul becomes terrified that he will lose his wife, but he's usually shocked at the intensity of her reaction, and he still remains mystified about any responsibility he might have for the conflict. Each time he feels like he is caught outside in a sudden thunderstorm. After the fight, relations between the two remain frigid, certainly for hours and sometimes for a day or more.

Step 2: Investigate the Triangle of Focus.

How do problematic character traits and unresolved issues with past objects impinge on this fight? We find out that Paul battled his older, highly intrusive sister for years and now, as an adult, never speaks to her. Could intransigent Paul be transferring his mistrust of his sister onto Maria?

We further discover that Maria's father suffered from paranoia and psychotic depression, for which he was hospitalized. He violently beat Maria when she stood up to him. Could her explosions toward Paul owe their stubborn life-and-death intensity to this unfortunate earlier trauma with her father? A character trait relates to family of origin, both of which connect to the fight. We've identified, albeit in most preliminary fashion, the three points of the triangle of focus for each of the pair.

**Step 3: Explore the Triangle of Conflict for Each Partner
and Diagram the Fight.**

Paul, suffering a lifelong fear of control by his parents and by his sister (A), becomes oppositional and ultrarational toward Maria (D), which keeps him from realizing the possibilities of cooperative give-and-take with another person (HF), a wish for a kind of relationship he probably has never enjoyed.

Maria, as a child physically abused by her father, erupts (D) when she feels utterly imprisoned (A) by her husband's rigidity. Still, she nurses the

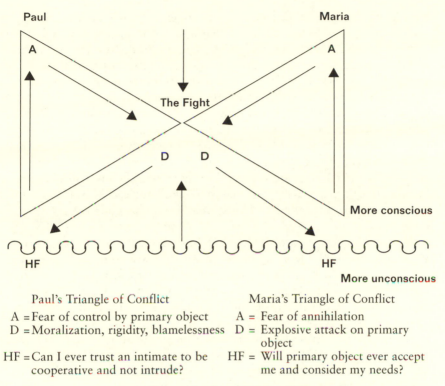

Paul   Maria

A   A

The Fight

D   D

More conscious

HF   HF

More unconscious

Paul's Triangle of Conflict   Maria's Triangle of Conflict

A = Fear of control by primary object   A = Fear of annihilation
D = Moralization, rigidity, blamelessness   D = Explosive attack on primary
                                                object
HF = Can I ever trust an intimate to be   HF = Will primary object ever accept
     cooperative and not intrude?   me and consider my needs?

FIGURE 1.5. Paul and Maria's Fight

wish that the primary object will love her but will accept her independence
and individuation (HF). At first, we thought we were treating a pair, but
now we realize that we are involved with at least an older sister and a
father as well. The marriage bed has become overly full.

Step 4: Alter the Triangle of Conflict: The Key to the Therapy.

As we study the diagram of the fight, again we realize why couple therapy
must work within a dual time perspective. Paul really is controlling toward
Maria, and we must intervene in the present with this behavior as a focus,
but Maria's father really did punch and kick her. We cannot understand her
furious reaction to Paul if we overlook those earlier, terrifying events.

Rearranging the triangle of conflict represents the key to many forms
of individual and couple treatment, but I think it remains poorly understood—a terrible problem because it often seems at the heart of the psychotherapy process. In chapter after chapter, we'll return to the complex process
of altering the triangle of conflict inside couple treatment.

As we begin to struggle with this triangle, we realize that we can enlist the necessary double-time perspective to our advantage, although it at first appears a burden to the therapist. The conflict in the present seems sufficiently complex. How can we ever address it and the past as well? But if we can coach the partners toward more cooperative present-day behavior, help them hear each other out and validate one another's emotional positions, we can create a more supportive atmosphere in the room, on which we will lean as we move back to the past and revisit the time when Paul learned to become oppositional and Maria terrified. (Most short-term couple treatment approaches seem to stop at Stage 1, the present, as we see when we review Dattilio's 1998a anthology, which may limit their potential for more lasting change, particularly with couples like Paul and Maria, who bring with them complicated pasts. Unfortunately, we have almost no research data on this point as yet.)

I actively, but empathetically, help both members of the pair to recreate their childhood dilemma and to outline the now-informed choice they have, whether to continue to try to solve their inner conflicts as they always have by projecting them onto the partner, or whether, for a few minutes, to attempt to trust the therapist and their mate enough to dare a different approach to the fight.

Let's try to capture Paul's individual object relations trap. Paul needs to realize, at some level, that because of his early impossible relationship with his sister, and perhaps, behind her, with intruding parents, he has become terrified by potential control at the hands of an arbitrary, interfering, sometimes malevolent object. His circumspect oppositional behavior would present difficulties for any partner, not just for his explosive Maria. Paul must come to acknowledge, in some sincere fashion, that he plays a role in initiating and maintaining the fight, a role about which, at present, he has almost complete denial. He must change his view that he embodies the innocent traveler suddenly savagely set upon by his wife.

Although the fight is clearly *interactional*, the first steps into and out of it seem just as clearly *individual*. If Paul cannot, in some way, confront his troubling objects, he probably cannot quell his anxiety, and his innocent defensive posture will not change. The fight will play on. But, as we'll observe in later chapters, this confrontation with inner objects need not require that Paul achieve deep cognitive and affective insight about those old relationships. The inkling, but the genuine inkling, of their effect may suffice for our work.

As we study Paul's dilemma, we grasp that two other important issues will come into play for him and probably for any individual caught in a couple fight. First, Paul and his therapist must follow the affect wound through his object relations. Paul does not appear anxious. He communicates an ultrareasonable, somewhat self-righteous, "Who me?" stance. Who could possibly blame him for his wife's incredible outbursts? However, we find that he has no best friend and few, if any, intimates, with the exception of his incomprehensible Maria. He is an isolated man, in terms both of his feelings and his social position in life.

Evidently, the relationship with his sister, and possibly with his parents, has left Paul profoundly afraid of close contact. One of the major challenges of this treatment will become to help him realize and wrestle with this anxiety. The A pole of his triangle of conflict looms very large for Paul, although he doesn't know it yet. Our psychotherapy textbooks demonstrate many strategies for moving clients closer to their anxiety, but Wile's script writing can prove a most helpful technique at this juncture. I'll take Paul back to the crowded New York City apartment with his sister and his parents, and I'll try to recreate with him this exasperating, frightening, and sometimes physically abusive sister. I want him to feel his anxiety, frustration, and rage. When he cannot speak of it, I will recount it for him and ask him if I've got it right. I will then try to help him feel that these same affects overwhelm him when Maria criticizes and protests against his rigidity.

Paul's sister, apparently somewhat paranoid, and certainly furious at her smarter, cuter, younger brother, represents a person impossible for Paul, and perhaps for almost anyone, with whom to empathize. He probably can't fix his relationship with his sister. But how much of the bad sister object has Paul projected onto Maria? How accurately does she really conform to this projection? Is his anxiety so great from this unfortunate sibling relationship that repressing and projecting the object represents his only choice to deal with it? I'll try to help him to see potential alternatives.

Now our trail has led us to the second of the important issues posed by the analysis of the triangle of conflict that affects any member of a warring pair—*personal responsibility*. Responsibility doesn't mean culpability. Clearly, we therapists cannot mimic our couples and assign blame to one or both members of the pair. Moralism of this kind would fatally short-circuit the alliance. Luckily, in almost every case, locating the blame also conflicts with the psychological reality of the fight. The partners' defensive poles simply interlock in unfortunate fashion, depending upon the specific anxieties, defenses, and internalized object relations of each member of the pair.

Until the therapy, each of the pair has remained largely unaware of most of the forces propelling him or her willy-nilly toward the fight. But once Paul has the opportunity to realize that he projects the image of his sister onto Maria, can he take responsibility, not blame, for this? He has a daily choice to make about his projection. For his marriage to grow, he will have to reabsorb some of this projection and empathize with Maria as a person of equal value to himself. Maria must assume her own responsibility, as we'll see in a moment, but without this sincere change in Paul's attitude toward his emotional life, the fight can only continue.

Turning to Maria, we realize that the central affect in her triangle of conflict revolves around trust. If she spoke up to her mad tyrant father, he would slap and kick her. This brutal man, literally ready to kill Maria should she resist his control, represents the internalized object that she probably projects onto Paul, a presence whom she takes on with the rage of a tigress. We must bring her into some contact with that terrifying father to help her realize his influence on her inner life. If she can address that object directly, some of her anxiety and fury may dissipate, at least to a degree, and she can become more free from her frozen triangle of conflict. She also needs to come to grips with her need to project that murderously controlling father image onto Paul. In Leigh McCullough-Vaillant's (1994) terms, she needs to recognize and relinquish her defensive need to attack anyone who poses a threat to her freedom. In a short-term therapy we certainly cannot complete all this work. We do need, however, to help Maria become aware of the process afoot inside her and the necessity of beginning to unwind it, particularly when she feels herself about to launch a "counterattack" at her husband.

Now Maria's sense of personal responsibility becomes all important. She, too, has a daily choice about whether to assume that Paul will automatically behave with implacable rigidity or whether to appraise him anew each time and sincerely work toward productive dialogue with him. Here we can introduce Eron and Lund's concept of the preferred view of self to great advantage. Does Maria wish to see herself as an adult person attempting to master her psychological life? What other difficult tasks has she conquered in her history? She survived a traumatic childhood. She emigrated to the United States to pursue graduate training and a successful professional career, all the while functioning in a foreign tongue. Perhaps she can take on the challenge of Paul with the same courage and determination.

I don't wish to make extravagant claims for this approach. I know that intimate relationships pose unique obstacles, even to those who have found the strength to confront considerable perils in other areas of their lives. Often, long-term therapy seems required to come to terms with early traumatizing objects. I do not see, however, an alternative direction in which to move with Maria that holds much promise. If Maria can take some responsibility for her triangle of conflict, as her husband begins to for his, then the devastating fights may lose some of their destructive intensity. Both members of this pair seem greatly concerned with fairness, because they feel, with justification, unfairly treated in the past. If one of them doesn't acknowledge his or her triangle of conflict, we can predict that the other one won't, either. The outcome of this therapy depends on both sharing responsibility for change.

Step 5: Work Through the Fight. Develop the Tools.

I need to help Paul and Maria to acknowledge to each other their past hurts and the influence of those early injuries, when their combat beckons. If Maria can say, "Yes, my father beat me to squash my independence. I know you're not violent, but I'm scared again. Can we talk about this?" she and Paul will have passed a great hurdle. Paul needs to forestall defending himself and to respond to Maria's request to discuss the conflict. "Okay, sure, I see the problem" sounds much better than "I'm not your crazy father." Working through the fight would take something like this form for Paul and Maria. I've tried to model such a dialogue for them, and they've initiated tentative, but very tentative, moves in that direction.

Tools may seem a concrete and even crude term to describe methods that couples develop to help them talk out their conflict, rather than fight it out. *Tools*, though, was the word offered by William, one of my clients whom we'll meet later, to name exactly the interchanges to which I now turn, so *tools* has become my term as well. When both members of the pair have explored their triangles of focus and relaxed their triangles of conflict somewhat, they can begin to develop and to use their tools. The practical problem about the fight is that it quickly gains momentum. Even when one or both members of the pair see it coming, they still often find themselves sucked into its vortex. Paul and Maria can explode in less than a minute. I usually suggest possible general tools but encourage the partners to devise others on their own. I need to teach Paul and Maria to call time outs and for each to respect the other's whistle for a break, no matter how much inner fury they must tolerate at the moment.

Sometimes I suggest that a couple propose a code word—for instance, "yellow card"—which would mean to both, "We have to stop now before we really hurt each other's feelings." If the partners find it useful, they could even construct yellow paper cards, which they can hand to each other at the crucial time. I've worked a lot with Paul and Maria to help them use any potential strategy to interrupt the fight before the conflagration begins. I've explained, emphatically, that the fight is bad for them and for their 3-year-old son. They gain nothing from it and only feel more hopeless and hurt afterward.

The function of the tools in this model is to help the clients to work through the fight. I counsel them to choose a time when they realistically will have an opportunity to start to unravel their recurrent conflict when it once again surfaces in their daily life, usually presenting as a disagreement over some decision or interaction. Some decide to separate for minutes or hours, before they start the work. Others prefer to sit down to begin right

away. Before they begin, I suggest an agreement that one speak for 15 uninterrupted minutes about the hot topic, while the other listens and asks only
for clarifications. Then the pair reverses roles. I also suggest that they refrain, as much as humanly possible, from blaming statements, because blame
nearly always provokes counterproductive retaliatory accusations. Usually,
the conflict has no obvious right answer, and when the partners share and
listen to each other's feelings about the matter, a reasonable course of action often presents itself.

The generic maneuvers I describe do not differ very much from those
offered by other couple therapists, such as Gottman, Hendrix (Luquet &
Hendrix, 1998), Christensen, and Jacobson and self-help authors who pre-
scribe couple exercises. I'll examine the differences between the five-step
model and other systems in some depth, and I'll begin with the issue of how
to time the introduction of the tools.

No implement works very well if you don't pick it up. Sometimes the
therapist gives in to the temptation of offering the tools from the outset.
I'm more impatient than most and have experimented with this rapid approach, but I find that the couple usually can't reach for the tools with any
reliability until later in the treatment, rarely before session six or eight.
Also, the partners need to develop and test their strategies in an individualized, trial-and-error fashion, which takes time. When the partners try these
methods prematurely, they often end up trapped in the fight all over again
and become even more frustrated. But many therapists, particularly
Christensen and Jacobson—and, to a lesser extent, Hendrix and Wile—try
to introduce their strategies in the first few meetings. Clearly, I haven't
often found this helpful, a major difference between my model and others'.
Susan Edbril (1994), in working with women in a year-long intermittent
model, likewise reports that introducing readings and homework assignments early in the therapy often backfires and leads the clients toward more
demoralization.

We've now touched on one of the points of controversy in short-term
couple therapy. As we continue through the book, we'll realize that considerable evidence suggests that couples probably cannot meaningfully resolve
the central conflict between them without taking decisive, voluntary, cooperative *actions* toward change. Developing and using the tools represent
clear examples of such actions, but I've found that the therapist and the
clients cannot effectively introduce the tools into the relationship until eight
or more sessions of therapy. Thus short-term couple treatment, as a general
modality, will probably require 12 to 14 sessions at a minimum. Much
briefer therapies will either have a different goal or, I think, run the hazard
of not working. We've begun, at least, to define the length of short-term
marital treatment. We can suggest more than that, though, and move ahead

to outline the necessary content of that therapy as well, which I'll turn toward now.

I've observed that the couple cannot devise effective tools early for two or three reasons. First, the partners must begin to constructively view the fight as a mutual psychological reality, with a life of its own, for which neither stands to blame exclusively, and as a major shared project upon which they both need to concentrate seriously. The narrative therapists have taught me this concept of acknowledging the conflict but separating it from guilt and blame. They call this agreement "externalizing the problem." Wile's script writing represents an excellent example of a maneuver to support the couple in this "externalizing," but it takes time to adopt this stance.

However, to review, before the partners can render the tools efficacious, they need to complete two additional tasks. The first of these I call accepting realistic responsibility. I've found that both members of the pair must not only feel but articulate, to their partner, a sense of personal ownership for their individual conflicts, which contribute so greatly to the fight. Yet in order to achieve such ownership, the husband or the wife must have come to understand enough of his or her object relations background and present character issues to render acknowledging these authentic. In other words, he or she must have engaged in some effective triangle of focus and triangle of conflict work before reaching for the tools can hold much likelihood of success. After the partners have learned more about themselves and their alliance to old inner objects from their family of origin, they can begin to work through the fight, or the impending fight, by initiating a helpful interaction about an emotionally loaded topic.

For example, "I know I'm hot-headed like my father, but I'm beginning to lose my temper about not eating dinner on time. Can we discuss what adjustments we both might make about this, before I get sarcastic?" Note that the speaker has included his whole triangle of focus here, his character feature of impatience, his identification with his father, and his habitual sarcasm. All these attributes represent his contribution to the potential spat. He's using the tools. Now that the husband has genuinely introduced his psychology into the dialogue and has taken responsibility for it, his wife will probably find herself less defensive and more able to join the process effectively. These conditions greatly increase the chance that the couple can devise a solution to the wandering meal time that can work productively and that will spark greater feelings of intimacy and cooperation between the pair.

Reducing defensiveness represents an important key to couple therapy (or any therapy), but you can't use the tools until you become less defensive. You can't behave less defensively until you've worked on your triangles of focus and of conflict. All five steps of the model become necessary.

Also, the couple probably needs to progress through the steps roughly in the sequence I've outlined. So, the development of the tools usually, though not always, must enter near the end of the therapy—again, an important difference between this and other systems.

I'm concerned that I may have misrepresented the five-step model along two important dimensions, and I want to clarify any misunderstanding now before proceeding. First, I may still have introduced my approach as too similar to perhaps Johnson's, Hendrix's, or Wile's, all interesting solid formats, because some of our techniques and our goals overlap, particularly at the end of the treatment. The aims of almost all responsible couple therapies seem, in fact, similar. We each attempt to move our clients away from an embattled stance and toward a collaborative one. Johnson, Hendrix, Wile, and myself clearly agree on that objective. In that connection, all four systems, and, for that matter, Nichols and Minuchin's, and even Guerin's, do appear somewhat alike. The difference between the models lies in what we conceive of as the necessary steps on the path to that common outcome. I'll explain.

The individual personality dynamics of each partner seem to carry a pivotal influence in the fight and in the therapy surrounding that fight, thus my concentration on the triangles of conflict for each partner (Donovan, 1998). The approach here includes almost as much individual as couple psychotherapy, a distinct difference from other systems. The five-step model represents an integration of a solo psychodynamic perspective with a couple intervention. Object relations theory allows us to bridge the gulf between the individual and the systemic, both theoretically and technically, as you'll see as we continue. The five-step model takes on the fight at all the important levels: the interactional, the historical, and the individual. It also includes an emphasis on the unconscious transactions within the couple and between the couple and the therapist. Other approaches, for the most part, do not display all these capabilities. In many ways this system attempts to combine some of the strengths of short-term formats with those of the longer-term object relations approaches. The more parameters we can include in our model, potentially the wider the spectrum of clients we can effectively treat. This approach seems particularly suited to include couples with complicated, chronic difficulties—in other words, with character problems deeply embedded in the triangle of conflict.

The model turns on Step 4, altering the triangle of conflict. If a couple cannot negotiate that phase, to some productive degree, in one fashion or another, then the therapy will probably fail. Luckily, it turns out that this crucial work can take many different routes. What follows then represents a psychodynamic detective story in which we will gradually discover the variety of pathways that couples, and the individuals within those pairs, find to confront their triangles of conflict and their triangles of focus.

I'm afraid, though, that so far I may have portrayed the triangle of conflict work a bit too simply, as if once the clients understood the content of the triangle and their personal responsibility for continuing or changing their defensive reactions, they naturally, and even somewhat effortlessly, would shift in a positive direction. Such is not the case. We'll observe much struggle, failure, and frustration in this endeavor, for both couples and therapists, as the book continues. We'll also learn a lot about what clients and therapists actually do to potentiate this work, and something about what both parties can't do, lest they undermine the treatment. The one impression I don't want you to carry forward is that wrestling with the triangle of conflict and the triangle of focus appears uncomplicated or formulaic. Both are rooted in the unconscious, which renders them resistant to change. Most of the last half of this book illustrates just how complex and frightening those triangles can become for clients and how confusing it can seem for the therapists as they try to derive strategies to pick their way through them. We'll see, however, that only small, though significant, shifts in the triangles of focus and of conflict seem required to support couple change.

THE NEXT CHAPTERS

The balance of the book expands on chapter 1. I'll devote one full chapter to each step of the model. I want to study what really happens in couple therapy, so I won't stray far from the data as I continue, and I'll introduce multiple clinical examples.

This model hardly represents perfection. I'm not arguing that it should do away with other proven approaches. Any new system of psychotherapy should not discard old knowledge, and we shouldn't have to learn an entirely unfamiliar language or radically different metapsychology to refine our methods. The reader already familiar with couple therapy can easily find in my system adaptations of the signature techniques of other writers. In different guise, Johnson's affective focusing, Wile's script writing, Minuchin and Nichols' boundary emphasis, and Hendrix's validation exercises all will make their appearance here, wrapped within a new overall model.

In closing this chapter, I want to reemphasize one further important feature of the model. I developed this system within an HMO setting, so it fits the patterns of treatment frequently dispensed in managed-care systems. It squarely confronts the core of couple therapy. The fight is the focus. Because this approach centers exclusively on the hot core of the problem, meaningful work can proceed relatively briefly in 15 to 20 sessions, clearly a difference from previous object relations approaches. Budman and Gurman (1988) tell us that most psychotherapies follow an intermittent pattern, regardless of the therapist's intention. The decision to end or interrupt treatment falls almost always with the client and with the unnamed third participant in most therapies, the third-party insurer. In as few as 6 or 8 meetings, we can apply the first phases of the five-step model, in which the clients explore the fight and begin to understand their triangles of focus and of conflict, developments that will offer the couple some symptomatic relief. The potential for relatively rapid application of the model represents an appealing feature for managed-care settings, in which clients revolve in and out of treatment frequently. This approach also guides our first actions when the couple returns for more therapy. Define the fight once again, and reassess the clients' insights into their triangles of focus and of conflict at the present time.

We can adapt the five-step model to group, as well as to solo couple, interventions, a final advantage. Eric and Judith Coché (1990), Fred Sander (1998), and Barbara Feld (1998) have offered us helpful descriptions of the strengths of couple group, particularly as a time-effective intervention. The group format provides the opportunity for mirroring between couples and for mutual support and accountability in a fashion that individual couple meetings almost never can. In the five-step approach, the individual couple sessions and the group meetings proceed from the same model, so clients can move readily back and forth between these modalities. Many of the pairs I'll introduce to you later I've treated in both contexts. These alternative formats, in which the partners can continue to confront their triangles of focus and of conflict, but with differing inputs and experiential possibilities, afford us maximum therapeutic leverage, using a relatively small number of treatment sessions. I'll devote chapter 5 to exploring the strengths of short-term couple group.

In chapter 2, I'll offer my understanding of object relations theory, which we'll see that we can adapt to deepen our work with both the triangle of focus and the triangle of conflict, to which we will return in chapters 3 and 4, respectively.

Object Relations Theory: Its Application to Understanding Marital Choice and Couple Therapy

The Contributions of Henry Dicks and David and Jill Scharff

Falling in love is the only socially acceptable psychosis.
—Elvin Semrad, in Rako & Mazer, p. 33, 1980

As I've worked with couples over the last 30 years, I've reviewed many models of treatment, and I've found that object relations theory, opposed to other approaches, more completely and more helpfully explains the data we encounter in each couple session. In chapters 3 and 4 we'll apply object relations theory directly to the five-step model by illustrating how that system deepens our understanding of the triangles of focus and of conflict. In this chapter I'll present my reading of object relations theory, after studying the work of Henry Dicks and David and Jill Scharff, and then attempt to illustrate its explanatory value to make sense of marital choice, couple conflict, and the interventions necessary to unwind that conflict within a time-managed therapy. To understand disruption in a dyad, we require some general theory of attachment, so first let's examine marital choice.

THE WORK OF HENRY DICKS

Dicks's Theory of Marital Choice

Before we can have marital conflict, we must have a marriage. Probably all couple therapists have, at one time or another, reasoned that if they could just understand what drew certain partners together and kept them together, they could grasp how the bargain broke, and the conflict arose.

To even the most experienced couple therapist, marital choice and subsequent marital interaction often appear mysterious and unfathomable. For example, when we desperately attempt to prevent the abused wife from giving it one more try with her violent alcoholic husband, we're forced to confront the issues of marital selection and marital longevity at their most dramatic and heart-rending. How could her judgment fail her once again and she return to him, her survival so obviously at stake? Along any number of more subtle dimensions, the decision to marry and remain joined seems ineffable. Almost everybody does it, at least for a while. Profound emotional forces clearly abound here, but the process defies any simple understanding. The previous Semrad quote sometimes seems to capture the situation. Falling in love does appear the only socially acceptable psychosis.

The depth, power, and supreme unreasonableness of romantic love have, of course, preoccupied our artists for centuries. The most important "decision" humans ever make seems controlled by utterly irrational factors. Romeo and Juliet, Western culture's most famous "star-crossed" lovers, only 16 and acquainted for just a few days, chose death rather than endure separation. In *Streetcar Named Desire,* Tennessee Williams's Stella rushes back to her drunken Stanley's embrace, even after his probable rape of her borderline sister, Blanche DuBois.

Is falling in love, and remaining in love, truly a psychosis that defies rational understanding? Any pursuit of marital attachment and the treatment of marital conflict must confront this question. H. V. Dicks (1967) and David and Jill Scharff (1991) help us wrestle with this dilemma, when they proffer us their object relations understanding of marriage and of its recurrent fight. Dicks, writing to us from postwar London, and the Scharffs, from modern Washington, D.C., represent the principal contributors, though by no means the only ones, to a grasp of the subtle, but incredibly important, object relations transactions that underlie marital choice and the subsequent intimate marital interaction. As I develop this chapter, I'll frequently refer to both writers and attempt to integrate their ideas, filling in the gaps with some of my own. Let's begin in historical order with Dicks, whose primary work in the 1950s so heavily influenced his later British and American colleagues.

Dicks used his practice at a public marital therapy clinic in London as one large clinical research project—the findings from which, illustrated through multiple lengthy case examples, he summarized in his 1967 book. Dicks's blue-collar couples, stumbling out of World War II, come alive in his clinical descriptions, even to us in America of 2003, the representatives of a vastly different culture and history. The fact that Dicks's picture of marital conflict, from long ago and far away, strikes us as so immediate offers the first clue that he grapples with unraveling profound human processes that have changed little across countries and across time.

We'll start near the middle of his book, with his examination of marital choice. Dicks observes that couples who marry engage across three "subsystems" (his word) of involvement (p. 129). I'll define them here. The first of these, the "public" subsystem, represents the realm of race and ethnicity, sociocultural values and norms, social class, and religious and educational background.

His second subsystem, "central egos,"

> operates at the level of the personal norms of the pair, their conscious judgements and expectations derived from the developmental background of object relations and social learning preceding the marriage.
> . . . As such they [the central egos of the pair—my clarification] may be expressions of a relatively unimpeded maturation of emotional and rational capacities through the incorporation of predominantly good objects whose norms and attitudes have been uncomplicatedly identified with.
> . . . The second sub-system, in so far as it works well, would correspond to Fairbairn's "mature dependence" characterized by a capacity on the part of differentiated individuals for cooperative-relationships with differentiated objects. (Dicks, 1967, pp. 130–131)

In other words, Subsystem 2 corresponds to the capacity for two adults to cooperate in terms of mutually held tastes, conscious personal choices, and positive identification with parents. These first two subsystems belong somewhat in the province of sociology and social psychology and deal mostly with conscious processes and choices. Dicks does not pursue them very far, because they do not pertain to inner psychological conflict.

In Subsystem 3, the unconscious fit between the pairs, the psychoanalyst Dicks finds his subject and the topic of his book. Dicks's central point is that in Subsystem 3 there must be *unconscious complementarity* between the partners, the details of which I'll explain in a moment, for the marriage to begin and to survive without major disruption. He does not ignore the other two domains, however, and he observes that marriages can tolerate incompatibility in one, but rarely in two of the three. A match in Subsystem 3, the unconscious fit, remains crucially important, then, but marriage can survive a major conflict here, if the attachment remains strong in the first two subsystems.

The drift of Dicks's thinking implies that depending on the subsystems through which the partners connect, we can predict the nature of their marriage. Recall that if the pair achieves compatibility in two of the three dimensions, the relationship carries reasonable promise of stability. For example, in a marriage stable within Subsystems 1 and 3, we find the couple in agreement about broad cultural expectations, and they mesh on an unconscious level, but this couple will conflict in matters of personal norms and decisions. How important is maintaining friendships for both outside the marriage, for example? But consider a clash at Level 1 and Level 3 and agreement only at Level 2. This will lead to a shaky relationship. The partners come from different social classes and do not complement each other in the unconscious fit. Their personal values and goals seem to mesh well, but they find themselves continually out of step, both in their worldview and in their intimate interaction.

Many, though not all, of the couples Dicks introduces to us meet relatively smoothly at Subsystems 1 and 2. The majority comes from working-class backgrounds, for example. These conditions obtain in most marriages across cultures, of course. Most of us marry people of similar social class, with roughly compatible individual values and goals. Subsystem 3, usually, though not always, seems to represent the site of the marital conflict. When Dicks begins to apply his three "hypotheses," which I'll introduce momentarily, to unravel the transactions in Subsystem 3, our education about unconscious exchange in marriage begins.

But before we start that education, I'll invite Dicks to summarize his observations on marital choice and the unworkability of matches that coincide in only one subsystem.

> Marriages may prove unviable at any of the three sub-system levels. It would seem necessary for at least two of the three sub-systems to function with credit-balances of satisfaction over dissatisfaction to both partners. Social affinity [Subsystem 1, my clarification] plus congruence of deep object-relations [Subsystem 3] can withstand strong divergences of personal norms and tastes [Subsystem 2]. Strong agreements over personal norms and values [Subsystem 2] plus deeper object relations [Subsystem 3] can override large cultural and social distance and incongruities [Subsystem 1]. Even social homogamy and good overlap of personal norms and values can endure, provided their defensive efficacy against "unwelcome" confrontation at deeper object levels hold. But if reality testing proves to one or both partners that the relationship was based on nothing but social interest [Subsystem 1]; or on nothing but seeing a potential parent figure or an exciting libidinal object as a guaranty against

essentially infantile loneliness [Subsystem 3]; then it is only a question of time before the need for broader-based merging of lives will become felt, and, in due course, acted upon one way or another. It is usually the case that, at this stage, the emotional content of the relationship is one of boredom, indifference and withdrawal of investment. Nothing of the self is any longer projected into the other. The institutional aspects of the co-habitation may be continued for rational or social advantages, but the marriage's interpersonal relation will be dead. The opposite to love is not hate. These two always coexist so long as there is a live relationship. The opposite to love is indifference. (pp. 132–133)

I'll provide a hypothetical example, from today's America, of relative fit within Subsystems 1 and 2 but conflict within Subsystem 3. Two people from similar suburbs meet. Their families both subscribe to liberal, democratic ideals, and both partners have professional class backgrounds and similar ethnicity. Each of our pair has graduated from college. Compatibility reigns in Subsystem 1, therefore. Both enjoy athletics and similar cultural activities, hold similar political views, want children, and agree that household chores and child rearing will be shared to a reasonable degree. Both consciously identify positively with the same-sex parent and both see the father as the principal breadwinner and the mother as the manager of the home. Each consciously wishes to meet the needs of the other and to support the partner. So we find complementarity in Subsystem 2—the central egos of conscious personal identity and norms and choices seem compatible.

But let's turn to Subsystem 3. The wife idealized her kindly supportive father and feels convinced that she has chosen a similar man for her husband, but after the marriage, she comes to bristle at his passivity. At this point, his soothing understanding seems to her more like passionless indifference. She wanted gentle but active. This represents an important example of Dicks's "Hypothesis (1)," the first of his well-known three principles to explain the roots of unconscious marital conflict, the exploration of which forms the core of his book. Conflict in the marriage results when a partner *fails* to play the prescribed, fantasized parental role for which he or she was selected. In Dicks's Hypothesis (1), "Many tensions and misunderstandings between partners seem to result from the disappointment which one, or both of them, feel and resent, when the other fails to play the role of spouse after the manner of a preconceived model or figure in the fantasy world" (p. 50).

Returning to our hypothetical case, mentioned previously, the now disappointed wife begins to rebel against her husband, as she did as a child against her father when he failed to fulfill her wishes. She starts purposefully disagreeing with her partner and then taunting him. Her husband had, in turn, counted on his wife to provide the apparently endless support that he enjoyed from his placid mother. He, too, brought an unconscious fantasy partner into the marriage. When his wife fails to conform to this model, he also regresses and becomes passive-aggressively distant. She pursues him, all the more provocatively, and the interactional spiral begins to career downward.

Note that the partners felt drawn together because of mutually interlocking unconscious needs based on positive idealized views of a parent, but when the partner fulfills these imperfectly, the match begins to unravel in disappointment. The ground for the attraction contains in it the seeds that now spawn the conflict. The partners choose each other on the basis of positive connections to a parent, but this view rests, at least in part, on idealization. Dicks describes the underpinnings of this kind of fight:

> in the absence of this fantasy likeness of the partner to the wished for compliant parent image, the deeper ambivalence towards the love object breaks surface in resentment and hate previously covered by idealization. The parties treat each other as if the other *were the earlier object* [my emphasis], and regression occurs in the means used to coerce or persuade the parent image with the old, childish resources for revenge or for getting favor. Forbidding and rejecting qualities are attributed and evoked each by the other. It is as if the "bad object" is shuttled to and fro in the contest which is indeed the essence of a collusion. (Dicks, p. 58) [This unconscious interaction represents the essence of projective identification, of which we will hear much more later.]

Alternatively, in Dicks's "Hypothesis (1A)" (pp. 59–62), the couple may marry to engage with a partner who plays a role the *opposite* of which they experienced in their families, only to find the same familiar objects underneath, once the idealization of the honeymoon passes.

> Tension between marriage partners can result from the disappointment that the partner, after all, plays the marital role like the fantasized parent figure, similarity to whom is denied during courtship. This often collusive discovery leads to modification of the subject's role behavior in the direction of regression towards more childish responses to the partner. . . . Even in the marriage by contrast (to the hated parent figure), there was the fashioning of an idealized object or role model by reference to rejected objects. (Dicks, p. 62)

"Hypothesis (2)" works somewhat differently. Partners may perceive in the other a repudiated, lost part of themselves that they have repressed. They recapture it in the spouse, but, once found, they eventually begin to persecute this lost piece in the other (p. 63). Here we encounter the seemingly inexplicable marriage of the learned, rational professor and his pretty, apparently scatter-brained secretary. Each discovers in the other the missing fragment to complete his or her own personality—a great relief, at first. But the denigrated part—for example, fun-loving lightheartedness—was discarded for a reason, and the professor soon comes to ridicule his wife for her "childlike" behavior, of course, the very characteristic for which he chose her in the first place.

Couple therapists seem to describe couple conflict 90% of the time and couple compatibility 10%. When we study the cases presented by psychodynamic marital therapists, we often come away with the assumption that the unconscious arrangement that the pair strikes seems inevitably doomed to failure. Considering Dicks's Hypotheses (1) and (1A), can any real person compete with the fantasy of the perfect partner derived from childhood or embody the opposite of the feared or demeaned parent, also the creation of early, repressed, fantasied object relations? The answer, surprisingly, appears to be "yes," with the caveat, "to some degree." We know that approximately half the marriages *do not* end in divorce, prima facie evidence that reasonable congruence in Subsystem 3, as well as in 1 and 2, regularly occurs. As we will see later, Dicks's work demonstrates, furthermore, that even quite disturbed couples can use insight about their unconscious wishes and assumptions to achieve greater mutual compatibility within Subsystem 3.

This discussion of an unconscious fit within the couple that might actually work over time lends us to consider the concept of mastery—an idea central to object relations couple therapy. From what we have learned so far about object relations within the couple, it now appears likely that one motivation underlying marriage may be the drive to master an unconscious conflict or a fantasied expectation. If, for example, a duty-bound man marries a more flexible woman, this match may represent an attempt by the man to grow in a more open way himself. If the challenge to master the self propels us to excessive degrees, however, it can carry with it the inevitable underpinnings of its own defeat. For instance, a man chooses an aggressive, rebellious, counterculture woman, whose chief appeal to him is that she defiantly stands up to his wealthy, conservative, controlling parents. When she also battles him at every turn, though, he realizes the futility of his unconscious strategy.

But in less caricatured choices, a man, afraid of intimacy, may marry a warm woman in a challenge to himself to develop his own tolerance of closeness. If she respects and can learn some of his self-confidence, all the better. Possibly, at the core of couples therapy, we will find pairs trying to master, in the other, split-off qualities in the self. When the somewhat-alien capacity of the other sparks admiration, not just fear or defensive denigration, it may turn out that with the help of life experience, and possibly that

of therapy, the pair can fashion a workable match. From the object relations viewpoint, coming to terms with unconscious object relationship expectations and the defenses surrounding these preconceptions seems to lie
close to the core of a general theory of attachment and of the treatment of
marital conflict. Throughout the book, we'll follow partners who gradually renegotiate their unconscious role expectations of each other.

Dicks's Application of Fairbairn's Metapsychology

Dicks's great contribution came when he applied the individual dynamic
theory of Fairbairn to grasp the two-person marital interaction—in other
words, when he unraveled the intricate workings of his Subsystem 3, in
terms of what we now call object relations theory.

Let's turn to Fairbairn, as Dicks summarizes his work (Dicks, 1967,
chaps. 3 and 5). Fairbairn's developmental theory runs as follows. Infants
receive all, or nearly all, of their pleasure and frustration in interaction
with early caregivers, particularly the mother. Under optimal conditions
the parents offer sufficient warmth, availability, and holding, which growing children can use, through identification with those parents, to control
and integrate their feelings of excitement and anger. This capacity for self-
control and self-soothing becomes most evident when children move into
the relative stability of the latency stage, perhaps the ages of 7 to 10.

But Fairbairn emphasizes what all of us clinicians well know, that
children's development may follow a sub-optimal path. Perhaps their growth
becomes marked by more loneliness, excitement, or fury than children can
manage, at a certain age, with their given capacities and with the resources
of their environment. Then children have no choice but to turn toward a
crucially important defense mechanism, repression. Children will have to
repress their rage, anxiety, or joyful urges, because they cannot integrate
these into their conscious ego.

A split occurs between the child's conscious and unconscious self. What
happens next? Here Fairbairn becomes even more helpful to Dicks and to
us. The child represses not just affects but *object relationships*, because
each affect remains tied to the important relationship in which it first arose.
Here Fairbairn diverges from Freud in significant fashion. Freud's original
psychic drive theory implied that affects such as sexual excitement represented the repressed phenomena, which inevitably then reappeared to form
later psychiatric symptoms, such as hysteria (see Slipp, 1984). Freud proposed that affects or energies made up the crucial repressed material, but
Fairbairn hypothesized that *object relations* composed the repressed experience. (For a particularly lucid discussion of the dialectic between drive

theory and the object relations stance in the development of psychoanalytic thought, see Greenberg and Mitchell, 1983.)

For Fairbairn, three crucially important psychological entities become repressed, intertwined together—an affect, perhaps anger at rejection; the object of that anger, perhaps the mother; *and* an experience of self in relation to that object, perhaps a guilty self. To repeat, every repressed object relationship has three dimensions: an affect, an object, and a self-representation. Some of the object relationships that undergo repression hold a frustrated sexual or loving valence, the experience of unrequited affection. These Fairbairn names *libidinal objects,* more accurately, libidinal object relationship experiences. Other repressed object relationships call forth feelings of rage or rebellion, perhaps a controlling father object image, coupled with the affect of anger toward that father, and a self-representation of a rebellious but frightened self. Fairbairn refers to these as "anti-libidinal" objects.

Clearly, a host of object interactions does not provoke enough guilt, anxiety, or excitement that these require instant repression. No split takes place here. These remain more or less in the person's awareness and available to him or her—the memory of warm soup served by a mother in a likewise warm kitchen perhaps recalls conscious unconflicted thoughts of a loved self, a giving mother, and the satisfying affect of dependency. Fairbairn calls this reservoir of unrepressed object relationships the "central ego." We recall that these conscious object relationships become part of the mature identity that Dicks locates within his Subsystem 2. Some repression, of course, clearly occurs in even a story of strong growth. Everyone represses oedipal love feelings, which are then projected, in compromised form, into later romantic partners.

But let's allow Dicks to summarize how this core developmental process of repression and splitting can proceed awry, when repressed object relationships dominate growth, and the split between the conscious and the unconscious becomes all important.

> The ego's identity is according to this theory preserved by unconscious defensive fission of parts of its inner world of objects, much as a lizard sheds its tail to a pursuing enemy. The earlier such a crisis of growth [the splitting and repression—my clarification] occurs, the more profound the effects on subsequent personality development. It results, according to phase of development as well as to intensity, in a more or less massive impoverishment of future relational potentials of the kind sketched earlier. This potential is fixated around the split of internal ego-nuclei locked in arrested combat with the original source of the rejection: the primary parental figures, who first evoked the flowing out towards them of dependent and libidinal needs, and did not satisfy them by requisite responses. One element—the unrequited love need, is described by

Fairbairn, as a withdrawing itself into a split-off enclave, which he terms *the libidinal ego*. If the split occurs very early in life, this ego part may remain exceedingly infantile—a poor little self who dare not show his presence. In this hypothesized structure reside the hidden wishes for dependence, for tenderness, for being loved. Here, also, are presumed to lie dormant the highly ambivalent sexual impulses towards the exciting frustrating object surrounded by the wall of the incest-taboo.

In another hypothesized split-off region are contained the frustration-rage arousing dangerous aspects of the relationship to the rejecting, frustrating object, which the child had to internalize in fear. To this other half of the split Fairbairn gave the name of *anti-libidinal ego*, related to and reacting in identification with the anti-libidinal object. (p. 41)

Now Dicks begins to adumbrate his signal contribution to the theory of marital interaction. He applies Fairbairn's *one-person* theory to the *two-person* situation of the marriage. The repressed libidinal and anti-libidinal egos of the pair will begin to interact in efforts at self-protection and in disguised forays to have long-repressed needs met. "His three hypotheses" represent ways in which couples frequently collude in this interactional bargain. Sometimes hate can be successfully expressed and sometimes love successfully sought in these unconscious couplings, but if not, explosive conflict and a referral for marital therapy often result. Consider Figure 2.1:

Husband's Object Relations Map   Wife's Object Relations Map

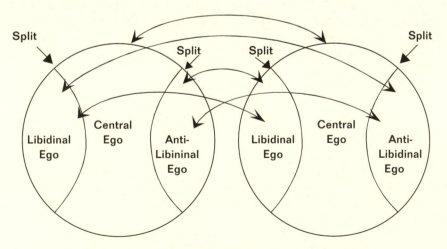

FIGURE 2.1. (Adapted from Scharff & Scharff, 1991)

If, in modern parlance, we substitute "object relations" for ego, a number of important ideas emerge. First, the historical timing and the size and rigidity of the split carry great significance for development. If the split occurs early and with great force, more of the personality will become walled off from any further maturation. When the split unfolds early and deeply in this fashion, the individual suffers a *basic fault,* in Balint's (1968) terms. The person's fundamental relatedness remains inaccessible behind the split, and that individual cannot deal with the self or with others through words. The person can't genuinely communicate. Therefore, the greater the ratio and the strength of the repressed object relations, the more these split-off presences will influence both partners in the marriage.

As maturity increases, the influence of the repressed ego states decreases proportionately (see Slipp, 1984). But everyone undergoes some ego splitting. However great or small the resulting impairment, we can guess that the fight within a pair will always take place at the location of the split for at least one partner, because this represents the precise relationship disability for each individual—the place, in an intimate interaction, beyond which he or she cannot go. In chapter 3 we'll study Paul and Maria extensively, and we'll find out that Maria cannot adequately separate Paul from her psychotic, abusive father. When he disappoints her at a key time, she becomes uncontrollably enraged. The location of her split falls at the exact point where she must trust that Paul differs from her father. She can say the words, but, emotionally, she doesn't believe the possibility. Behind the split lies the unconscious affective conviction that all men will transform into the same sadistic, utterly unreliable madman that was her father. As we continue through the book, we can identify the locus of the split for each member of each couple, a crucial step in defining the developmental tasks that each must take on, in his or her own way, in the therapy.

To summarize—if, in developmental terms, a given person has not worked through and mastered a critical conflict situation or phase with his or her parents in early childhood, defensive repression and splitting will occur. According to this concept of the unconscious split, not only does the internal image of that object and the feelings surrounding it become repressed, but a part of the ego itself, which is in relation to the threatening objects, must become split off also.

> What is essential about this way of looking at marital life is that it is not feelings, not impulses as such, but affective relationships between self and some figure outside the self which are repressed. This splitting necessarily involves also a portion of the reacting self, which then becomes less, if at all, available to the central ego. In this psychological theory the split-off object relation remains charged with psychic energy. . . . Therefore if my split off internal relation to a forbidden or dangerous object

takes its quota of ambivalent cathexis, and preoccupies part of me unconsciously, I have that much less investment of self to offer to an adult
relationship. (Dicks, p. 70)

We can guess the next step in Dicks's theory. The energy in the repressed object relationship surges toward expression—the anger, excitement,
and condemnation must all have their say, but these affects endured repression for a strong reason originally: their danger. Enter the mechanisms of
defense, which allow expression of powerful feeling and which simultaneously guard against it. Perhaps the most important of these is *projection*.
If I have a repressed object relationship of a rejecting mother with a needy
child, I can readily project this onto my wife. She becomes the cold mother
and I, the deprived child. In other words, numerous unconscious projections, represented by the arrows in Figure 2.1, can and do take place between the repressed object relations of one partner and those of the other.
As Ogden (1982) explains, we recreate our inner world with each new object we encounter. The more intimate the encounter, the more powerful this
recreative process.

We can now appreciate that Dicks has offered us a giant step in understanding the marital puzzle. Partners who, in other sectors of their lives,
can function at high levels become embroiled in bitter, apparently incomprehensible disputes, which defy resolution but which they seemingly endlessly repeat. Couples have only one fight, but they have it hundreds of
times. We can grasp that this compulsion to repeat the fight simply means
that the same repressed object relations come into play each time. The man
with a repressed object relationship of an infantile demanding mother can
hold an accurate view of his probably reasonable wife for a while, but
before long he finds himself "inexplicably" snapping at her understandable
requests. By explicating these unconscious transactions between intimate
partners, Dicks makes a brilliant contribution to a general psychoanalytic
theory of psychological functioning. (See Greenberg & Mitchell, 1983, and
Pine, 1985, 1990, for extended discussions of the importance of such a
theory.)

Applying the Fairbairn and Dicks models to live couples, we can more
deeply grasp how everyday misunderstanding and conflict enter the interaction. If the husband's unconscious libidinal ego contains a rejecting mother
object, he may experience a *transference* reaction to his independent wife
when she chooses to pursue activities on her own. The husband's reaction
can be codetermined, if his early life with his mother has also led him to
become somewhat afraid of intimacy in general. He will then all the more
likely translate his wife's "distance" into the projection that she, too, avoids
closeness with him (Berkowitz, 1999). From the other side, his wife may
crave independence from a repressed, "anti-libidinal," angry father object.

She cannot grasp why her husband does not experience the world simi-larly—why he doesn't want more autonomy in their relationship—her trans-ference reaction to him.

Repressed objects do not just persecute, reject, cling, or demand. They also influence us in more subtle but often even more powerful ways. Con-sider separation and survivor guilt. Perhaps, in our hypothetical example just mentioned, this independent wife has also internalized a mother object who always seemed sad and unhappy in her marriage. The wife may expe-rience unconscious guilt about herself enjoying a fulfilling relationship when her mother could not—an example of survivor guilt (Weiss, 1993). This unfortunate guilt writes a scenario in which the wife may become all the more tempted to pull away from her husband and perhaps to angrily (guilt-ily) disengage from his somewhat desperate embrace. As we study this hy-pothetical, but familiar, case we can understand a little more about the concept of transference in couple interaction, and we can also learn to rec-ognize and follow the footprints of unconscious guilt and begin to see how one affect can defend against another. Here the wife's anger protects her from her gnawing unconscious guilt about her mother's apparently empty marriage.

Notice, though, that underlying all these complex affective transac-tions between the partners stands the Dicks-Fairbairn model of split-off object relations. The crucial affects—the rejection, the wish for indepen-dence, the guilt—all seem tied to three-part, repressed object relations: (1) repressed experiences of self; (2) of parental objects; and (3) the accompa-nying affects of the repressed relationship. In exciting fashion, Dicks and Fairbairn, writing decades ago, have offered us a theory of marital interac-tion that can thoroughly explain the couple conflicts of today, brought to us in our 2003 offices.

Dicks does not spell this out concretely, but we can observe that Figure 2.1 represents the unconscious marital transaction in only the most general sense. In real life we encounter couples who sometimes project around a few, but not all, issues and may possess some, but hardly complete, aware-ness of where and what they project. We can now understand the objective of object relations marital therapy. Its goal is to soften the arrows and the splits in the diagram, in order to reduce the harshness and the rigidity of the automatic interactions that this schematic pictures.

Clearly, when the repressed material remains most deeply hidden and the object relations involved are most primitive, the worst case scenario can result. We open the newspaper to read that an estranged husband, who needed complete dominance over his wife, continued to track her every movement despite restraining orders. Finally, unable to influence his wife in any other way, he breaks into the house and shoots her and then himself. Obviously, this man's central ego has remained critically undeveloped. He projects his libidinal ego (object relationship) onto his wife. She represents all the love he never received as a child, but he mistrusts her and assumes she will reject him. Therefore, he cannot allow her out of his sight. She can't stand her imprisonment and seeks a separation. He must control her at all costs, lest she spurn him and offer her perfect love to someone else. On the point of losing her, he cannot tolerate the abandonment. He kills her, but unable to live without his idealized libidinal object, he then kills himself. Like the atomic bomb, the repressed object relations in the marital dyad can release great energy in a small space and create havoc when they do.

The process of projection takes on added metapsychological complexity when we realize that the second partner, into whom the old object relationship becomes projected, has repressed anti-libidinal and libidinal object relations of his or her own, among which the projection may fall. Let's study another hypothetical clinical vignette. An ACOA (Adult Children of Alcoholics) man assumes that his wife demands perfection of him. If her development has progressed quite optimally, her central ego will have grown very broadly. She will unconsciously absorb her husband's projection within that central ego, evaluate it as inaccurate, and probably offer him reassurance to assuage his anxiety about her judgments of his performance. We can recognize this as a more or less optimistic outcome, but it obtains thousands of times in more stable marriages and, from time to time, within less stable ones. Partners regularly check possible distortions of perception with one another and receive realistic feedback.

However, let's return to Figure 2.1. The projections launched from the first partner toward the second might not land in the area of the central ego; the narrower this space, the less likely such a landing. The repressed libidinal ego or the anti-libidinal ego of the second partner may now become involved. If the wife, in our previous example, has a repressed view of self that she is suffocatingly demanding, she will become threatened by her husband's explicit criticism. She will furiously reject her husband's projection and possibly attack its author. In more primitively organized couples we can see this pattern play out incessantly. They regularly hurl accusations back and forth at each other, most of which seem unfounded to the more objective therapist, standing outside the projective system, who initially sits amazed at the vituperation that suddenly emerges. More developed couples restrict this behavior to their worst fights.

Therefore, when we review Figure 2.1, we note that the arrows go both ways. Our hypothetical ACOA husband receives projections from his wife and reacts to those, even as he sends his own. He feels her his exacting father, but perhaps she experiences him as her guilt-inducing mother. The fight ensues. The process of marital projection can become circular and continuous. We can also see that the couple's fight represents the analogue of the concept of repetition compulsion in individual psychology. Unconscious relationships with repressed primary objects compel the pair to battle over the same ground again and again, in self-defeating fashion. The couple relives familiar relationships in an attempt to keep continuity with and master the past, but that quest becomes frustratingly futile. Later in this chapter, when we begin to consider therapist technique, we can see that a major issue in couple therapy centers on when and how to intervene in this projective cycle and thus in the couple's shared repetition compulsion.

The Role of Other Defense Mechanisms in Marital Conflict

At this point we can grasp why Dicks and the Scharffs emphasize the centrality of projection in marital interaction. We'll return to a discussion of this central maneuver in a moment, but first I must note that additional defense mechanisms play crucial parts in marital life as well. In *idealization*, the first partner protects the second as "all good" and represses his or her negative attitudes toward the partner. A wife explains to her child, "Your father loves you very much. He's a wonderful man. He just never talks about his feelings," thereby repressing and converting into idealization her own wish for more warmth from her husband. Or, what about *denial*? "My husband only drinks too much because he doesn't have a job." (Perhaps he has no job because he drinks too much.) Both of these mechanisms, idealization and denial, based on prior repressed object relations, often figure prominently in strained marital relationships, which then become stilted and ultimately unworkable. The defense crowds out intimate contact.

Projection, though, remains the key mechanism that must concern us, because of the phenomenon of *projective identification*. David and Jill Scharff (1991) propose a model of unconscious marital transactions similar to Dicks's, but their thorough exploration of projective identification goes beyond his and helps us understand unconscious marital transactions more deeply.

THE CONTRIBUTION OF THE SCHARFFS: THE CENTRAL ROLE OF PROJECTIVE IDENTIFICATION IN MARITAL CONFLICT

The Scharffs (1991) represent the modern successors to Dicks as the primary proponents of object relations marital theory. They draw upon and integrate the earlier work of Fairbairn, Klein, Bion, Ogden, Racker, and Zinner, as well as that of Dicks, to, at last, offer us a clear, helpful summary of the often invoked, but almost as often misunderstood, process of projective identification and its role in unconscious marital life. We'll see that the

Scharffs' careful exploration of projective identification specifies and extends Dicks's beginning work on unconscious marital engagement.

According to the Scharffs, projective identification unfolds in eight steps (Scharff & Scharff, 1991, pp. 55–59): (1) Projection—the projector projects an image of self or object onto the projectee. (2) Object induction—the aspect of the partner to which the projection corresponds, responds affectively to the projected material. (3) Introjective identification—the partner increasingly identifies with the projection. (4) Transformation by the object—the partner transforms the now-accepted projection according to his or her own personality and history. (5) Valence of the object—when parts of the partner's psychic structure seem strongly consistent with the projection, he or she will more readily accept it. If I have an unconscious conviction of fault—for instance, I feel I'm a nag like my mother—I readily accept the role of the blamed one. (6) Complementary and concordant identification—a part of the *self-image* or the *object image* may be projected and identified with. In the case of an object image, we call the identification complementary, and in the case of a self-image, concordant. For example, a man has a punishing father. If he projects this object onto his wife, he may see her as his critical parent (complementary identification). But if he projects his cowering self onto his wife, he may experience her as frightened and timid, his reaction toward his father (concordant identification). (7) Introjective identification—the self reidentifies with the projected self or object image he now sees in the other. In other words, "identification," in the term *projective identification,* refers to the partner identifying with the projected material but *also* to the projector reidentifying with what he has expelled. (8) Mutual projective identification—even as he projects, the partner also receives and transforms projections from his spouse, so the process becomes mutual, circular, and continuous.

As we carefully study these eight stages of projective identification, important conclusions tumble forth. First, this process shows us that marital pairs change one another. The mechanism creates or recreates the inner world of each within the marital pair. The husband projects his angry mother onto his wife, and she accepts it as a complementary identification. Now she really does feel angry. An affect has been inserted into one marital partner, perhaps absent previously. When the husband accuses her of anger, his observation is correct, even though he has projected that anger onto her in the first place.

Now we must ask the question of why people seem so prone to engage in the process of projective identification. Ogden (1982, pp. 21–24) helpfully outlines four functions of projective identification: (1) Projective identification as a defense—projective identification creates psychological distance from the unwanted, disavowed parts of the self. (2) Projective identification as a way of communicating—projective identification provides a method through which feelings like one's own become induced in the other person, which the other then identifies with, leading to a sense of being understood. (3) As a level of object relations, projective identification represents relating to another object, although only a partly separate one. (4) As a means of psychological change, projective identification becomes a method through which I can watch another wrestle with my own feelings in a slightly different fashion than I do, and I can identify with that person and reinternalize that new process. This last point carries particular importance for us, because a client can project feelings into the therapist and gain psychological growth by identifying with the therapist and with the manner in which he or she struggles with what began initially as the client's own conflicts. I add a fifth function of projective identification. The mechanism can embody a way of telling a story from the past. One partner treats the other with harsh condescension, so that the latter can understand the difficult childhood of the former.

At this point we also need to consider why projective identification takes place in families much more than elsewhere. Remember, we occasionally fight with our neighbors, but we more often fight with our spouse, because our neighbor usually does not stimulate our repressed, libidinal and anti-libidinal, object relations, that is, hoped-for expressions of love, fear of control, and so on.

Although we're studying couple interaction here, we can readily see that projective identification almost inevitably involves the children in the family as well. Jill Scharff (1989) has edited a book summarizing her research and that of David Scharff, Roger Shapiro, John Zinner, and others, demonstrating that psychopathology in adolescents, particularly the borderline syndrome, may represent the acting out of parental projections by the teenager. If a father cannot resolve his own conflicts over independence, he may project the negative side of those struggles onto his separating adolescent and may view that teenager as evil for wishing to individuate. The unfortunate adolescent identifies with the projection and acts out his or her wishes for independence along antisocial, self-destructive avenues, such as failing in school, becoming promiscuous, or abusing drugs. Thus the mechanism of projective identification in the family has created, in large part, the borderline syndrome in the adolescent. These researchers found this dynamic to predominate in the families whose "borderline" adolescents were hospitalized at the NIMH residential unit in the Washington, D.C., area. Samuel Slipp (1984) makes many of the same observations about the role of projective identification in the development of psychopathology in teenagers and young adults.

The Scharffs do not emphasize this corollary to their thinking, but the primitivity of the projected material clearly represents a critical factor in the marriage. For example, if the repressed anti-libidinal objects threaten constant persecution within one partner, then any marriage that this person enters would have to contain great protective distance, were it a possibility at all. Or, if the partner suffers from repressed libidinal objects that threaten abandonment, a clinging marriage seems the only arrangement that could readily operate, before treatment has resolved some of the pressure from these repressed objects.

We can now observe that the attraction of couples in Subsystem 3 may represent an unconscious attempt to solve in the marriage some difficult prior inner conflict with repressed libidinal and anti-libidinal objects. Put otherwise, pairs become attracted when their mutual projective identifications complement one another, a central insight contributed by Dicks and the Scharffs. A woman whose father deserted the family, the abandoning libidinal parent object par excellence, becomes drawn to a protective man. If this man also provides flexibility and support, Dicks would predict relatively smooth sailing in the marriage, providing Subsystems 1 and 2 fit. However, the fatherless woman may also have enjoyed a measure of personal autonomy without parental control, and if her new husband, initially idealized, also becomes dominant as well as protective, the honeymoon could jolt to an abrupt end. Here the husband initially seems nurturing, unlike the father deserter. Thus we have an example of Hypothesis (1A), the object appears to embody the opposite of the absent parent, but then he ignores his wife's genuine welfare, though in very different fashion from her father. He doesn't desert, but he strives to control.

At this point we can see again how our object relations model of marital interaction can explicate matches that work, as well as those that don't. Not all unconscious bargains seem fated to unresolvable conflict. For example, a woman whose angry mother and distant father left her with an inner, repressed self object, suffused with low self-esteem, meets an outgoing, enthusiastic man, but one burdened with a repressed, suffocating, tantalizing, but ultimately frustrating libidinal mother. (Our lady, fleeing her disappointing parents, has grown into an independent, if not altogether trusting, woman.) Relieved that she does not attempt to envelop him, her new boyfriend can offer her the warmth that she craves. This scenario provides us with an illustration of Dicks's Hypothesis (1A) that functions constructively—partners choose each other to fulfill a role opposite to the repressed libidinal and anti-libidinal objects, and here the unconscious bargain seems to work for both.

THE FIGHT ACCORDING TO OBJECT RELATIONS THEORY

As we explore and try to apply our fresh understanding of object relations psychology to couple therapy, we can begin to view the repetitive fight in

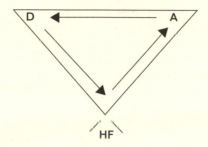

FIGURE 2.2. The Triangle of Conflict

something like its true complexity. Let's return to the triangle of conflict, introduced in chapter 1, to see how object relations theory deepens our grasp of this important schematic.

The anxiety pole (A) represents the fear that repressed libidinal and anti-libidinal objects will return to reject, threaten, guilt-induce, shame, or persecute the self. The D pole represents the response to those objects. Usually, though not always, the mechanisms of projective identification now come into play. Let's again study a case from Johnson (1999). Sixty-year-old Clara suffers from cancer and senses abandonment by her husband, Len, of the same age, who won't talk with her about her fears but attempts to minimize her anxiety. Len once again controls Clara and downplays her concern over the cancer. Clara defends herself through anger. Her anxiety at rejection embodies her (A) pole and her fury the defense pole (D). Now we enter the realm of the hypothetical. Perhaps Len had a critical, unsatisfiable mother who exasperated him. He projects this object onto his wife. Clara then experiences that projection and identifies with it, and she becomes all the more overwrought. Len's expectation appears confirmed. The anxiety that he can never win with his wife-mother overwhelms him (A). He bursts into fury (D). The fight is on. Clara shouts that he's never been able to help her. His identification with his unsatisfiable mother's projection now completely takes him over. He unravels still further. We progress to rounds two and three.

Clara's hidden feeling or hope (HF), that she can receive support and acceptance when she's in need, represents her lifelong wish that her libidinal objects would change and no longer desert her. Len has bitterly disappointed this hope and thus her desperation. Len's hidden feeling (HF), the wish that he could offer real love and have it warmly received, becomes similarly dashed, lending more frustration to the already disheartening fight. The projective identifications of the pair have locked into an automatic, repetitive, retaliatory battle grip. Otherwise reasonable, competent people find themselves screaming accusations at one another that they literally did not know (unconscious) lurked inside. The fight occurs at the point at which each has endured his or her repressive split. Len cannot master his old fear that he can never help Clara or any other woman, and Clara can't trust that he, or any man, will support her.

The Scharffs' theory of marital interaction places projective identification at its core, and their grasp of this central mechanism helps us understand intimate contact and intimate conflict in new dimensions. In a moment we'll observe how the Scharffs' metapsychological theory translates into their technique of marital therapy. First, though, I'll illustrate the added perspective that object relations theory offers us as we study the array of short-term couple treatment approaches.

AN OBJECT RELATIONS PERSPECTIVE ON THE SPECTRUM OF COUPLE THERAPY TECHNIQUES

We can begin to see that this object relations model of marital interaction allows us to reanalyze the foundations of a number of couple treatment schools that I mentioned in chapter 1. For instance, if the reader, like myself, experiences discomfort with systems such as Christensen and Jacobson's behavioral couple therapy, which depend mostly on coaching the couple toward more constructive behavior, perhaps the reasons for our uneasiness have now become apparent. Although the couple tries to cooperate with the exercises, the partners also inevitably trade, at an unconscious level, significant numbers of self and object images, projected, partially identified with and reintrojected. For example, if I suffer from a repressed image of a withholding father, it may prove awfully difficult for me to believe that my husband will deal fairly with me in any behavioral exchange task. Christensen and Jacobson confront this problem, somewhat successfully, apparently, by incorporating trust-building exercises as the first phase of their new integrative couple therapy (Lawrence, Eldridge, Christensen, & Jacobson, 1999), but I still wonder whether many couple treatments can progress far without some exploration of the repressed libidinal and anti-libidinal objects that each partner brings into the relationship and for which the marriage was the intended cure.

Moreover, it appears possible that a general object relations conceptual framework underlies most schools of couple treatment, however unacknowledged by the authors. For example, when Hendrix (Luquet & Hendrix, 1998) and his coworkers introduce their validation exercise to their clients, in which they teach the partners to listen in uninterrupted fashion to each other, they attempt to reverse the influence of the repressed objects, although, of course, Hendrix would never use this descriptive language. In the exercise, both members of the pair can experience in real life that their primary object can listen to and empathize with their position, not act like the old object and rebut or dismiss.

As I mentioned, Christensen and Jacobson's trust-building exercise carries the same thrust. Before they begin their social learning interventions, they attempt to neutralize the influence of previous uncooperative objects by introducing the trust-building sessions. When the solution-focused experts Steven Friedman and Eve Lipchick (1999) help the couple search for an "exception" to the old pattern, they could almost communicate, "See, the repressed frustrating objects do not have to reign supreme with you. You can solve a problem together constructively, without regressing into shrieking, mutual recriminations." As I have already explained, it appears to me that Susan Johnson tries to restructure the affective responses to old objects by helping her couples understand and empathize with each partner's present feelings, but Johnson rarely focuses explicitly on the childhood objects.

The thrust of my discussion in this chapter implies the one general criticism I have of some of these other methods of short-term couple therapy. They appear to assume and hope that each pair will function mostly within Dicks's Subsystem 2. Their methods seem to depend on the ability of the couple, to a large degree, to remain in contact with their conscious mature identities, in order to cooperate in the difficult tasks of the therapy. However, Subsystem 3 exists and will inevitably enter the room. To a greater or lesser extent, these other models do not account for Subsystem 3, and I think the unconscious transactions, if unacknowledged, can subvert the therapy. Projected mistrust, infantile anger, and the need for control often make their appearance, and I hypothesize that when these alternative models fail, they do so because of undetected turbulence within Subsystem 3.

Although this reanalysis of contemporary couple therapy approaches remains cursory, we can begin to see that couple therapists ultimately do not disagree very much about the generic problem in marital therapy. Preconceived expectations influence the marital interaction in destructive ways, and the therapy needs to address and mitigate those expectations. The theoretical explanation of the origin of these preconceived sets differs markedly from system to system, of course, which, in turn, dictates very different technical approaches to facilitate change in the couple.

MARITAL TREATMENT FROM THE OBJECT RELATIONS PERSPECTIVE: THE CONTRIBUTION OF DICKS AND THE SCHARFFS

Dicks's Model of Treatment

Dicks's format for couple treatment remains somewhat difficult to describe, because his approach evolved into different forms over time. In addition, for the most part, Dicks illustrated his treatment model through his case studies and stopped short of spelling it out completely in any one place. I will summarize my understanding of his therapy strategy, relying as much as possible on his concrete examples.

Dicks offered one or two evaluation sessions at the start. Historically, he originally began his work in a format in which one therapist interviewed the couple, usually in separate individual sessions. Later on, he usually arranged these evaluation meetings as joint interviews (JIs—in his terminology), which included both members of the couple. Sometimes one or sometimes two therapists led the meetings. In the evaluation sessions Dicks concentrated on the recurrent conflict between the partners and tried to formulate an object relations, psychodynamic understanding of the case, using his three hypotheses as possible starting points. For instance, was this partner chosen to repeat the idealized role of a parent and had that partner failed in this expectation?—Hypothesis 1.

Following the evaluation sessions, Dicks made the decision of whether to offer the couple marital treatment. He did not specify the length of the proposed therapy to the clients, although he implicitly planned that the treatment would last 1 to 2 years of weekly meetings. It appears that Dicks did not extend treatment to a significant number of his original referrals. He apparently declined therapy to at least half of his potential caseload. Many of these clients he referred to individual treatment, and others did not continue in the marital work for a variety of reasons. In fact, because of practical necessity, many of Dicks's therapies seemed shorter than he had planned. Although his outcome statistics remain confusing, at least to me, he may have treated a number of couples in less than 20 sessions per year, for 1 or 2 years, thus meeting today's definition of short-term couple therapy, whatever his original intent.

As I just noted, Dicks's evaluation and treatment format changed over time. As his approach developed, he used more and more JIs, in which he alone, or he with a co-therapist, treated the couple conjointly. Various experts at the time, apparently including Balint and Ackerman, warned against this joint arrangement of including both members of the marital pair as too combustible (Nichols & Schwartz, 1998), but Dicks persevered and thus invented what we recognize as today's psychodynamic marital therapy.

What did Dicks actually do in his evaluation and treatment hours? In the first two sessions he delved into the patient's childhood and marital history to form working hypotheses to understand the present conflict. He then began to draw parallels between the individuals' childhood conflicts and their present marital distress, and he offered these interpretations remarkably early, usually in the first few meetings. For instance, in the second joint interview with a 45-year-old couple, Dicks interprets a battle for control based on internalized objects from childhood. The wife tries to "improve" the husband, as her father had her, by inspiring her intellectual interests as a child. The husband resents her attempts at control, withdraws, and becomes sarcastic with his children and impotent with his wife. Here, Dicks presents us with a clear example of Hypothesis (1) operating within Subsystem 3. The husband fails to live up to the idealized father image (pp. 243–244).

Dicks did not coach his couples. He refused to offer practical advice and relied on clarification and interpretation as his exclusive treatment interventions. When the clients sought his counsel, he pursued the transference meaning of the request. Why didn't the pair trust their own opinions and resources? Dicks's classically analytic stance in this regard differs from my approach and from those of many contemporary couple therapists, save the Scharffs. Reading through his cases, we can grasp that although Dicks's orientation deprived the clients of his advice, which they might or might not have used, it does provoke the emergence of the transference material that he sought. For example, did the clients experience him as an omniscient but withholding parent who could help them more, if he only would?

Dicks conceived of his therapy in two parts. Very early, he grasped the central themes underlying the couple conflict. For instance, a woman has endured a mastectomy. How do she and her husband come to terms with this damage to her attractiveness, particularly when, due to his depression, the husband also feels damaged? (p. 248). In their childhoods, each had lost or couldn't identify with a parent, and they furiously attack each other for failing to become the perfect substitute for the lost objects—Hypothesis (1) again. For Dicks, working through represents the second phase of each marital therapy (p. 268). The partners struggled with their aggression, loss, and disappointment, which were identified very early in the treatment—by the therapist, at least. The length of the therapy appears to have been dictated by the vicissitudes of the working through.

Dicks describes these two phases of treatment as follows, and in doing so, he also touches upon the curative function of the therapists.

> There are two chief aspects to long therapy shown in the above case descriptions. One is the rapid emergence of the main dynamic of the dyadic interaction; the other is the working through phase. As in a symphony, the chief themes are stated early, the rest of the movement is occupied with their development and working out, ending with a restatement. It is the working through period which takes the time. In the cases quoted we have tended to give quite major interpretations early, almost in the assessment phase. The objective of an interpretation is to facilitate emergence of fresh material, forgotten or repressed or ignored, and to mobilize feelings hitherto anxiously denied. These are likely, but not certain, to be expressed in transference. If this happens, acting out (in mood, words, or actions) outside the consulting room diminishes and

the JI (Joint Interview) becomes now the main arena of conflict while the actual life of the couple improves, and the two personalities also feel better. This can be seen in the last record; the couple report better relations but have tense angry sessions with us. The therapist(s) thus becomes the catalyst and mediator and also serves as a new, more adult, transitional object to be internalized. Apart from his function as a symbolic object first feared and idealized, then denigrated or attacked and finally seen more realistically, the actual job of the therapist is quite repetitive: to reinforce the early interpretations by further glosses, by reminders of what had already been said, using different words or new variants of the older material. For a time he becomes a "counter-dyad," the dyad's joint auxiliary reality ego assimilating the meanings of what they externalize towards each other and towards him. He feeds it back to them as interpretations and reinterpretations. (pp. 267–268)

Dicks has just shared with us as complete a picture of his psychoanalytic object relations couple therapy as I can find. Carefully rereading this passage, we note that Dicks has incisively defined the role of the couple therapist within his system. The therapist functions along at least four dimensions. (1) At the beginning of the treatment, he or she actively and exclusively works to understand the unconscious object relationship conflict in the couple. Without question, couple treatment for Dicks stands as a focal therapy, and the focus will always fall on the unconscious object relations bargain gone awry. (2) The therapist will interpret feelings, memories, and assumptions previously forgotten or ignored, which bring fresh data into the therapy. (3) In this way, the therapist serves as a catalyst for activity, but he or she also becomes a transitional object whom the partners internalize as they struggle to confront their unconscious lives in more adult ways. (In chapters 5, 6, and 7, we'll see examples of how couples productively use the therapist as a transitional object but in a short-term treatment format.) (4) The therapist becomes the object of projections by the couple. He or she takes in the projected material, reacts to it (countertransference), and offers it back to the clients as a clarification or an interpretation. We can apply object relationship theory to the interaction within the couple but also between the couple and the therapist. Please note that Dicks functions here as a classical psychoanalyst, in that he apparently uses interpretation of unconscious material as his primary, almost exclusive, method of intervention. We will return to this therapist job description at important junctures later in the book. We will ascertain whether we should amend it, as we study more and more couples in subsequent chapters and gain greater understanding of the change processes in this kind of treatment.

Dicks also gives us several clues about how to fashion a model to undertake couple work in a shorter format, although at the time he had no such goal. He tells us, first of all, that we require, early on, a veridical assessment of the underlying object relations themes, which roughly corresponds to the exploration of the triangle of focus and the triangle of conflict in the five-step model. This assessment need not approach perfection, but we have to center our formulation in the right areas at least. We can refine the understanding of the object relations bargain as we continue. Dicks then hints that the differences in shorter- or longer-term models will come during Phase 2, working through, parallel to Steps 4 and 5 of our model. The length of the working-through phase will vary a great deal from couple to couple. The more the therapist can help the partners to take on this task themselves, during and after the therapy, it follows that the more likely is a shorter and possibly a more successful treatment. If we hope to practice object relations couple therapy within a briefer format, the onus falls on the practitioner to devise active intervention techniques in the working-through phase to shorten it without undermining its power. In the balance of the book I'll suggest and illustrate a number of those techniques.

The Scharffs' Model of Therapy

Now I will try to piece together the Scharffs' model of couple treatment—a similar one to that of Dicks, though still unique in important ways. As I summarize their approach, I can contrast the two and later formulate ways in which we might adapt these models to a shorter-term format.

The Scharffs use a different language, but their treatment approach, like Dicks's, centers on the concept of projections within the couples. The Scarffs do not make use of Dicks's three hypotheses to explain unconscious conflict, but they do emphasize and reemphasize that the couple represents a small group in which each member of the pair twists and turns to induce the other into carrying important unconscious aspects of the relationship.

In chapter 7 of their book, for example, David Scharff describes a couple in which the husband utilizes passive-aggressive defenses, particularly silence and denial, to avoid control at the hands of his primary objects. He projects the hostility in the relationship onto his wife. She consciously rejects the projection but ends up feeling frustrated, shut out, and defensively compelled to criticize her husband, fighting off his projection. Once again, the reader can see that these complicated maneuvers within the couple rob the pair of spontaneity and intimacy. Equally clearly, the underlying meaning of the fight and the resulting alienation remain murky to the couple. The therapist's job is to make the unconscious conscious and to help both members of the pair grapple with their own conflicted affects *without* the necessity of projecting these onto the partner. When this man can speak up and voice his anger directly, he, his wife, and the therapist can understand it and deal with it. In other words, when the therapist interprets this projective identification process, the couple experiences some immediate and, often, some long-lasting relief.

The Scharffs use the analysis of their own countertransference as the principal method of investigation into these unconscious transactions of the couple. In the previously mentioned pair, David Scharff feels the passive-aggressive anger of the husband as he smiles and looks at the therapist in his helpless, "What can I do?" fashion (p. 144). Once the therapist feels the anger in his countertransference reaction, he can interpret this to the client. I'll explain more shortly about how the Scharffs pursue countertransference analysis.

As the therapy progresses, the Scharffs and their couples come closer and closer to the basic anxiety against which the defensive projections in their relationship protect them. Here the Scharffs find the concept of the "because clause" particularly helpful—(1) a required relationship defends against (2) an avoided relationship, because these arrangements both seem preferable to (3) a calamity (p. 115). The couple just mentioned has worked out an arrangement in which the passive-aggressive husband forever rebels and the wife remains all reasonable and all good (the required relationship). This avoids the direct expression of anger on both their parts (the avoided relationship) and the ultimate calamity that their anger would explode the marriage.

Like Dicks, the Scharffs explain that the basic themes, captured within the projective identifications, appear very early in the treatment, and the bulk of the therapy entails analyzing layer after layer of resistance. The twice-weekly format allows the Scharffs to put consistent pressure on the resistances and to watch carefully as the characteristic object relations transactions come to the surface.

The Scharffs, like Dicks, use interpretation almost immediately in the treatment, often in the first session. For instance, "Each of you is inhibiting the other's development in order to avoid anxiety and aggression" (the Scharffs, first session, p. 96) or (to paraphrase) "You [the wife] have to be the good one because you both agree that your angry husband is the bad one. If you became bad, too, there would be no goodness left" (the Scharffs, third session, p. 136).

The Scharffs center their approach on projective identification and on countertransference investigations much more explicitly than does Dicks. Dicks's treatments appear shorter and less intense. He never met couples twice weekly, for example. Otherwise, the two models, although explained in different language and undertaken in contrasting cultures and historical periods, seem perhaps surprisingly similar.

Let's look in more detail at the techniques that Dicks and the Scharffs use to drive their therapies. We'll start with their opening moves. In their case reports, Dicks and the Scharffs always begin with a discussion of the recurrent conflict. We note once again that the reason for the stunning repetitiveness of the fight has become obvious. The repressed libidinal and anti-libidinal objects in each partner remain frozen in time within the unconscious. When each partner begins to sense anxiety about the behavior of the other or when external stress impinges, the characteristic projective identifications and attendant defenses become activated, and the fight enters its opening phases.

In contrast to Dicks and to myself, the Scharffs do not commence with a direct exploration of the clients' history. They start with the clients' associations about their conflict, but they remain intensely interested in history with past objects, although they wait patiently for the details of these relationships to emerge in the natural course of the treatment. They also make immediate use of transference and countertransference fantasies and of dreams—more about these techniques later. Both Dicks and the Scharffs, well-trained psychoanalysts, knew what they sought. All three have a well-worked-out theory of therapy into which they quickly begin to insert the pieces of the puzzle as these emerge from their clients.

Their case reports, inevitably incomplete, seem to show us something quite surprising at this point. I would have expected the clients to respond with denial and confusion; after all, transactions with their internalized objects have undergone repression for good, and still relevant, reasons. The frightening, competitive father (anti-libidinal object) or the titillating but rejecting mother (libidinal object) reactivate painful experiences, shameful or denigrating to the self. The child never can best his father or entirely possess his mother. He can only feel defeated or rejected. One of the Scharffs' patients, for instance, isolated from her unavailable parents, engaged in sex play with her older brothers, behavior that excited and partly satisfied her, as well as plunging her into sickening guilt and shame. This unfortunate history inevitably complicated her sexual relationship with her husband. Will she really hasten to divulge these experiences to her husband and to her therapist?

In fact, Dicks's, the Scharffs', and my clients do respond quite rapidly to our object relations interpretations. At first, many may seem confused, but when clients are pressed, the material often readily spills forth. They acknowledge anger at a heretofore idealized father, hateful competition with an also-loved sibling, or identification with a controlling mother. Of course, these revelations do not take place immediately or with great release of affect each time, but within a few sessions we find ourselves in the midst of them. In other words, the affect and the unconscious relationship assumptions become real enough, and present enough, for the clients and the therapist to work with the material.

The role of psychotherapy for married couples becomes clearer. Dicks and the Scharffs tell us that the therapist must help the partners to accept

their own difficult self-images and to project them less or, at least, to acknowledge when such projections may be afoot. We can readily discover
this central principle of object relations couple therapy throughout their
case reports. The split-off object relations and the attendant mechanism of
projective identification reside in the unconscious. The repetition compulsion toward the fight operates because each member of the pair continually
attempts to recreate, to communicate, and to master that old world of objects. To Dicks and the Scharffs, the principal role of the therapist is to use
interpretation, clarification, and counterprojection to help clients lift their
repression, to confront the relationship with the past objects, and to understand the interactions that this relationship compels clients to recreate in
the present. In each intervention the therapist strives to render the unconscious object relations more conscious.

If this represents the object relations model of couple treatment, then
the hallmark of successful therapy, in its closing stages, arrives when we
observe both members of the couple spontaneously illustrating that they
acknowledge more of their unconscious object relationship history. For
example, "Maybe that's my problem, maybe that's my mother, maybe you
aren't mad at me after all." When Wile attempts to construct a "shared
platform," upon which his couples can exchange their honest feelings of
jealousy, deprivation, competitiveness, or anger, he tries, in object relations
terms, to create a context in which projection becomes less necessary.

Resistance

Naturally, the repressed object relations do not break out into the open in
any complete way. Now we confront the problem of resistance—to my
mind, the single most important therapeutic issue in all couple therapy.
What if the partners do not buy what the therapist has to sell? Return to
the previous examples. The wife from the Scharffs' case, in discussing her
reluctance to be the "bad one," could have responded, "Well, my husband
is the bad one. What else can I do?" Or, even less helpfully, "He's not that
bad. I guess I'll try more patience." Then the conflict goes back under-
ground, and even if the partners enjoy short-term improvement, the basic
interaction of their unconscious worlds remains unchanged.

Resistance quickly becomes an equally important problem in other
types of couple therapy. What if one of Christensen and Jacobson's pairs do
not practice the behavioral exchange exercises at home or fail to see the
point of them in the first place? What if Hendrix's couples cannot genuinely validate each partner's experience? "So, your mother was critical of
you. I'm not, so what's the problem?" What if Wile's people cannot learn
to speak out their feelings honestly or if they can't stop arguing with Wile

about his rendition of those conflicts? I find that in the majority, short-term couple therapists seem disingenuous when they discuss, or fail to discuss, resistance in their clients. Understandably, they have to focus on proving that their method can work briefly. They have little time to explain what to do when the clients resist the method. In my experience, couples inevitably do resist, to a greater or lesser extent. Dicks and, particularly, the Scharffs discuss resistance and how to deal with it at great length.

The Scharffs confront the resistance as Freud did, by making it the focus of their treatment and attempting to gently, but firmly, understand it in greater and greater depth. Why can't the previously mentioned wife bear the experience that sometimes she could become the bad one? What in her history, or in her firmly held sense of herself, prevents this? If she occasionally becomes the bad one, can her husband tolerate this? If not, why not? As we review the Scharffs' cases, we see that, gradually, both members of the couple can allow themselves to consider more and more of these initially distressing object relations possibilities. As the treatment continues, their psychological life becomes wider. The longer and more intense the therapy, logically, the greater the chance of this desirable process deepening. In a moment I'll discuss the particular problems with resistance in short-term couple therapy.

We can read and write entire informative books on resistance, so my continued discussion of it remains foreshortened, but, to me, three important sets of circumstances seem to influence whether the resistance will sink the treatment. First and most crucially, as mentioned, the couple brings a level of collective resistance to the treatment. If this looms too large, no intervention will work. We'll discuss this point at length in later chapters, when we study Prochaska's stages of change model.

Second, the training and the experience of the therapist play an important role, although some pairs do spontaneously flee treatment, even with senior therapists like the Scharffs. In studying brief therapy, Hans Strupp (1981) found that the training and background of therapists, in comparison to "naturally helpful" but untrained college faculty, could bring about better therapeutic outcome, especially with less-disturbed clients.

How do experienced therapists confront resistance? When we read and reread the Dicks and Scharff reports, we get to know veteran practitioners who patiently, confidently weather the resistance and who continue applying their method without losing heart. This neutral, nonjudgmental, but steadfast attitude certainly seems to affect the clients. The tone of the reports indicates that the couples feel "held," understood, and less loathsome about and frightened of, their transactions with their inner repressed objects and with those of their spouse. This psychological message of the therapist appears optimistic, that he or she can calmly understand the partners and accept their struggle and that, in time, they will come to understand it

themselves. The "in time" clause resounds particularly loudly for brief therapists, and we'll return later in this chapter, and in subsequent ones, to show
how we might adapt the object relations approach to a shorter scope.

The third factor rendering the analysis of resistance possible has to do
with the nature of the repressed object relationships themselves. The pain
and shame bound in the repression seek acknowledgment. Freud has shown
us that the nature of the human condition dictates that the repressed material cries out for expression. Previously, this expression has assumed indirect, guilt-laden forms—the essence of psychological conflict and projective
identification—but in therapy, the participants gradually can experience
the comfort and greater freedom of movement that occur when repression
lifts. Increasing intimacy in marriage then becomes an actual reality for the
couples that they can see and feel. If we could not count on this self-rein-
forcing drive toward growth, clearly, couple therapy, or any therapy, would
remain an impossibility. Now let's examine resistance of a special type,
transference and countertransference.

Couple Transference to the Therapist

Up to this point, my discussion has taken on the complicated transactions
between the partners at the level of their unconscious repressed objects and
views of self. Indeed, these comprise the sub rosa fit within the couple and
also inevitably become the battleground for the partners' recurrent fight.
However, in therapy, the couple becomes a threesome. Each member of the
pair experiences transference to the therapist. Inevitably, the projective identification of the couple will not stop in the marriage; it will find expression
in some form toward the therapist, a second intimate object relationship.
In this way the pair forms an unconscious couples transference to the therapist, both as a couple and as specific individuals. The most obvious of these
transferences toward the therapist and one that, in my experience, arises in
nearly every couple treatment occurs when the pair places the therapist in
the role of parental arbiter. Where does the fault lie? Whose behavior seems
incorrigible to the therapist? Does the therapist agree with me that my husband is paranoid and impossibly controlling?

Many other transferences can, and do, come and go. The couple may
experience the therapist as the permitter of pleasure or as the punisher of
pleasure as a competitor seeking to steal one or the other member of the
pair, or as a representative of the adult world, looking down judgmentally
at the partners' immaturity and dysfunction. Therapists must clearly keep
on watch for these special forms of resistance and make use of the valuable
material they communicate. Moreover, we can glimpse the possibility that
the therapist could use the transference to push one or both members of the

couple toward greater growth. This potential source of influence becomes all important when we're attempting to work in time-managed formats, as we'll observe later in this chapter and in chapters 5, 6, and 7.

Therapist Countertransference

We must remember that projective identification changes the projectee. He or she experiences feelings and thoughts induced by the projector. Therefore, countertransference, the unconscious reactions of the therapist, will inevitably occur in this projective identification melange. Dicks concentrates only a little on the countertransference reactions of the therapist, though reading between the lines of his reports, we can pick up that in many of his subtle insights about the couple, he probably uses his countertransference responses as first clues.

The Scharffs, by contrast, make countertransference the center of their couple therapy technique. They feel that the only direct contact available with the unconscious messages from the client's world comes from the therapist's unconscious reaction to what the members of the pair verbalize, how they say it, what their bodies express, and how their silences and glances communicate. In other words, the therapist's countertransference reactions to the clients, at many levels, become crucial data.

For instance, in an early evaluation session, David Scharff feels discomfort as the husband angrily criticizes his wife for her apparent judgmental disdain. Previously, Scharff's attempts to engage the wife about her anger have fallen flat. She bristles and withdraws. The therapist feels stymied here and a little angry himself. In his helplessness and discomfort, two important observations leap into his mind. First, he identifies with the husband, who can never seem to approach his wife in the right way. But Scharff also feels the husband's reluctance to confront his wife because he understands her discomfort over her anger. She hates becoming an angry person. Clearly, the therapist has happened upon two important, highly significant unconscious transactions that beleaguer this couple. The wife experiences shame at her anger, and the husband can't confront her because of this and because of his own defensiveness. This therapy will turn on following how the anger card gets passed back and forth between the members of this couple (pp. 140–144).

How do therapists listen for the unconscious meaning, though? A moment's reflection clarifies that therapists must engage their unconscious with that of the client to understand the meaning of the communication, so therapists must first clear their conscious and unconscious mind as a receiving field and allow the client to register messages on that relatively clear slate. Here David Scharff introduces the concept of "negative capability," an open state in which the therapist absorbs the patient's affects and un-conscious object relationships in order to grasp them without actively search-ing for a concise definition of these phenomena.

I have come to a similar conclusion and have found that not looking directly at the clients often abets this process (Donovan, 1989). The thera-pist can then listen for the metacommunications from the couple without becoming drawn into the immediacy of the fight and of the present drama of the couple's bodily and verbal interaction. When I am working this way, I hunt for affect, affect, affect, but always affect tied to objects. For ex-ample, a 41-year-old businessman seems extremely controlling and argu-mentative toward his 32-year-old attorney wife. Does he feel compelled to repeat here a repressed relationship with a parent?—a relationship in which he suffered as the belittled child? If so, has his earlier humiliation at the feet of his father been so strong that he must now destroy his marriage to even the score? As I absorb the client's affect states, I feel the wife's humiliation as her husband belittles her, and I also experience the desperation of the husband's defensive compulsion to criticize.

This search for the affect that ties the present relationship to the origi-nal repressed ones depends on the openness of the therapist's conscious and unconscious presence. A potential difficulty now arises. What if the therapist's unconscious field remains encumbered by any number of unanalyzed personal assumptions or projections? Jill Scharff, for example, meets a couple in which the wife dresses and speaks like a New Age, overly aggressive, termagant—quite the contrast to her more sedate surgeon hus-band. Jill Scharff analyzes her uncomfortable reaction, a judgmental thought that the client didn't act or talk like a doctor's wife (p. 111), "hardly an appropriate wife for a doctor." What if Dr. Scharff were unable to acknowl-edge and place her thought into perspective? We can predict that this therapy might go quickly off track, with the therapist attempting to tone down this garish, somewhat foul-mouthed, unsophisticated lady and defend her smooth, more accomplished husband, who also, I might add, is a physician like the therapist. Dr. Scharff would miss the crucial fact that the wife car-ries the unmetabolized aggression for this couple.

The Scharffs observe that to check overly personalized countertrans-ference intrusions, the therapist requires a past personal therapy, leading to a less judgmental attitude toward the self and toward his or her own inter-nal objects. They add that self-supervision, supervision with colleagues, and review of work through writing and presentation also represent ways of exploring countertransference. Some of these avenues of self-analysis stand open to all of us, and some do not; we can't all publish our work, for example. But I find implicit in these instructions the need to constantly scan our internal reactions, as we sit with clients and think about them before and after meetings, to correct our prejudgments and search for helpful clues to the meanings of personal fantasies stimulated in us by the clients. When agencies work as a team, and one or both members of the couple participate in contemporaneous individual therapy with fellow staff members, I find the reports of colleagues who treat the individual partners helpful in gauging my reaction to some of the couple material.

The Scharffs have extended and refined Dicks's pioneering work, particularly in their study of projective identification and in using counter-transference exploration. But at the core, both Dicks and the Scharffs present quite similar approaches to couple therapy. I'll try to integrate and briefly summarize their methods. Both observe that conflicted, repressed object relations lie at the center of the marital conflict, Dicks's Subsystem 3. These therapists appear to focus their theory of change on the need to make the unconscious conscious. They take as their primary goal, in other words, to support their clients in lifting repression. These clinicians use one basic method to achieve this end—interpretation, often interpretation based on material brought to light by the countertransference. Dicks and the Scharffs, then, seem to represent psychoanalysts in pure form, because they rely quite exclusively on interpretation of the unconscious and do not coach or otherwise overtly influence clients to drive the therapy.

But the picture becomes more complicated. Dicks introduces, though does not pursue very far, the idea that the *therapist* might play an active role as an object in the treatment. He suggests that the therapist acts as a "transitional object," whose function the clients internalize, or as a "counter-dyad," who responds to the couple's projections with realistic feedback. These observations imply that therapy may not depend entirely on the power of interpretation but that the therapist exerts additional influence through his or her presence and activity as an object.

We may also have to admit the possibility that interpretation may have particular limitations as a mechanism of intervention in a brief couple therapy. Many couples or individuals may resist or fail to understand or constructively respond to that interpretation for a number of meetings. Then the curtain may fall on the therapy before the actors have the chance to play productive parts. It follows that in brief object relations couple therapy, the therapist's role as an active object may loom very large, because interpretation alone may have its short-comings.

I have summarized the work of Dicks and the Scharffs at considerable length because they communicate so revealing and so detailed a picture of the unconscious marital transaction in the marriage. They've proved to us that this must represent one important field of operations for couple therapy. They've also spelled out the role of the therapist in that field and illustrated any number of interventions therapists might make within Subsystem 3. I don't think we can proceed to study object relations couple therapy without this kind of complete picture that Dicks and the Scharffs have offered us. How to adapt their long-term intervention models to a shorter-term perspective necessarily becomes the focus for the balance of the book.

SHORT-TERM ADAPTATIONS TO LONG-TERM OBJECT RELATIONS COUPLE THERAPY

Any number of challenges abound for the intrepid clinician who attempts to reformulate the longer-term object relations models to the requirements of briefer work. Where resides the point of entry into this complex problem? Dicks points out that couple therapy consists of two phases, assessment and working through. No one can instantaneously evaluate a couple, of course, so we cannot contract this first phase very radically. We'll have to introduce our alterations in technique mostly in the second phase, confronting and working through the resistance. The shorter the treatment, probably the more necessary therapist activity. Chapter 1 included a summary of some possible techniques, such as actively coaching the couple in more constructive behavior, initially speaking out the partners' lines for them, and including other relevant family members in the treatment. But we can think of additional maneuvers, methods based within object relations theory that also might prove effective.

For example, the five-step model focuses the treatment and points the therapist toward the next move. First, we learn about the object relations history within the triangle of focus; then we push for change in the client's orientation to those objects, past and present. Beyond adopting this or some similar brief treatment model, based on object relations theory, what other general strategies might we pursue to shorten the therapy? First of all, returning to our discussion of the therapist as an object, it seems as if we could attempt to broaden the relationship possibilities between client and therapist and could experiment with assuming different personal stances toward the clients. This action might reassure or support them along specific lines suggested by the history. In other words, we might make precise relationship offers to our clients. I will explain much more about this in a moment. In addition, we could create "enactments" in the sessions, direct confrontations between the partners over their core issues, or we might assign readings and homework to support or challenge the clients in particular planned ways. The reader can quickly perceive that active modifications in techniques, such as the ones I've just mentioned, carry great promise but also can potentially implode in the unconscious of the couple and distort the transference unproductively. I will discuss these positives and negatives as I continue.

How might an active object relations short-term couple therapist actually proceed in the sessions? Searching for and interpreting transference and countertransference data represent important specific technical methods in pursuing object relations couple treatment. But in observing my own work, I find, particularly in shorter therapies, a somewhat different approach more generally helpful. The emergence of distinct transference and countertransference material and the opportunities to interpret that material tend to oscillate in and out of the treatment. Sometimes I can pinpoint important themes in the transference, and sometimes I and my clients draw blanks. Nothing germane seems to come to mind. We need to assume an ever-mindful querying attitude toward particular countertransference phenomena, but I find that I cannot count on precise transference and countertransference reactions, and the accompanying interpretations they suggest, to propel, on their own, a short-term therapy.

The Scharffs and I disagree on this point—probably because they ply their trade in an intensive, often twice-weekly format, and they meet their couples usually for 2 or more years continuously. But the Scharffs also report on cases that move very slowly, and in which the countertransference observations take many weeks or months to focus productively. As brief therapists, many of us don't have the luxury, or probably the temperament, to wait so patiently. (Recently, the Scharffs [1998] and their colleague Michael Stadter [1996] have experimented with using the object relations approach in a brief therapy format for focal issues. To my knowledge, they have not as yet applied this model to brief couple work.)

I have found three reliable methods of active approach that I can use each session: (1) counter-offering a focal relationship; (2) constructing the object relations map; and (3) coaching the clients. In the discussion that follows, I want to clarify that I'm not abandoning the traditional object relations couple approaches that I've just described at some length. I'm adapting those to the requirements of a shorter-term format.

1. Offering a Focal Relationship

As my most consistent therapeutic tool I try to use *empathic inquiry* to help formulate a relationship counter-offer to each partner. Here I try to grasp the exchange extended to me implicitly, by each of the pair, and then make a counter-offer of an interaction that will push the client in a growth-promoting direction. A theory underlies this stance, which I will explicate further on, but let me illustrate the approach first and then the conceptual thinking will make more sense. Marital exchanges, particularly the recurrent fight, can appear fantastically unreasonable, even shocking, right up until the point that we put ourselves in the moccasins of the participants. For example . . .

Mark and Joanne

Fifty-nine-year-old Mark, a short, powerfully built businessman, chronically dissatisfied with his success, joins the ranks of day stock traders. At first he enjoys phenomenal success. He invests his children's college funds and then the profit from the sale of the couple's home. Disaster strikes. The NASDAQ plunges. Forced to liquidate his leveraged positions, he loses $250,000. His wife, Joanne, explodes. He admits his error but does not appear mortified, nor does he swear off day trading. "I'm sorry. I screwed up big time. I learned a lot. It won't happen again, but do I deserve to be in your dog house, and the children's, forever?" This financial debacle drives the warring clients into still another couple therapy.

Speaking of countertransference, I find myself becoming furious with this man who has gambled away family money, not really his, and who seems so reluctant to take responsibility for his actions. In fact, he did do the wrong thing, and his rashness will have long-term consequences for his entire family, to say nothing of his marriage. I can't overlook this, but berating him in any way will tip the balance of the alliance of this just-beginning therapy toward an acute angle, from which it probably could never recover. I must try to recreate the facts and feelings of this crisis from inside his skin, as well as from inside his wife's.

Joanne's father and the husbands of her two sisters, all three successful lawyers, have each apparently amassed significant fortunes in the stock market. Our client, Mark, runs a moderately profitable service business but has never enjoyed and will never enjoy the material success of his in-laws. I also reflect that although short in height, my client is an excellent natural athlete. In his late 50s, he still plays competitive softball several times a week in the summer. Physical exercise represents a good health regimen, but what else might he be trying to prove? As he relates to me, another male of similar age, a professional like his in-laws and also possibly more financially successful than he, he seems competitive, truculent, and defensive. Using my countertransference empathy, I hypothesize that Mark has a conviction of inferiority compensated for in his bristly, provocative style.

Joanne, of the same age, looks roly-poly and somewhat sad. A lock of hair continues to fall across half her face, whose function may be to hide her expressions. Perhaps unfortunately, Joanne works in the business with Mark. She keeps the books and suggests numerous cost-saving strategies, which he always dismisses as unworkable. The provocativeness played out with me stops only when Mark begins to passive-aggressively engage with Joanne in parallel fashion. He meets each observation from her with a countermove, subtly blaming her for some of their various predicaments. She usually bites and shoots back undermining criticism toward him. This appears the destructive interactional pattern, the fight, which has now brought them to the brink of separation and to the counseling.

If I cannot empathize with this thoroughly embattled man, I will have little chance of helping him alter his self-defeating, pugnacious style, his major resistance, and I will not support this couple to break its deadlock. The therapy will fail, and the pair will slip into even greater unhappiness. High stakes!

At least, I can formulate a tentative plan. Mark extends me a relationship offer to fight with him. He invites my criticism, which I know he will smilingly deflect. In my countertransference, I do feel anger with him over his irresponsibility, but a battle now will help none of the three of us. I decide to relate to him by circumventing his defense and attempting to join him in his vulnerability, a particular strategy to deal with a powerful resistance.

Now I begin my empathic questioning and responding. I observe how galling it is to have a rich father-in-law, whose level of wealth I can never reach. Who can, and does, swoop in, a white knight, to repeatedly rescue Mark and his wife from financial crisis. No sale. My client answers that his father-in-law has been lucky in the market, bought IBM early, and now gets most of his stock advice from his barber. "All the worse," I say. "The guy has made big money in stocks, and he didn't even know what he was doing." A glimmer of response from my client. "It's incredibly disheartening to work so hard to keep up, to realize considerable gains and watch them crash," I add. "It's so hard to feel failure once again. A man wants to show that he can do as well for his family as his relatives did for theirs." Of course, most of us never do dramatically succeed in stocks, particularly lately. The successful ones sure do stand out, though, especially if they're your in-laws.

I want to do whatever I can to connect with the defeated part of this warrior man so that he can come to accept some setbacks and not immediately punch at me or at his wife, when we suggest alternatives to his often impulsive schemes. "Even CEOs of large corporations have consultants and seek the advice of boards of directors," I offer, as a gambit to help him accept input from others. I must also give him positive feedback about his tenacity and courage. If Mark cannot grasp that I do genuinely like and respect him, he will never relax his guard and suspend his major defense of provocativeness—his primary impediment to personal change. "You've worked hard in a tough business," I say. Whatever misgivings I may have about some of Mark's behavior, direct interpretation of his strong defenses will ricochet off this man, who appears and acts not unlike a miniature Sherman tank.

At the same time I must offer similar empathy to his despairing wife, or she will conclude, rightly, that I've moved to his side. "How frustrating and frightening it must feel to live shut out, to watch your husband flail after success. You want to help, and each time you feel only rebuff. You're both very angry and with reason. You're both frightened so you lash out."

If I try to bypass the anger and disappointment, they will experience me, correctly, as sentimental and naïve. They know they both feel great pain in this marriage. But if I only get in touch with my countertransference anger and the frustration provoked by this situation, I will fan these affects in my clients even hotter.

When I intervene in this fashion, I use a technique akin to Wile's script writing, employing my empathy to capture and speak out the feelings for each of the partners. If they can follow my lead and begin revealing a little more of themselves, we're in business. If they don't, I can't let my empathy slip but must return to the fight and ask why they cannot move toward more constructive empathy themselves. Now I must stay with the pain, or they will feel judged. Once again, they will assume their familiar roles and be unable to cooperate, unless I can feel with them and touch some wish inside of each to grab for a constructive alternative—in other words, for them to contact some corner of their positive hidden feeling within the triangle of conflict. The slide into frustration, so easy for this couple, represents a journey on which I cannot accompany them.

This treatment, only three sessions old as I present it here, may not succeed for Mark and Joanne. I hope my initial attempts to bond empathetically with them and to counter-offer relationships will see us through to a point where they can contact the repressed objects so central in each of them and so central in their struggle. Already, you, the reader, can detect one method I will use to render this a time-limited treatment. I'm highly participatory. I share much of my empathic reaction to the clients' story directly with them, and I have specific aims in doing so. This approach represents my initial attempt at pushing them to suspend major defenses and more toward deeper and deeper feeling.

A theory of therapy somewhat similar to Dicks's and the Scharffs' underlies this intervention. As the defense lifts, more fresh material and old memories will enter into conscious play for Mark. The repressive barrier becomes more porous, and his need to act out and project his conflicts with internal objects, repeatedly, in the same intense fashion, will diminish. He will have the opportunity to exercise more choice about his behavior with intimates and with strangers. A difference in emphasis between Dicks, the Scharffs, and myself perhaps lies in the qualification that I have not found it necessary for the client to largely become consciously aware of the specific repressed material. Clients only require the experience of greater freedom of movement and openness within. They don't need to understand most of their repressed object relations in detail. We'll investigate this picture of effective psychotherapy more fully in each succeeding chapter.

What does the phrase *relationship counter-offer* really mean? Mark seems ready to fight with me at every turn. This pugnacious style protects his vulnerability, but I won't strike for the bait. Instead, I'll extend him a relationship with a male teammate, a man who understands his insecurity, but I won't call direct attention to it. I could commiserate with him about life's challenges to men who must always seem strong. I do not criticize or confront him but indicate that I think I know what the world is like for him and try to communicate that understanding in my approach to him. I hope that once Mark feels safe with me, he can consider some relaxation of his major defense, truculent aggressiveness. At that point he might construct a behavioral alternative. I've moving into the five-step model here. I've learned something already about his object relations history and certainly about the anxiety → defense dimension within his triangle of conflict. But my relationship offer represents, in some ways, jumping ahead to Step 4. I'm trying to support him to soften these rigid defenses and to become more open to alternative courses of action.

The obvious shortcoming of this approach intrudes when I'm wrong. What if my empathy does not match the inner reaction of the client, and I offer a relationship that unwittingly repeats the transference fear of the client and quickly undermines the therapy? I hope that I've helped to create an open, collegial atmosphere in which one or both partners could correct me, should this occur. But I must remain vigilant for the possibility that I've failed the client, that I'm extending a counterproductive interaction similar to the traumatizing aspects of the negative parental interaction. In this case, the client's worst unconscious fear would have come true (Weiss, 1993). High therapist activity represents the risk I feel I have to take in order to introduce the possibility that we can circumvent the resistance and accomplish a good deal of work in a short time.

The theory behind my countertransference-based relationship interventions derives from James Gustafson's (1981) and Michael Balint's (Balint, Ornstein, & Balint, 1972) earlier work. They, like myself, find that in a shorter-term format, clients often seem unable to use interpretations, particularly transference interpretations, which they receive as perhaps too threatening or too confusing, but they can productively respond to relationship interventions focused on the central conflict. In a famous case, Michael Balint (Balint, Ornstein, & Balint, 1972) allowed the paranoid stationary manufacturer, obsessed with a delusion of his wife's infidelity, to control the therapist and use him as a "sounding board," because the client felt profoundly helpless in his marriage and utterly unable to influence his wife. This relationship transaction with the therapist, in which the client felt powerful and secure, led to a stabilization of his inner state and to a diminution of his paranoid symptoms and his hostile irritability.

My tact in couple therapy often pursues a similar strategy. I contact Mark's vulnerability, demonstrating to him that I, too, have vulnerable feelings, because I can so readily empathize with his. Then I can perhaps help him move out of his fort-like defense of the rebellious adversary, at least long enough to begin some genuine dialogue with Joanne. I'm guessing that any interpretation of his fears of fragility and inadequacy would only provoke him to drop his portcullis even more securely and probably to fire a few arrows over it for good measure.

Following Gustafson and Balint, I'm attempting to reach Mark through a focal relationship offer, guided by my countertransference reaction to his style, and not through focal interpretations, which would call direct attention to the meaning of that style. When we review Dicks's instructions to the therapist, noted earlier, he encourages us to use interpretation with a couple in order to facilitate the expression of "fresh material" and of "feelings hitherto anxiously denied." I have the same aim but try to use a different method to achieve it. I want Mark to relax his defense so that he can remember thoughts and feelings about past objects and can experience new feelings about present objects, but I'm not going to employ only interpretation as my primary means to facilitate that outcome.

2. Constructing the Hypothetical Object Relations Map

At the same time that I formulate my counter-offers to Mark and Joanne, I'm attempting to construct a map of the repressed object relations of this couple, a best-guess guide to the partners' unconscious world, which will dictate my next relationship offers to them and my behavior as I move through the five-step model. So far, I've learned the following: Joanne, the older of three sisters, grew up in an overly protective home dominated by her controlling lawyer father. We've heard nothing, as yet, about her mother, except that she now suffers from end stage Alzheimer's. The mother will prove, no doubt, a central figure in the drama, and I underscore the importance of her anonymity thus far.

I also notice Joanne's anonymity. Hair falling over her face, she diplomatically pulls her punches and keeps intense feeling back. Joanne tells us that "I was allowed to do nothing in adolescence. I escaped at 18, when I went to college in Rhode Island, and I never returned home." From exactly what or whom at home did she escape? From her demeanor and self-presentation, I assess the somewhat overweight, sad-looking Joanne as an intelligent, well-educated, hesitant woman, low in self-esteem but struggling to control a great deal of anger engendered both long ago and in the present. Mark talks nearly nonstop; Joanne speaks very little and then softly. Evidently, her family sat on her. I need to make a relationship move that recognizes her voice as she speaks up in therapy. If I contribute to conditions that silence Joanne, I will repeat the original traumatic family environment, and I will lose my client's participation.

I'm also attempting to piece together Mark's unconscious object relations map. Mark's father owned a variety store in a poor urban section and could never make a success of it. His mother, the more energetic of the two parents, also assisted in the family business and continually criticized her husband's business acumen, apparently an exact parallel to Mark and Joanne's present difficulties. Mark recalls feeling sympathy for his timid father's plight, the object of his mother's daily "suggestions." Mark reports, as well, that his maternal grandmother lived rent-free in the parental home, complaining and criticizing almost constantly. Despite her son-in-law's generosity to her, the grandmother remarked on the day of his death, "None of those Stern men were any good."

What educated forays can I entertain about Mark's repressed inner life? So far, he seems identified with a devalued, helpless father and suffers from an internalized critical mother and an even more undermining grandmother. He uses denial about these negative aspects of his childhood and states that he felt "happy—my parents loved me a lot." We can begin to conclude that Mark's truculent stance probably represents an attempt to counterphobically master his bond with the damaged father, to possibly identify with the aggressor and become an attacker like his mother, or to do both.

Remembering Dicks's three subsystems, I reflect that although of different economic backgrounds, Mark and Joanne share a strong Jewish heritage in Subsystem 1 and seem to agree almost completely within Subsystem 2, their central egos of conscious personal values, ideals, and choices. This may explain why their two children have—perhaps surprisingly, given the chronic parental conflict—enjoyed great early success, Ivy League educations, and the like. In Subsystem 3 the unconscious fit appears to be one of an underconfident woman drawn to an overly confident man, who expresses enough aggression for both of them. From his side, Mark may have, at first, found in Joanne the admiring, supportive, nonthreatening wife, an antidote in fantasy to his mother and grandmother. Now, however, provoked by Mark's dangerous impulsiveness, Joanne has become the critical mother once again, and he must do battle with her. We can glimpse the repressive split in Mark's consciousness. He's unable to trust the other enough to take advice when he's confused—the developmental task that he could not, for obvious reasons, resolve with his parents.

In this reading, Mark and Joanne's marriage may represent an example of Dicks's Hypothesis (1A), the partners chosen to play roles opposite of primary objects fail to do so and end up resembling those old internalized objects all too closely. For Joanne, enthusiastic, warm, outgoing Mark, the cure for her cold authoritarian father, now has become tyrannically controlling of her and her future with his financial speculations. For Mark, sweet, accepting Joanne has transformed into his undercutting mother and grandmother. Of course, each partner has colluded in recreating the initially ideal objects who have now snapped back into becoming the equally unrealistic, threatening, original object images.

Dicks's Hypothesis (1A) helps us with more than categorizing the marriage, however. It points us toward the critical issues we need to focus upon to alter the destructive interaction in the relationship, and it helps us formulate the crucial moves, on the part of each partner, that we will probably require to propel this treatment forward. For example, at some level Mark needs to admit to himself that he provokes Joanne, onto whom he has projected his undermining mother. He jousts with her in order to master his fear of women. Joanne must acknowledge, at least to herself, how liberating she finds Mark's daring aggression, so that he will not have to act it out so frequently for both of them.

In constructing the object relations map, I'm clearly using history to speculate about the nature of the repressed objects. I'm more interested in the flow of the feeling about the objects than I am in concrete facts that describe them. I actively pursue this historical information once I have an opening, although I find structured history taking, such as genograms, not particularly helpful. Sometimes crucial data from the past emerges later in the therapy, when repressions have lifted. I'll accept this information whenever I receive it, but the sooner the better. I know that my initial map is indeed "hypothetical." I can't afford to wait as long as the Scharffs to draw conclusions, so I have to remain open to revise the map, maybe radically, as I continue. My emphasis on history differentiates my approach from most, but by no means from all, current short-term couple models. Wile, Christensen and Jacobson, Friedman and Lipchick, and the strategic experts do not pursue history at all. Johnson and Hendrix make some use of it. I focus on it.

Building the object relations map leads me directly from Step 1 into Step 2, the triangle of focus, which connects the fight to the family of origin and to problematic character features in each of the pair. The fight for this couple turns on two central character attributes, Mark's provocative argumentativeness and Joanne's protesting victimhood. I've partially succeeded in understanding how each of these features relates to the respective families of origin. Next I'll attempt to fill in my map and formulate a better picture of Mark's and Joanne's individual triangles of conflict—that is, how each defends against his or her primary anxieties. I've already begun a relationship move with Mark's triangle of conflict by empathizing with his vulnerability. This may help him relax his automatic need to provoke and attack (Step 4, alter the triangle of conflict). As well, I'm trying to offer Joanne a chance to gain a voice in this therapy. This may support her to come out from behind her soft tones and obscuring lock of hair.

In later chapters we'll catch up with this interesting pair to find out how the balance of the treatment unfolded, a drama that took some remarkable turns. Now, though, I'll conclude this chapter with a discussion of my third initial intervention strategy, coaching. To do that I'll introduce another couple just beginning treatment, Ming and Cathy, who if anything offered a greater challenge than even Mark and Joanne.

Coaching the Clients

Because of the urgency accompanied by "time's winged chariot," brief couple therapists probably must actively coach their clients in a fashion that long-term therapists rarely would. The time pressure forces us to dare risks that can add weight and value to our work, but whose possible negative consequences we must never overlook. Active coaching can easily spark interaction with repressed object relationships, and every definitive intervention potentially changes transference and countertransference transactions. We can coach, but we cannot forget the potential influence of our behavior on the inner object relations world of our clients. Relationship offers can also subtly, or not so imperceptibly, retraumatize our clients. That's why we need to construct the hypothetical object relations map as soon as possible and to use that to guide our interventions. Otherwise, we'll risk the trap into which, as I predicted earlier, some other short-term couple therapists may fall—coaching prematurely before we've assessed the impact of that intervention on the object world of the client.

Ming and Cathy

> Ming, a 45-year-old Asian American man, timidly follows his Caucasian wife, Cathy, into my office—he, a college educated contractor, and she, a real estate underwriter with an MBA. Married 20 years, they have two teenage sons, a 16-year-old and a 13-year-old. Cathy complains that their marriage has collapsed. They rarely speak, hardly ever agree on how to handle the children or on any household decision, and have not made love in 2 years. She feels divorce imminent. Ming smiles shyly at me, apparently in embarrassed agreement, but says only, "I guess it's like she says."

Already, I'm stuck. I sense that Ming feels intimidated by my authority and probably by hers. I quickly guess that the partners find themselves locked in a passive-aggressive battle over control—their fight. If I push him to participate, won't I just reinforce myself as a threat and drive him further into himself and away from any helpful therapy? The two confident whites gang up on the shy Asian. Wonderful!

As I often do with reticent couples, I decide not to enter the zone of their cold war right away, other than to empathize with the difficulty of this conflict for both of them. I explore their backgrounds first (Step 2, the triangle of focus). This approach will potentially benefit the treatment in two ways. I will learn more about the primary objects in both their heads, who have interacted to produce their couple, so I can start work on the map. Also, almost anybody can talk about his or her personal history. This conversation may put my bashful man slightly at ease and may help him to join in more later on. It's worth, a try anyway.

I hear that 1 year after Ming's birth in Vietmam, his father was seized by the Communist government and executed. The father's father gathered his clan, including the patient's mother, and immigrated to Boston. Because of the paternalistic control wrapped within the culture, the mother had no option but to join the exodus. Her children were going; she could accompany them or not. Free choice!

In America, the grandfather predictably ruled. He began several businesses, real estate and restaurants, which employed many of the family members. He financially supported the group and sent Ming to college, but the grandfather's word remained law, in large matters or small. My client now works for his cousin, under the cousin's contracting license. Ming apparently takes most of the responsibility in the company but feels he can never speak up to the cousin, who appropriates large sums from the business for his personal needs. My client protests only mildly about the lack of freedom in his life, past and present. "It's the way it is. What are you going to do?"

Cathy, to our American eyes, lived a much more conventional life when growing up. Her parents, alive and well, still married, seem to cooperate with each other. Cathy enjoyed an upper-middle-class Midwestern upbringing as the star of four siblings: cheerleader, student government, all As in high school, now a master's degree, successful at a large Boston firm. How can she possibly empathize with her husband's amazing history? Not so incredible by Asian immigrant standards, maybe, but incredible enough for her or for me. I ask her reaction to her husband's story. She replies that she senses its harshness, but, as with everything else, he says little about it.

I quickly realize that Ming will have to alter his inhibited stance, if I'm going to help this couple snatch its marriage back from the brink. From earlier experience with a few Asian patients, I also know that his blank expression and appearance of naiveté reflect cultural roots and generations of character identification. I cannot hope to dislodge his impassive stance with interpretation or repeated confrontation.

Now I construct a bare-bones object relations map for Ming. Control probably represents his central dynamic issue and certainly lies in the middle of the couple conflict. From before his birth, and until now, authoritarian figures have determined Ming's fate: first, the Communist assassins; then his grandfather, his cousin, and his wife; and now, potentially, his therapist. I sense that he's frightened of me already. To survive, Ming has adopted a defensive stance of overt compliance balanced by inner rebellion. His disorganization and lack of cooperation at home probably express his anger toward his methodical, definitive wife. We can immediately identify the split in Ming's repressive barrier. He can't genuinely cooperate with intimates, because he's afraid of becoming enslaved.

Ming slumps in his chair in front of me, hair over face, blue jeans and work boots muddy. Cathy sits upright in a chic business suit, makeup exact. How can I help them to bridge the gaping distance between them, and how can I do this in some brief fashion?

I sense that I need to make Ming a relationship offer, and I need to do it soon. Somehow I have to support him to participate in the treatment. I need to do this, though, without in any fashion demanding that he take part, which would only provoke a passive-aggressive backlash.

Now I take a chance, but the only chance I feel I have. I start to coach. I conjecture that I can ask Ming, in a friendly, noncoercive manner, to talk and to negotiate more directly with his wife, and because of his strong tendency to obey authority, he will comply. I take the risk, and a big one, that this tact will not reinforce his unconscious fury at a succession of authority figures now personified by a demanding therapist. If I'm not careful, I will repeat Ming's trauma and capsize the therapy. He may outwardly cooperate, but the repressed inner objects may become all the more persecutory in their control. He may then have to invoke his major defense of silent withdrawal, to destroy the treatment and to defeat those objects. I'd better start by disarming myself.

I'll have to speak directly with him and ask sincerely for his participation as a colleague. I begin, "I'm guessing, Ming, you've felt somewhat pushed around and controlled by many people in your life, particularly your grandfather and now your wife. I can feel how hard this has been for you and the great effort you've put into doing the right thing. Now I'm going to ask you to make some changes. I understand how you might resent this. Please feel free to express your anger, if you sense I'm ganging up on you with your wife. Is it okay if we try to work this way?" He smiles, I think with some genuine acceptance of my offer. He responds, "Okay."

I then tell him that although the strategy may seem unfamiliar, I think that he can help his marriage by talking more with his wife and systematically discussing each of the problems in the family. I say that I know that neither he nor Cathy could be right every time, and he probably has just as many good ideas about courses of action as does she. He answers, "Okay." I continue, "Great, let's start. Now what's the first problem?" I sense that only concrete results will appeal to Ming. Diaphanous discussions about feelings will probably mean little to him.

The partners begin a halting discussion of how to manage the behavior of their son, Jerry. A canny teenager, Jerry has located the power vacuum in the family and has evidently become a self-taught expert at playing one parent off against the other. I suggest that first they talk alone about what they need from their son and then present Jerry with the outcome of their deliberations.

I offer that they, as a couple, might not actually disagree on every subject, even though often they think they do. Because they have difficulty discussing some issues in depth, they might be quite surprised that they share expectations for their son, once they delve into the subject without arguing. I counsel them to let first one talk for 15 minutes without interruption, except for clarification, then to let the other one speak for the same period. They agree to try and leave with their first homework assignment. I suggest that they can call me between sessions, if they get stuck. Here I play the transitional object role suggested by Dicks earlier. The couple can project the capacity to resolve conflicts into me, experience me as a resource, and identify with my capabilities in this regard.

Two weeks later they return, both smiling. They have attempted the new approach with some success. I congratulate them on their constructive open-mindedness. I continue the therapy in the same fashion, focusing on one family problem after another, finances, getting the house in order, and restarting their sexual life. The approving parental object, I enthusiastically offer positive reinforcement.

My strategy could have failed, of course. Then I would return to the specifics of how their talk got off the track, and I would pursue their issues of anger and mistrust. However, the treatment so far has, maybe surprisingly, progressed positively. After four sessions Ming appears to appreciate the improvement of his marriage, so he's willing to take part in these new discussions with Cathy and with me. He has not spoken of or demonstrated, to my eyes or ears, anger at me for my controlling stance. Perhaps my candid introduction, speaking to his probable transference, proved helpful.

As I continue to coach these partners, I do so with their map of internalized object relations in mind to guide my forays. My information about their repressed objects remains, unfortunately, so far sketchy. I do feel that Ming has internalized anti-libidinal images of a tyrant-like, controlling grandfather and a repressed libidinal mother who manipulates him to take care of her. However, I know that he identifies positively with the grandfather as well. Several times, Ming has mentioned his admiration for this tenacious man, who was wealthy in Vietnam, had lost everything, and then rebuilt his fortune in a foreign country. Perhaps he feels an unconscious connection between his assertive, protective therapist and his grandfather who displayed some of the same characteristics. On the other hand, I also speculate about his internalization of his father, a rebel, executed for his beliefs. Can Ming expect the same fate if he speaks out for himself? Does he fear Cathy or me as potential executioners? The unconscious message seems clear: Overtly rebel, and you may die.

Ming rarely mentions his father, whom he never knew, but does talk about his brother, who apparently rarely works and lives with the mother, exploiting her financially. If the mother has a household repair, she calls Ming from across the city to fix it, while the brother, who lives in an apartment adjacent to the mother, purportedly does not budge. The functions of industry and passivity seem split in the family. Ming may transfer his anger at his mother onto his wife. He never overtly defies either, nor does he genuinely cooperate with either.

Cathy seems identified with her executive father and appears one of the more successful of her high-achieving siblings, but why has she chosen so unconventionally in her marriage? A Vietnamese immigrant contractor hardly seems a match for this Midwestern cheerleader. On Subsystem 1, common cultural background, Ming and Cathy appear far apart, but in Subsystem 2, central egos, personal goals, values, and identities, they seem much closer. They met as members of the same college social fraternity and share many personal, conscious norms, such as the value of education, hard work, and individual competence.

The fit at Subsystem 3 remains more of a mystery. Oddly enough, despite Ming's traditional Asian upbringing, he explains that he feels neither Vietnamese nor American, and his unconscious expectations of his wife seem quite unconventional by the standards of either culture. Having grown up working in restaurants, he's become an expert chef and does all the family's cooking, apparently happily. He has no objections to his wife's demanding 50-hour-a-week job or to the fact that her projected earning power and employment status seem greater than his. "She does her work with fiber optics. I do mine with wrenches. My office is my truck." I hypothesize that Cathy found herself drawn to Ming's liberating lack of American middle-class expectations an antidote to her straitlaced family background. However, Ming's free-flowing style leads him to become disorganized personally and to make decisions in haphazard fashion, which has now alienated the orderly Cathy. This conflict in character styles then becomes the foundation of their many disagreements.

For his part, Ming may have found himself unconsciously drawn to Cathy to provide some of the self-discipline he lacks, the role his grandfather played in the past. Now, of course, Ming feels her to be manipulative and controlling. In other words, this marriage appears to be a possible example of Dicks's Hypothesis 2. Each of the pair perhaps married the other to recapture a repudiated part of themselves, but later they find they cannot stand that lost part in the other. Ming wanted Cathy's self-discipline, and she his free-spiritedness, but now these character features have become oppressive, rather than liberating, for the respective partner.

In the therapy I will need to help this couple toward somewhat more conscious awareness of the dynamics of their choice and toward more acceptance of their split-off subidentities that they have projected into their partner. Ming probably must become more self-directing and organized, or at least acknowledge his limitations in these areas. He cannot leave all the family management to his wife and then resent her for taking over. Cathy needs to become more accepting and supportive of their differences and of Ming's strengths. She cannot continue to denigrate and to admire, simultaneously, Ming's laissez-faire freedom. (In addition, Ming displays a number of signs of ADHD—particularly, procrastination and a scattered style. I have referred him for psychopharm evaluation.) With relatively slight alterations in their triangles—not defensively dismissing the other, for example—Ming and Cathy may regain respect for each other and gain competence in unraveling their impasses.

In sum, the relationship offer I extend to Ming is one of respectful coach or mentor. I can teach him something about relating to his wife and his son and about organizing his family, but only if he genuinely wants to learn from me. The offer I make needs to include the option for Ming to decline my services, and I explicitly include this possibility in my approach to him. If he does not feel free to turn down my suggested contribution, this will activate his passive-aggressive defense,

*and he will continue to project malevolence onto his wife and his mother
and now probably onto me. If he doesn't feel free not to join with me,
he will arrange to defeat each of the techniques I suggest, and I will
prove an unhelpful teacher.*

Note that I'm using the five-step model here but in an abbreviated
form. I doubt that this highly defended couple can productively make use
of extensive explorations of their triangles of focus and their triangles of
conflict. Even though I don't pursue that exploratory work in depth with
this couple, I draw my own conclusions about both triangles. Then I begin
to coach the partners toward changes in their triangles of conflict, toward
a shift in their automatic defensive reaction to each other. I've also broken
my rule about introducing tools early in the treatment. I felt I had no choice
except to move fast, but I did so in terms of my understanding of the object
relations map. Evidently because of my initial relationship intervention with
Ming, he, in particular, could suspend his defense somewhat and engage in
genuine negotiations with Cathy, which made the treatment possible.

Although I offer almost no direct interpretations in this therapy, I guide
my interventions with an object relations map and with roughly drawn
triangles of focus and of conflict. To paraphrase Gustafson (1981), I'm
pursuing focal aims but not employing focal interpretations. I've embodied
some, though definitely not all, of the functions Dicks outlined for couples
therapists. I don't interpret, but I do function as a mediator and an adult
transitional object with whom the pair can identify.

This case illustrates three central issues in brief couple therapy. First,
therapists can proceed productively with active coaching, as long as they
keep their object relations guidebook in mind, and the partners may respond productively without working directly with their repressed objects.
Participants vary greatly in their capacity or willingness to explore the unconscious territory. I doubt that these partners, particularly Ming, in the
foreseeable future can or will want to confront their inner lives more intensely. As Dicks suggests, further change here will probably come as a
result of the couple identifying with the therapist as a transitional object in
the transference. The therapist can serve as a consultant and a mediator,
whose presence the couple can internalize. Change will probably not come
from the insight generated by interpretation of the unconscious. Ming and
Cathy have spoken relatively little about their families of origin thus far,
and my information about their unconscious identifications remains specu-
lative. But they have improved with only four sessions of treatment up until
now.

Second, from this introduction to Mark and Joanne and Ming and
Cathy, we begin to appreciate that we can accommodate a wider spectrum
of couples in treatment, if we use relationship interventions as well as inter-

pretive techniques. Sometimes highly defended couples like Ming and Cathy can benefit from these kinds of object relationship interventions; sometimes they can't. It's hard to predict. Offered empathy and a relationship response to their standoff, given the opportunity to have their anger held by the therapist in the session, so that it does not swamp them, and using a few simple guidelines for mutual discussion, couples often can suspend their triangles of conflict somewhat and interact more constructively together. So far, Ming and Cathy have utilized the treatment productively. We'll rejoin them later to discover how their therapy turned out. The coaching in couple therapy represents the analogue of educating the individual client about psychodynamic functioning explained by Pine (1985).

Object relations therapy helps us a great deal in our understanding of therapeutic impasse. When the shutdown occurs, I have found that one or possibly both partners struggle with their repressed object relationships in a conflict on which they can make little progress.

For example, it turned out that Mark, the impulsive businessman, was probably an unplanned child. He was perhaps an unwanted one, too, 10 years younger than his sister, born at a time when his parents had undergone financial ruin and did not have the psychological or monetary wherewithal to raise him with care. Both parents worked long hours, and he was left to fend for himself under the slipshod supervision of his disturbed grandmother. Mark has foraged for himself ever since and has never learned to negotiate with others or to think out his judgments realistically. While he was growing up, such skills meant nothing because no one sat across the table with whom to interact. Now he careens through his life, making decisions like the headstrong child he psychologically remains. If he cannot come to terms, in some fashion, with the fact that his early primary objects ignored him, he will probably never realize that something remains missing from his experience. This is a skill that he needs to develop for himself. If he can't, he will remain the "bull in the china shop" and ultimately will not become able to listen to his wife or to his therapist, and the treatment will then founder.

I hypothesize that Mark does not need to gain this insight into his family of origin in any absolutely clear way, but he does need to encounter the true nature of his inner objects in some emotional reality, for him to alter his style—in other words, for the necessary triangle of conflict work to usher in behavioral change. We'll meet Mark again in chapter 3, to see how he ultimately used his treatment to develop new insights that worked for him. In sum, object relations theory can guide us toward the required steps of a brief therapy and will help us to explain the success or failure of that treatment.

As we close chapter 2, we can feel that Dicks and the Scharffs, with their expertise in object relations theory, have developed for us a compelling explanation of couple conflict, an understanding that rings true to my clinical experience, and I hope to yours. Their work will represent our basic theoretical texts as we proceed to later chapters. Their emphatic message— Don't forget Subsystem 3. Partners engage in complex unconscious trans-actions with each other and with the therapist, based on their repressed, internalized object relations. Before we attempt any intervention, we must place any move within our best estimate of the object relations context for each of the pair.

Dicks and the Scharffs, though, function as psychoanalysts. They use transference and countertransference interpretation as their principal—at times, almost their only—instruments of intervention. Our discussion sug-gests that this technique may stand as too narrow a choice of options for therapeutic activity. I've introduced the additional strategies of offering counter-relationships, mapping the object relations field, and coaching the couple. In later chapters, particularly 5, 6, and 7, we'll learn more about the potential of these and similar techniques. Dicks and the Scharffs, then, have comprehensively explained the fight, but their treatment models do not exhaust the possible ways to address that fight.

As we move into chapter 3, I will explain the concept of the triangle of focus more completely, a concept that accompanies me in my search for the crucial opening material that I will need to orient the therapy and construct the object relations map. The balance of the book depends upon the under-standing of object relations theory that I've developed here in chapter 2. It's tricky and complex. If you do not feel confident in at least an introductory grounding in that approach, take time now to go back and review the ma-terial in chapter 2. I'll meet you in chapter 3.

Step 2: Investigate the Triangle of Focus

When we study what couples actually say and do during the opening treatment sessions, meetings that proceed in a free-form manner—not structured, for example, by behavioral exercises or strategic assignments—the pairs almost inevitably gravitate toward three topic areas: (1) the fight, (2) the problematic character features of each of the pair, and (3) the family-of-origin dynamics of each. I call this naturally occurring, tripartite confluence the *triangle of focus*. The psychoanalytic principle of free association suggests that if these three subjects usually emerge intertwined with one another, as the clients speak spontaneously in the first few meetings, the three relate to each other in the unconscious of the participants.

In addition, if the content of the early couple sessions deals predominantly with these three matters, then perhaps they provide most of the information we require to undertake our task of understanding the fight and beginning to unravel it. Our job has narrowed. If we can grasp the fight in detail, and the influence on the fight of the important character conflicts of each member of the pair and of unresolved issues in the family of origin of each, we've probably found our focus for short-term couple therapy. This explains why I've called this three-part inquiry "exploring the triangle of focus." As we continue, it will become clear that when we start to investigate this area, we're not just gathering data; we're also formulating and experimenting with relationship interventions as we proceed. We need the information, but we must also focus on the interaction between couple and therapist.

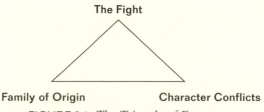

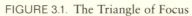

FIGURE 3.1. The Triangle of Focus

PAUL AND MARIA REVISITED

I'll illustrate exploring the triangle of focus and the close connections between issues from the family of origin, character features, and the fight by returning, at some length, to the battle between Paul, a 40-year-old scientist, and his wife, 40-year-old Maria, also a scientist, who grew up in Southern Europe. Paul, a short, trim, youthful, bearded man, stands only slightly taller than his petite, rounded, dark-haired Maria. Their diminutive physical proportions seem ironic, in contrast to the thunder of their many fights. At the time of this interview, they had been a couple for 10 years, had been married for 5, and had a 1-year-old son.

This excerpt allows us to trace their fight, step by step. In addition, it demonstrates, particularly from Maria's side, how her role in the fight connects to tragically unresolved matters in her original family. These have, in turn, left her with a major personality conflict—autonomy versus subjugation—that she imports, at nearly every turn, into the marriage and into the fight. This powerful session, which occurred as a follow-up to a course of couple group work, also helps us to understand the role of early trauma in later marital discord. As we will see, object relations theory allows us to penetrate, at considerable depth, into all three points of the triangle of focus.

Paul: It's [the couple treatment] working more with us.

Maria: Yes, it's working, but again, like we said last session, that's the pattern. It goes nice, nice, nice. Then it just blows up. And then we suffer and cry and come here and talk about it. And then it becomes nice again and then blows up again. [The therapist here seems to play the role of mediator and soothing transitional object. So far, the partners cannot perform these functions for themselves.]

JMD: What do you make of that?

Maria: Maybe we could think about what happened over Christmas. We were like nice, nice, nice, nice, very busy. The usual happened. I'm doing my stuff. Paul is helping, and then I have three weeks of break. As soon as the class is ended, I felt very depressed, weird, and very irritable. I told Paul about it, and then we started fighting.

JMD: Class has ended. I felt depressed. Holidays. From that point on, things really deteriorated.

Maria: There was something about the holidays, definitely. I feel very like foreign, very lonely over the holidays.

JMD: Something like missing your home country, your family?

Maria: Missing my home country, my family.

JMD: What about missing Europe?

Maria: Well, because it's Christmas.

JMD: Sure.

Maria: Yes. Christmas was always full of mixed feelings for us. Because nobody at home likes it. It's very sad for us. But, at the same time, we want to be together. [Maria's unable to separate from her primary objects. She still reacts to Christmas in the exact style of her family. We need to know why.]

JMD: No one in your family likes Christmas?

Maria: No. I think it's very sad. I have a sister who died.

JMD: I didn't know that.

Maria: Oh, you knew that. Yes. I had a sister who died, when she was 13. And my father was driving. He was not drunk, but it was more or less his fault.

JMD: Was he at all under the influence of alcohol?

Maria: No, he was not, from what we know. He goes without drinking for 2 or 3 years. Once he was without drinking for 10 years, and then he goes back, really bad. Anyway, he was driving, and he did something stupid. He was going to cross a highway. And he looked to one side, and he entered the highway. He didn't look at the other side. And it was a horrible accident, and she died. And before she died, they stayed on the road waiting for the ambulance, and nobody would stop. So my brother and my mother and him, they stayed there with her dying, basically, and trying to make people stop to help them, so it was horrible. I was not there.

JMD: She was terribly injured.

Maria: It hit her in the head, basically, and then she was in the hospital unconscious for about 2 weeks. And it was very hard for everybody to deal with that uncertainty, because they thought that, even if she survived, she would not be a normal person ever. So my parents were debating what they really wanted. If they wanted her to live or to die or what. And then finally she died.

         And everybody feels very guilty about that because my father and my brother, for some reason, they didn't like my sister at all. They were very cruel to her for some reason. They would pick on her all the time. I don't know if they were jealous of the attention that my mother was giving to her or what, but you know, she was like their favorite target. It was very cruel.

JMD: Was she the baby?

Maria: She was.

JMD: How old were you when she was 13?

Maria: I was 18. So anyway, so when she died, there was that sense of guilt. We [Maria and her sister] have a very competitive relationship. [Does Maria suffer unconscious survivor guilt?] But I was not cruel to her, so I felt guilty but not too much, but they felt really guilty. That was very traumatic, and then again there was always that question, how guilty my father actually was.

Paul: It was Christmas time?

Maria: No, it was not Christmas. It was January 16th. So Christmas was not great, and after that it became more . . .

JMD: Somebody was missing there for Christmas?

Maria: Yes.

JMD: Your story is heart-rending.

Maria: Yes.

JMD: What was her name?

Maria: Sophia.

JMD: It's a beautiful name.

Maria: It is a beautiful name. It was very funny, because she was very different from us, very different. Very, very social. Very, very outgoing. I think she didn't find the resources inside the house, so she went to get [these] from the world [as Maria has]. She was very likable. She had many friends. On her funeral we were surprised to see how many different people come like from all walks of life. So it's funny how she, instead of staying in the family and agonize, she decided to go out and get from the world what she needed. [But if you leave the family, you die.] This is all painful, but I don't see direct relationship with our fighting because we fight other times of the year. That is not Christmas. [Her resistance to realizing the connection between sister's death and the present marital fight.]

JMD: Right. But you must be very angry about your sister's death.

Maria: I have this general anger over a lot of things. Why all this shit happens. And I feel that at the same time that it causes me a lot of problems, at the same time, my ego has a lot of energy in it. I think it does fuel for a lot of changing those things. [What is she trying abortively to change in her marriage?] I think if I were not that angry, I would still be in Portugal going around, you know, my father does this, my father does that.

JMD: It gave you the impetus to get the hell out of there.

Maria: Yes.

JMD: And it's a better life?

Maria: Yes.

JMD: But still this isn't exactly the way we want our development to go. Right? [Therapist begins to question if flight from original objects and continued anger projected onto the present object represents the optimal path of growth.]

Maria: But see, at the same time it was a big progress. When I first came to the United States, with my first therapist, we worked for years that I was unable to feel anger, to feel angry. I was just shut down, depressed. [Does her anger represent warded-off depression?]

JMD: Right.

Maria: So when I started expressing it, we thought it was great progress. (laughter)

(We glimpse here, in starkest terms, some of the harsh unconscious dynamics of Maria's upbringing. The family represents a pitiless battle-ground for attention. Those who receive more than their share get tortured in retribution. Those who seek autonomy and a life outside the family risk punishment by death. What aspects of this vicious calculus has Maria transferred into her marriage?)

Maria: Last night I'm very tired, and the computer didn't work. It would print four copies of an entire document. I was going crazy, but then I went to the kitchen and counted to 10, 20, 50, and 100, and I came back, and we didn't fight. But I was very angry. So you see the progress? (laughter) I'm developing some control over it. [Efforts at behavioral self change.]

JMD: This is very positive. I was just thinking more about this. I mean, things were not going well in the family, anyway, and for some reason the men were very mean to Sophia. Now, was she a particularly pretty girl? [Inquiry into family-of-origin pole of triangle of focus.]

Maria: Very.

JMD: Very pretty and very popular.

Maria: Yes.

JMD: So, possibly they were envious?

Maria: And my mother liked her very much.

JMD: So, that's probably more to the point. That she was maybe your mother's favorite and that the men were jealous?

Maria: And also a very easy target, right? A woman, the youngest.

JMD: And what did they do to her?

Maria: It was very mean. It was extremely mean. For example, my father would go through the trouble of writing songs, saying bad things about her, that she was annoying, that she was ugly, that she was a pain in the butt. So he would like write a song, and he's a very smart man, so the songs were very clever and extremely mean. And they would sing those songs.

JMD: The two of them?

Maria: The two of them, again and again.

JMD: Did anybody tell them to stop?

Maria: Oh, yes. My mother would just come to defend her, but it didn't work. This is far beyond a normal teasing.

JMD: It's sadistic. [Therapist accompanies Maria back into the affective horror of her family.]

Maria: It is. And then I was not there, but the night before she died, they had been very bad all day long, and she told the maid, who was her friend, "I cannot live this life any more, I wish I would die." A 13-year-old! And the following day this happened. So you can imagine the effect that it would have on everybody, but the guilt part nobody talks about. This is taboo. Nobody ever mentions it. [Has Maria repressed her guilt as well?]

JMD: The guilt being that they wanted her dead?

Maria: No. Guilt about the things they did.

JMD: So you would say, stop teasing her?

Maria: Oh, yes.

JMD: And then he would get very angry?

Maria: Yes. And then I was the target.

JMD: Then he hit you?

Maria: Yes, he hit me, really bad. But you see, I had that sense that I was doing something right, that I was absolutely right. And I started screaming at him, telling him exactly that I was right, and he knew that I was right and that he was a lousy father. [The fight with Paul seems to assume this same form.] You know, but it went on and on. So that made him even angrier at me. But it was a very funny story because the more he hit me, the more I would scream. It was amazing. I don't know where that was coming from. I could not feel the pain or anything. I would just scream, scream, scream.

[Precisely Maria's behavior in the fight with her husband.] Saying everything I thought about him. So it was very interesting.

JMD: He punched you? [Reestablishing that unlike Paul, her father was a violent, sadistic man.]

Maria: Yes, he would punch me. Now, in the beginning of January, one day we were driving here with the baby, and a guy started doing silly things in the traffic, and he's trying to beat all the cars. I think he was drunk. [Stranger stands as the anti-libidinal father object to whom Maria develops an instant violent transference.] And the guy would not let it go, and he was trying to hit our car. And then we stopped at the red light, and I opened the door, and the guy opened the door, and I think he wanted to confront Paul.

Paul: Yes.

Maria: Yes, but he could not get to him. I got there first. [Maria protects Paul from insane drunken attacker, as she protected her sister.] And I would scream at the top of my lungs, and I would tell him go away. You know it was like a wonderful scene of me on Beacon Street, screaming.

JMD: It happens a lot on Beacon Street.

Maria: So it was very funny. The guy was kind of puzzled. He was telling me Paul was a bad driver. And I was telling him to go away. I thought the guy was going to hit me. This was a big guy [Maria's father?], mean looking, and he was very close to me. It was funny. I was not afraid. I just screamed go away, so that happens sometimes. [Maria becomes depersonalized in her fury and demonstrates poor judgment.]

Paul: You were also so overwrought already because your classes began, and we were fighting very badly anyway, and you were very tense before.

JMD: This guy on Beacon Street sounds crazy. [Like her father]

Maria: Yes. He seemed to be very violent.

JMD: But, I mean, there's so many interesting things about it, because he could have been your father. He was out of his mind.

Maria: Yes, he was, but he was wrong, too.

JMD: Oh, yes, but so was your father. Completely wrong.

Maria: Yes. Someone had to tell him.

JMD: Right and you're a rather tiny person. And I can see you in his face, screaming at him, and I don't think you were one bit afraid.

Maria: No. (laughter)

JMD: My question is how do we link this [confronting the tyrant] up to your father and your husband. [The triangle of focus connects a character trait to the family of origin and to the fight.]

Maria: You may find this extremely funny, but I feel that this is a disease, my reaction to abuse of power. [Maria recognizes for a moment how distorted her reaction to male authority can become.] You can't do anything that you want and just plain get away with it. You are bigger and meaner and more powerful and all that, but I'm a person, too.

JMD: Right.

Maria: There's something very important that you cannot walk over me like that, just because I'm a child, or because I'm a woman, or because I'm a whatever. You cannot. You know, I'm not going to take it. You can hit me. You can even kill me. But you know, I'm going to tell you. So sometimes this feeling may take very mean twists, but the basic idea is that people cannot do this kind of abuse and just get away with it. The problem I see is that when this happens with Paul, at that particular moment, I see Paul as very mean. Complete jerk. Try to make me suffer. [Maria's projection changes Paul into a brutal maniac like her father.]

JMD: Make you suffer?

Maria: You know that *he's abusing his power* [same phrase she used to describe all male tyrants], that he's being a pain in the neck, criticizing me. He's so jealous all the time and controlling. When it goes away, I feel okay. Maybe Paul was a pain in the neck tonight, but, you know, he's not mean. He's not trying to destroy me, but at the moment. . . .

JMD: He's all black.

Maria: Yes.

JMD: At that moment he's the black knight.

Maria: Complete jerk! Yes. [Maria gets stuck in her projection and the resulting depersonalized state of fury.]

JMD: I mean, it's pretty clear that with your father, you saw your identity as a person utterly, completely threatened. And the reason that you were able to stand up to him, despite savage beatings, and even your life being threatened, was that something inside of you said you're fighting for your life and when someone's fighting for their life or for their sister's life, nothing matters.

Maria: Yes.

JMD: I imagine, down at the Biotech Center, your boss there, you were about ready to strangle him? He sounded horrible.

Maria: Yes, he was.

Paul: I never heard you describe him with the kind of anger or with that kind of blackness. Your description of the time that your father was beating you, and you were defending your sister, brings to mind one of the fights in September, when no matter what I would say, anger just kept coming out of you. Just angry, attack, attack.

Maria: I don't think he [the former boss] was sadistic. He was the power type of guy, control type, really tough but really open. I didn't think he was going to hurt me. He was defending his surgical interests.

JMD: And he also didn't have life and death power over you. You could do what you did, which was quit.

Maria: Yes. It was very painful, but it didn't hit my core identity.

JMD: Right.

Maria: With Paul, like, say, the big fight that we had when we moved to the new apartment. I felt he left me alone with a young baby, in an apartment, full of furniture and just to clean out the old apartment, the old basement, that went to my core.

JMD: Right. It had something to do with being in a new place. I mean, not only was it a total mess, but you were starting at a new place, you were anxious. [Maria completely vulnerable—Paul has life and death power to help.]

Maria: With a new baby, who wouldn't stop screaming, so I felt powerless, so poor me. Here, raining outside, I can't walk around. The baby doesn't stop crying. I felt so *powerless*. Oh, my God! So that went to my core. And then I was absolutely mad. I was mad the first day. He did it again the second day. And on the third day we had a huge, horrible fight.

JMD: So he was all black?

Maria: Yes.

JMD: But the signal, the totally important part is that because of your vulnerability, new place, baby, rain, that your core identity was threatened?

Maria: Paul had abandoned me and the baby. He was there polishing someone else's basement. I felt we were not important. It's more important to be the perfect ex-tenant than to be here with us.

JMD: I'm thinking your father couldn't possibly have behaved toward the general public as he behaved toward the family?

Maria: No.

JMD: Of course, what he was doing to your sister was unspeakably destructive. It was terribly destructive to her core [and to Maria's], I think. With his clients I'm sure he was okay?

Maria: I had a friend at school, and my father was a member of the Rotary Club. One day she came to me, and she said, "Oh, I love your father so much, he's so funny, he's so friendly, he's so outgoing. Must be a lot of fun to be his daughter." I swear to God, I thought, she has the wrong person. She's confusing me with someone else. We're not talking about the same person.

JMD: And a great many of your fights come when Paul concentrates on outside people, doing work for school on the weekend or looking after his mother and father, right?

Maria: Dr. Donovan, we don't have to go through psychoanalysis to conclude that what my father was doing was not right. But what Paul is doing isn't right either. Paul doesn't do the important stuff for us, I feel. I think Paul does it for reasons that are different from my father. I think Paul does it 'cause he feels that it's the right thing. This is a very vulnerable point for me, to be nicer to the people outside than you are to the people you love. [Maria distorts Paul's realistic external obligations as cold rejections of her.]

JMD: Right. But with your father it must have been a real question about whether he loved you or not? [Interpretation of complete rejection by primary object.]

Maria: I always thought I was boring, that we were boring, compared to his glamorous clients. One of his clients had a daughter who was the same age as us, and he was talking about buying her diamond rings. My mother kept on saying, "None of your two daughters ever had diamond rings." So I remember thinking, "Why are you looking at their kids? We are your kids. Why are they so interesting, and we're so boring? Now his clients are all dead. Just the big three clients, they're all dead. Yes, this is the hardest thing. [Primary object prefers someone else, leads to fury.]

JMD: I'm not saying that Paul is perfect and blameless, and that all you're doing is reliving the past. I'm not for a moment saying that. But what I am suggesting is that the total blackness comes from before. [The triangle of focus. Character trait, fury, connects to family of origin, connects to the fight.]

Maria: I've been trying to come to terms with it for a long time. And I think I've made a lot of progress. I'm not just sitting there, and everything's fine, and then Paul does a little thing, and I just blow off and start throwing a tantrum at him. The dynamic is that I'm usually upset about something, and then Paul does something. I'm already unbalanced [rejected?] for some reason. I don't feel good about something, and then Paul does something, and I show that I don't like it, and then Paul does the same thing again. I say I don't like it a little louder, but there is always a process that goes like that and grows and grows and grows. I think we're so used to these dynamics that Paul doesn't stop, either. I do, he does, I do, he does. [The unstoppable momentum of the fight.]

JMD: At some point it turns the corner from irritation, and then it becomes he's completely controlling, it's my core identity that is on the line, and that's when it gets really serious.

Maria: When we look back, our big fights are usually over because I felt abandoned or because of his mother [her father?] did something, that in the past did something, feel like he was not on my side. This thing with the apartment, I felt abandoned because we were there with the baby. It's usually something that I feel close to the core. When I ask myself, *Does Paul* [her father?] *really love me?* That's when shit happens. When I doubt it, if he really loved me, would he do this? [Rejection by primary object ignites the fight.]

JMD: And then you nuke him!

Maria: Yes.

JMD: Obviously, you looked, and you saw your father treating your sister in a way that we had to conclude that, in part of himself at least, he hated her, right?

Maria: Yes.

JMD: Out of jealously, probably, he was trying to destroy her. Then you identified with her. You stepped in, and the two of you were a team, and he tried to destroy you, too. At that moment he didn't love you, he was beating the crap out of you, right?

Maria: Right.

JMD: And you knew you were fighting for your life. You were screaming at him, and he was hitting you. This was a standoff to the death. I don't think anything could make you stop screaming, do you?

Maria: No, but it also teaches me something about how and why because even after the fight, I would feel very clearly who held the power.

JMD: Who did?

Maria: He did. All the time. And now at school we're dealing with these issues of power and powerlessness in women, and I told Paul I'm going to cause a revolution. I feel like the professor says we're powerless, and students say, Yes, yes, we're powerless. I just can't stand there. I raise my hand. I have this very interesting interaction with the dean because of power. It keeps coming back, power, power. It's like I don't have much, but I have the power to talk or to scream or to say that I don't agree. [Maria's fighting follows a self-defeating pattern. She feels convinced that she will lose but must speak up. Her battles with Paul represent the same stand for her rights that she took with her father, but because she never expects to win, she assumes an exaggerated position and, sure enough, the fight never ends satisfactorily for her. Her stance seems more like a symbolic last stand than a realistic negotiating posture.]

JMD: I'm thinking about something you've already thought of. These arguments do not burst full blown, there's a prodromal phase, and you can see it coming. I would try to interrupt that, and I would say, "Time out." [Therapist senses that after this long emotional exploration of the fight, the couple may be able to respond positively to coaching.] You know when you're heading into something. I would try to interrupt it, because when it turns the corner, it's very upsetting for everybody.

Maria: Yes.

JMD: These big fights don't bring you closer. I mean, I don't think they're healthy for either of you.

Maria: Yes. I think I have some awareness of that, and I think that's why things have been getting better.

This extended case excerpt teaches us a great deal about the three poles of the triangle of focus.

The Fight

Let's look first at the ferocious fights into which this otherwise polite academic couple so frequently descends. The roles never vary. Paul, the conscientious scientist, son, and husband, feels he must return to his office to work or travel to Chicago to care for his aged, ill parents. Maria, already feeling overwhelmed by career and family issues, now feels utterly abandoned by a man (a primary object) who chooses to "ignore" her and to shine in his performance toward others, just as her father did. She explodes and attacks Paul, as if her "core identity" has come under mortal threat.

In his role, Paul always professes his innocence. He never intended to abandon her or to overlook her needs. He simply had to finish his research proposal or to attend to his mother's real estate tax situation. He would prefer to spend the time with her but sees no choice but to fulfill his commitments. Maria almost never feels reassured by Paul's protestations about his obligations. She continues the attack even more vociferously, and Paul does not know where to turn.

As with nearly every couple, the fight does not begin and end with little leftover reverberation between episodes. Paul works frantically to avoid confrontations with Maria by taking on large amounts of child care and household duties to reduce her stress and by rising early in the morning to work, before she wakes up. He lives in fear of emergencies or unanticipated requirements that will disrupt this family routine. So, the fight and its influence on the daily atmosphere remain extremely costly. The fight markedly inhibits the capacity for these otherwise quite well-matched partners to grow in their relationship and to raise their lively son.

Character Features

The character features of each member of this pair also figure prominently in the triangle of focus. Maria is sparkling, smart, and humorous. Her extensive scientific background and high intelligence allow her to understand Paul's work and converse knowledgeably with him about it, as he understands her and her profession. But Maria, a good communicator and well aware of feelings, is volatile, and once she becomes enraged, her consciousness becomes "black" indeed. Like a threatened wolverine, she simply will not back down and retreat from what she feels to be a war to the death. She seriously misperceives rather mild situations as these mortal threats, and she locks into an adversarial posture that she cannot easily shift away from.

Paul, on the other hand, strikes us as much more on an even keel. He virtually never raises his voice, except in the final stages of the fight with Maria. He demonstrates many of the attributes in mild form of the anal-compulsive character—not humorless or dull, but very concerned with duty and with guilt. He fears he may not do a conscientious enough job for his wife, for his employer, for his son, or for his ailing parents. Consistent with this orientation, Paul also frequently feels concerned with what is fair, right, and just. He would not wear a tie in high school, despite the regulations, because he thought it a ridiculous rule. He did not retreat, no matter under what pressure the high school dean put him. Paul's stubbornness, unfortunately, matches Maria's desperate aggression. Paul appears never to start the fight but not often to back away from it, either.

The Family of Origin: Maria's Object Relations Map

This case illustrates for us the precept that we can't understand the meaning and the persistence of the fight unless we delve into the repressed object relations of each member of the pair, which in turn relate to their problematic character features and to the roles they instantly assume in the recurrent battle.

Maria has had a good deal of therapy, both in the United States and in Europe. She can feel and talk about her traumas from the past—a great advantage for us. Our excerpt teaches us much about Maria's tragic family, and we can infer from this history a good deal about her repressed inner objects.

Maria and her younger sister, Sophia, were assigned the part of scapegoat in her family. We know nothing about the father's earlier life, although, clearly, great disturbance probably abounded there. Evidently, the father could not tolerate individuation in his children and projected onto his two daughters the theme that they were indifferent to him and to his wishes because they demonstrated strivings for independence. By contrast, her brother still lives close to the parents and works as the father's partner in the same profession. In the father's eyes, the family sin was separation, to go to outsiders for attention and care. The father hatefully punished his daughters who tried to individuate. He systematically tortured both girls verbally and savagely beat Maria, when she stood up to him.

Jill Scharff and colleagues (J. Scharff, Ed., 1989) have extensively explored this theme of the parent, unable to tolerate an issue in himself—here, independence—who then projects it onto one or more of his children, who act it out, which throws the parent into turmoil. The psychiatric literature contains few reports more chilling than Maria's story recounting her father and his ally, the brother, composing songs ridiculing Sophia, who ultimately dies in an automobile accident for which the father bears some responsibility. Sophia has become a martyr, executed by the power of her father's psychotic projections.

We can readily hypothesize that inside, Maria carries a repressed antilibidinal object of a murderous father bent on her destruction, should she dare to individuate and express her own needs. We cannot forget that Maria also must feel burdened by an inner object of a mother, her female identification, who watches helplessly as her husband verbally abuses and then punches, kicks, and ultimately kills one of his female children. Maria will evidently fight to the death to protect her "core identity" and not emulate the powerless feminine object who fails to protect herself or her young. The other female inner object, with whom Maria lives, is the sister, Sophia, left broken on the highway, her head smashed, the symbol of what happens to vulnerable women who don't, or can't, fight back.

No doubt Maria immigrated to the United States, in part, to prevent herself from murdering her father or he her. But inner objects move with us. In this country, the war goes on with supervisors, with department heads, and with the apparently unsuspecting Paul. In each seemingly trivial domestic dispute, Maria feels compelled to stand up for herself, and her dead sister, and to fight without quarter. At these times her opponent becomes "all black," the embodiment of the dark, hate-filled, abandoning father. She's recreating a familiar set of objects and also trying futilely to master her conflict with them.

Paul and Maria's case contains two possible wild cards that may heavily influence its outcome and to which we'll return in later chapters. Maria behaves in an ultimately self-defeating manner. In Portugal she married a violent alcoholic, like her father, whom she divorced. In the United States, at job after job, she becomes embroiled in fights that lead to multiple changes from position to position and even now to a new profession. She knows Paul isn't all black, but she repeatedly treats him as if he were. We must remember the sad fact to which her unconscious reverberates every day. Her sister died, and she escaped. She cannot relinquish her anger, no matter how out of proportion it rages, because this would mean that her sister died in vain and that the tyrant has triumphed. Possibly, Maria's survivor guilt grips her so strongly that she's forced toward self-destructive behavior, challenging dangerous strangers on the street and fighting almost nonstop with her husband.

Although her father's exact psychiatric diagnosis remains unclear to me, Maria obviously comes from a family with a history of mental illness. Her extreme irritability and reactivity to stress and to loss may represent symptoms of a depressive spectrum illness, post-traumatic stress disorder, that might respond to antidepressant medication. I haven't pursued this strategy because for the last 2 years, Maria has undergone hormonal treatment for infertility, which in itself may contribute to her volatility. In other words, to understand and treat this complicated case, we may have to gauge the power of factors outside the dyadic interaction between Paul and Maria. I pursue this last point in chapter 7.

Paul's Family of Origin: His Object Relations Map

The themes from Maria's family of origin and the inner objects that still embody those themes seem all too clear. Unfortunately, try as I might, I cannot map Paul's inner object relations with anything like the same clarity. Paul, the physical scientist, seems not psychologically minded and tells little about himself and his past, even when I persistently question him about these matters. I do learn that his father died when he was 2, likewise his first stepfather 16 years later. The mother is now married to a very elderly man, Paul's second stepfather, of whom Paul seems very fond. Paul felt protective of his twice-abandoned mother and tried to help and support her as much as possible. This explains his attraction to Maria, perhaps, a second petite woman of pluck, left alone in the world.

Paul's character, however, displays another side, related to another set of inner female objects. He continually warred with his 6-years-older sister through his childhood. The battle seemed over territory. He entered her bedroom or played his records too loudly, bothering her. She attacked. He defended. Each "aggression" became the occasion for another skirmish. Now, as middle-aged adults, Paul and his sister still do not speak and interact only with the placid brother-in-law as intermediary. Paul seemed equally obstinate at school, refusing, as I've said, to bend to rules he thought arbitrary.

Whether his stubbornness developed as a result of his protecting himself against the loss of father after father; as a way to defend himself against a jealous, hostile sister; or as a maneuver to fend off a loving but intrusive mother, I cannot say. His obdurateness does clearly represent a lifelong character feature and probably a reaction to unresolved family-of-origin issues. I can't pinpoint which issues, though, and I can't explain why Paul must participate in endless vendettas with women. Like a Middle Eastern conflict, the fight with his sister and now with his wife never stops, atrocities piling up on both sides. Regrettably, I cannot grasp many more of the details of Paul's development, and I can't pursue this stubborn repetition compulsion to its point of origin. If I could, I might help Paul more with his role in the fight.

We can predict what will come to pass when the stubborn Paul marries the bellicose Maria. It seems like a Hypothesis (1A) match. The unconscious bargain, in Dicks's terms, probably originally ran as follows. Paul found an attractive, energetic woman, like his mother, who, alone in a foreign country, needed his protection. But Maria promises to contribute additional positive features for Paul. Because of her professional training, she stands as a less helpless, more independent figure than his mother, and one who could fully understand and appreciate his scientific work. In return, when she received his protection, Paul probably expected that Maria would offer the interest, admiration, and gratitude that his mother had evidently showered upon him. For the most part, he's still waiting, although Maria can sometimes offer him warmth and affection.

Apparently, Maria chose Paul, again following Hypothesis (1A), as a man opposite to her brutal tyrant father. Paul seemed a soft-spoken gentleman who would respect and applaud her independence and never abandon her. Paul fills these requirements admirably, but, unfortunately, he also obstinately battles her over control. Here the bargain breaks, and the fight begins. The intense, recurrent battle, which sometimes ends with Maria hitting Paul, shows us the depths of disappointment these partners feel that their fantasy joining has not come true from either side. Maria isn't the mother Paul expected, and, in turn, Paul, as an unconscious father figure, persistently disappoints Maria.

Paul and Maria embody the dilemma of short-term object relations couple treatment in almost pure state. Maria's paranoid father and Paul's almost equally paranoid sister represent unmanageable inner objects. We must wonder if one unconscious meaning of the marriage stands as the opportunity to resolve a relationship with a paranoid inner presence. But neither Paul nor Maria, despite their sophistication, can grasp this possibility at the crucial moments. They cannot add the perspective of the past to the present conflict. Since the events mentioned in our previous excerpt, they have weathered great additional stresses together; job conflicts, the death of Paul's beloved stepfather, and seemingly interminable infertility treatments that physically and emotionally undermine Maria's already fragile inner state. They remain together, but they keep fighting the same battle. Maria feels that Paul overlooks her needs and fails to respect her autonomy. She blasts him for his lack of support. He defends himself.

Further treatment, including subsequent work with an individual therapist for Maria and another couple therapist for the pair, has failed to bring them into meaningful contact with their inner objects so far. If we cannot induce some direct or indirect resolution with these objects, we're stuck with a chronic standoff. I can't imagine Paul and Maria cooperating, even briefly, with a CBT, strategic, or behavioral approach, although, of course, I could miss the mark here. The case might require a long-term, intensive format like the Scharffs', not a practical possibility for them and not a plan that guarantees success, in any case. When I apply the five-step model to Paul and Maria, it seems to explain their predicament, but up until now, at least, it has failed as a practical intervention to treat their profound difficulties.

However, our study of Paul and Maria helps us understand, with almost crystal precision, the triangle of focus and its three interacting apexes: the fight, character features, and the influence of unresolved issues in the family of origin. Paul and Maria, then, illustrate for us the kind of complex object relations matrix that underlies the fight of which every couple complains when its members seek treatment. Today's fight appears embedded within a broader psychological and historical context. Each partner undergoes real conflicts with a real contemporary person, but the pattern of that conflict and its vehemence seem strongly influenced by the past unresolved family issues of each one.

Even though I have thus far proved unable to complete this work with Paul and Maria, the triangle of focus points us toward the task we probably need to accomplish in order to help this complicated couple ameliorate its fight. Each partner suffers from the repressive splits we studied in chapter 2. Because the split renders much of the conflict unconscious, neither of the pair can explain a lot about the problem, but each displays a characteristic impairment in relatedness. Maria, because of her traumatic history, cannot tolerate any infringement on her independence, and Paul rigidly bristles at any unfairness. Just beneath the split of each, we can find an unmanageable object relationship: Maria's destructive interaction with her father and Paul's experience of tyranny at the hands of his sister. Each must tolerate the anxiety to lift a defense surrounding that split, to undertake triangle of conflict work, in order to become open enough to develop more constructive behavioral alternatives.

As we'll observe repeatedly, exploring the triangle of focus represents the content of the therapy, but altering the triangle of conflict, that is, suspending a major defense, reflects the necessary process of the treatment. Unfortunately, because of their deep splits, Paul and Maria both appear somewhat paranoid in intimate relations. Both view the other with suspicion and remain vigilant lest the mistrusted partner try to take advantage. However, if Paul and Maria can dare some shift in their triangles of conflict, they would then return to their triangles of focus and acknowledge that, for most part, their fight is with past and not present objects. This realization would render constructive behavioral experimentation and possible conflict resolution much more likely.

Although I've seen this couple for 20 sessions or less per year, I cannot present Paul and Maria as a short-term treatment. I met them first some 5 years ago and treated them intermittently in a couple group and then in a solo couple format. I've included their material here because it graphically illustrates the triangle of focus, which we need to explore in the opening stages of any couple case. I also want to state my appreciation for the length of time some couples require for their treatment.

TED AND ESTHER: INVESTIGATING THE TRIANGLE OF FOCUS WITH A NEW CASE

Now let's turn to Ted and Esther, whom I've seen only three times, but whose troubled relationship also demonstrates for us the centrality of the triangle of focus.

An attractive, well-dressed, 38-year-old pair, Ted and Esther met in business school. They married 14 years ago and have two sons. Ted has embarked on a successful consulting practice. Esther, for reasons yet unexplained, never did pursue work with her professional degree.

Their fight is silent and frosted. Esther feels that Ted does not demonstrate responsibility in household tasks, in reliably depositing money into the checking account each week, and in regularly attending to her activities and to those of the children. She has literally turned a cold shoulder to him. The pair expresses little affection and in the past 5 years has rarely made love. Esther feels let down and Ted unappreciated and angry.

In the few months prior to our first meeting, Esther received a diagnosis of depression, for which she now takes the antidepressant Celexa. Esther feels less irritable and more optimistic, but the pair talks little about intimate matters, and Ted seems to have a limited understanding of the ramifications of Esther's depression. He does know that he feels lonely in his marriage, and he wonders if they belong together. Each blames the other for withdrawing and cannot forgive the abandonment. They have begun to lose respect for each other as people, which we know from Gottman (1994) represents a negative prognostic sign for the marriage. Neither believes the other one makes more than a minimal genuine effort to change the atmosphere between them. This sad state of affairs represents the fight (more of a cold war) apex of their triangle of focus.

The Families of Origin: Ted's and Esther's Object Relations Maps

In our first session I inquire with Esther about her family, the second apex of the triangle of focus. Esther can draw on little insight from her previous therapy, but as so frequently happens, the salient emotional conflicts of her original family tumble immediately from Esther and her preconscious.

Esther: My father was a pool contractor. He worked hard, but my mother ran the house and managed the finances of his business. He was a nice man, but he was quite uneducated. He seemed so self-centered and childish. It was all about him. He would read his newspaper at the dinner table. Because my sisters were 6 and 10 years older, I was practically an only child, and he didn't pay attention to me or to my mother. I wouldn't ever talk with him about anything important. My mother made the decisions about the family. [We've learned already that in Esther's unconscious, families represent matriarchies. Woman run them and men act as additional, troublesome children, who offer no adult empathy, closeness, or guidance.]

JMD: This sounds very difficult. Your father's self-centeredness must have made you very angry.

Esther: When we visit them now in California, he shows us off to all his friends, but then he doesn't stay around. He goes off and spends time with those friends. When I was growing up, it was cards one night, bowling another. He never gave it a thought.

My mother has had a stroke, and she doesn't walk very well. You have to walk with her and help her up the stairs. But he's impatient. He just goes ahead of her and dashes into the apartment, because he's hungry or whatever. I get mad at him and tell him to help her. For the moment, he acts a little better, but the next day he's the same again. He's not mean, but he just never thinks of anyone else, what they might need. [Has Esther projected her father's characteristic self-centeredness onto Ted?]

My parents had a 50th wedding anniversary. My father spoke and thanked everyone for coming. He talked about the children and grandchildren, but he never mentioned my mother. She just died. I pointed it out to him. He just got angry and stood up and walked off.

My mother seems more adventurous. She might want to go to a more intellectual movie or to a Chinese restaurant. But if it's not the same meat and potatoes, not only does he not like it, he just won't go. Very self-centered and childish. He says, "I see better movies on TV. Let's stay home." Very much a child. It's so frustrating. I was also a little afraid of his bad temper. He's difficult to reason with. You just can't contact him. [Does she experience Ted as similarly distant?]

JMD: This part of your family life sounds very sad.

Esther: I don't know if it's sad. He's very irritating, though. I don't really like to be around them; I guess that's sad.

JMD: I think this background influences your present marital problem.

Esther: Well, I certainly didn't need a man like that, who didn't pay any attention to his family. Ted seemed like such a sweet guy—a real friend. He didn't let anyone down. When we were going out, he seemed so interested. [At first, Ted appeared the opposite of her father.] He wanted the same things I did, but now he doesn't pay the bills, he doesn't care about decorating the house, he just leaves it to me. [Like her mother Esther feels left to run the family.] I just feel so *frustrated*. [And scared?]

JMD: That's the same word you used to describe your relationship with your father.

Esther feels devaluement at the hands of her oblivious father. This anti-libidinal object relationship, particularly the affects embedded in it, and the damaged sense of self-connected with it remain mostly repressed. Esther describes her father in the uninvolved tones that an anthropologist, and a cynical one, at that—might use, observing a curious, befuddled primitive from an alien culture. So Esther does not appear in direct touch with her fury at her self-centered father. As yet, she cannot connect her repressed anger with her father to her rejection of her husband, Ted. Ted appears self-involved and overly talkative to her, someone she now has trouble warming up to and enjoying, but the parallel to the father remains mostly unconscious. However, Esther now does know that she's depressed, complaining of aches and pains, chronic headaches, low libido, and irritability. She seeks reassurance of her husband's love and of her self-worth by requesting a series of major home renovations and expensive parties for the children. Hoping to finally gain her love and esteem, Ted complies.

Ted, from his side, feels overt hostility toward his mother. "She's an asshole. If you call her and say I hurt my leg, she says, 'Let me tell you about my leg.' She has no concern for you, and she doesn't even realize it. It's crazy." (Ted's brother married a discontented woman, like the mother, but has finally divorced her.) Ted's father worked long hours in poorly paid retail, his wife continually complaining about lack of money. Now Ted, whose income equals 10 times his father's, finds himself in the same prison as his father, trapped with a wife who requires more and more material expenditure. Long ago, Ted learned to turn a deaf ear to his mother's litany. At present he speaks to her as little as possible, and on those few occasions, it appears that his attitude has barely disguised disrespect. Unfortunately, he now may address Esther in similarly sarcastic tones.

Esther and Ted seem to live in a Hypothesis (1A) marriage. Each chose the other to embody the opposite of a parent figure, but up to the present, the bargain has failed. Ted regards Esther as selfish, cold, given to somatic complaints, and obsessed with lavish spending, just as he sees his mother. Esther experiences Ted as oblivious, unrelated, and irresponsible, like her father.

As Dicks has told us, we can often make the diagnosis and uncover the central themes quite easily in the first two sessions, and with this couple we can do just that. Both partners have to realize, at some level, that they're disillusioned with the opposite-sex parent and then they have projected this deep disappointment onto the spouse. What is my next therapeutic move, though? First, and this represents a step not emphasized by Dicks or the Scharffs, I need to assess how much awareness both partners have about the unconscious life of their match, about their triangles of focus. I'll start with Ted.

Ted certainly acknowledges and feels his rage at his mother. He has begun to realize that he reacts to his wife's somatic complaints and requests for money in the same dismissive way that he deflects his mother's many woes and wants. At this point he's aware of the wife–mother connection, but, feeling cheated and angry, he can't see any role that he might play in provoking his wife's sour stance, nor does he grasp why he must continually chase an apparently unsatisfiable woman.

For her part, Esther consciously feels her irritation, although not her rage, with her father and also with her husband, but does not consciously connect her fury at her father with her anger at her husband. From what I can gather thus far, it appears that Esther's characteristic annoyance represents a major affect state for her. Her whole life seems to irritate her. Many tasks remain undone. Husband and children often seem a burden. She seems to think, "I'll enjoy the family later, when I finish the work"—but later never arrives. Here we might find ourselves encountering what Christopher Bollas (1987) has called the "unthought known." Esther becomes annoyed about someone or something so often, as if she lives a memory of many hurts but cannot connect these past events to her present mood. Life never seems to measure up for Esther. She didn't use her MBA, her children frustrate her, and her husband falls short. If Esther cannot come to acknowledge, in some way, the unthought known that she's continually grumbling inside about past and not necessarily about present disappointments, she will continue to live the memory. Neither she nor Ted will find warmth in their relationship.

Esther's depression represents another key factor in the therapy. At least in part, she's irritable for biochemical and not just object relations reasons. She had received psychopharmacological treatment for the depression for only a few months, but the therapist abruptly interrupted the therapy without explanation, just before I began with this couple. Characteristically, Esther did not seek additional treatment and let the medicine lapse. I found her a new clinician with whom I can communicate regularly to assure that she will receive individual psychotherapy and adequate medication. Perhaps, as her depression lifts, Esther will become less unsatisfiable and more available emotionally to Ted and to herself.

But what if the medication remains only partly effective? Now, as with Paul and Maria, we encounter the dilemma of short-term object relations couple treatment in real time. Esther probably needs to uncover more and more of her feelings about her father and about herself for the therapy to work. Recall that a repressed object relationship encompasses three entities—an object (in this case, the father), an affect (so far, irritability), and the self (thus far, an angry self, but under that, probably a devalued, sad self). From Esther's side, the success of the therapy will depend on whether I can help her come into contact with more and more layers of her repressed object relations. In other words, following the five-step model, Esther needs to become more open to engage in triangle of focus work, relating her character features of irritability and withholdingness to her relationship with her father and then to her cold war with her husband.

I need to undertake a parallel exchange with Ted. I'll try to help him experience that he's projected his disappointed libidinal mother object onto Esther. Now he ignores her wishes because he assumes that she can't be satisfied anyway and will never return to him the attention he craves.

The pace of the therapy will depend on how constructively Esther and Ted can pursue the working-through process. But maybe they will not undertake this journey. Although I can support, coach, and offer homework assignments, I can't make the trip for them. The length and outcome of the treatment, given a "good enough" therapist, always remains under the unconscious control of the clients.

The therapist's principal tasks to abet working through seem clear: (1) maintain an active positive alliance, (2) analyze resistance, and (3) construct productive relationship counter-offers. This first principle seems an obvious starting point for any therapy, so I'll move to number 2. The analysis of resistance focuses on the client's reluctance to associate to his or her repressed conflicts but also on the client's unproductive, more general interactions with the partner and with the treatment. For example, Esther seems broadly self-defeating. She finished business school but failed the accounting licensing exam and never retook it, never practicing professionally. Although apparently depressed for at least 5 years, she only recently sought psychiatric treatment and then only because her husband insisted. She has not pursued the couple therapy with me with great determination and has already missed two of our sessions because of avoidable last-minute schedule conflicts. Probably in the next session, I will help Esther focus on her disinclination to help herself, but she quickly feels shamed and blamed, so I can't move fast into this territory.

Ted exudes likability and good cheer. He reports, and I believe him, that everyone, except his wife, responds warmly to him. He's almost compulsively generous. He overpays his business associates and lends money freely to relatives. Ted's lighthearted, friendly style may represent a complex resistance in itself. Perhaps he expects the world to return to him, right away, the love that he seems so enthusiastically, or so desperately, to offer. When his wife fails to mirror his beaming grin, perhaps he gets miffed and refuses to empathize with the details of Esther's severe conflicts and debilitating depression. I need to explore this possible resistance with Ted soon.

Finding the correct relationship stance to this couple remains a quandary to me. I've tried an early interpretative approach, suggesting to Esther that she feels the same "frustration" with Ted that she did with her father and connecting Ted's feelings about his mother with his attitude toward his wife. This strategy has struck no remarkable chords. Little new material has emerged, and the relationship remains stuck in icy standoff. Esther misses sessions. Ted sometimes attends by himself and continues to express his dissatisfaction with his marriage but can gain little insight into his contribution to the checkmate. I could refuse to meet with Ted alone, but then I fear that this troubled pair might slip away entirely, and I would have no chance to help either member.

I've found this halting progress not uncommon in the beginning phases of short-term couple work. I can clearly grasp the triangle of focus for each member of the pair. They agree with me intellectually but, initially, can't use the interpretations to break through into an increased awareness of their marriage. I have two choices: Keep on interpreting, taking on the resistance frontally, or attempt to move through it with relationship interventions. Usually, the second strategy works more quickly and effectively. In couple treatment it is easier to change the doctor than to change the clients.

With Esther, if she does return on any regular basis, I'll try to empathize warmly with her pain and bring her out to talk more about how she has given up on her frustrating, hurtful father but has lost a part of herself in doing so. Chic, sophisticated Esther has hidden her true self behind her elegant sweater, coordinated slacks, and Mercedes SUV. Esther reminds me of Dicks's description of the poor little child, deprived of loving response, trapped behind the resulting ego split, who fears to reach out genuinely in any way. I'll try to speak to the repressed little girl self struggling so hard for her father's attention that never came.

Boisterous, amicable, loquacious Ted, much easier to talk with than Esther, presents as great a challenge as his wife does. I need to work behind his shield of affability to contact his sadness and rejection over his depriving, repressed, frustrating mother, as well as to work with his more available rage at her. Ted also has an identification with a downtrodden father, and I'll need to reach that, too. Anxious Ted has trouble staying with one feeling for long, so I must persist in making him stick to the topic. In my countertransference, I also must keep in perspective my reaction to him as the loving one rebuffed by his cold, rejecting wife-mother. Ted expresses real pain over his situation. If I ally too strongly with him, I will lose my credibility with mistrustful, easily disappointed Esther. I can throw my support to Ted, but this won't help their marriage. I must offer Ted a more stern, demanding relationship than he's become used to. He's a warm, generous man, but he does tease and provoke prickly Esther, and he needs to stop that. As she suggests, he could pay more attention to the details of his adult responsibilities to the family, such as the checking account, schedules, and so on.

We can readily identify the repressive splits for each, the place beyond which they cannot go, the relationship theme they have such difficulty in negotiating. Esther implodes when she feels overlooked, Ted when he's unappreciated. The charge for the therapy is to introduce our model to help each partner tolerate and express these vulnerabilities to the other, rather than to go on the attack automatically, when the relationship rubs the split raw.

THE TRIANGLE OF FOCUS REVISITED AT THE CLOSE OF TREATMENT: COUPLE GROUP EXAMPLES

In this chapter I've suggested that a key step in the treatment occurs when couples acquire some genuine affective appreciation of the connections wrapped within the three parts of the triangle of focus and thereby gain the freedom to experiment with fresh constructive behaviors. I'll offer two examples of pairs, from later in their therapy, who've worked toward that understanding of their triangles and of the object relations underlying those triangles. We can observe these pairs in the midst of resolving their fight as they use their new knowledge. We can see and hear how the treatment begins and finishes with the triangle of focus, but, by termination, that triangle looks and feels very different than it did at the start for each participant.

The Triangle of Focus in Short-Term Couple Group

Short-term couple group therapy, which I will describe in greater detail in chapter 5, represents a particularly helpful context in which pairs can study the influence of the family of origin on the character conflicts of each member of the couple and on how and why each participates in the fight, following his or her persistent fashion. In the first few meetings of these three- to four-couple, 15-session groups, my co-therapists and I help the pairs identify the major themes in their fights. In these early meetings we draw parallels to unsolved issues in the families of origin, but, understandably, the individual group members at first resist these connections. This resistance takes a characteristic form. The members do not flatly deny the relationship between the present conflict, their past family history, and their problematic character stance, but their response tends toward the neutral. They treat our clarifications and interpretations tentatively, as ideas worthy of consideration, but hardly as revelations leading to significant new insights. Little new important material emerges.

However, meetings 5 through 12 offer the chance for the couples to work through the possibility that present and past really seem affectively connected. By session 13 or 14, often, though not always, some repression lifts and many members, though not all, break through into powerful affects that undeniably link the difficulties of the fight to the libidinal and anti-libidinal objects from the past, to traumas connected with those objects, and to problematic character features inherited from early family interactions. In these sessions, the workings of the triangle of focus—the relationship between family of origin, character stances, and the fight—become very real for some of the participants. Dramatic shifts in the marital interaction often, but not always, immediately follow, as we'll see in the next two case examples.

In a recent group, two couples experienced epiphanies in session 14. One of these pairs we've met previously—Mark, the bull in the china shop, and his reticent wife, Joanne. This couple reported major changes at the end of meeting 14. Our new pair, Jack and Eileen, had their breakthrough at the start of session 14, so I'll introduce them now.

JACK AND EILEEN

Handsome, athletic Jack, age 45, a lawyer, and his pretty, slender, graceful wife of the same age, Eileen, a teacher, lived a marriage apparently marked by Jack's withdrawal and Eileen's furious reaction to it. Jack really does step back, and at these times he's silent, aloof, and uninvolved. When Eileen senses him slipping away, she lashes out at him and then sadly withdraws into herself and becomes depressed— feeling frightened and hopeless. Eileen tried antidepressant medication some 2 years ago but didn't find it helpful and has discontinued it.

Jack's family represented a psychiatric disaster area. Both parents suffered major depression and were hospitalized intermittently through his adolescence. In recent years matters have deteriorated still further, and at one point recently, the aged couple entered the same psychiatric hospital together. Jack lives in fear of the phone call that his parents, who reside some 20 miles away, find themselves once again in crisis. Jack rarely speaks to Eileen about his parents, never talks to his children about them, and has only recently discussed family issues seriously with his younger sister, his only sibling. The two siblings have colluded to ignore the frustration and sadness of their parents' endless despair. The problematic dynamic between Jack and Eileen became clear in the early meetings of the group.

(Group Session 2)

Jack: I found my mother the worst to deal with. Whenever I wanted to do something like go and play basketball with my friends, she would get angry and start yelling at me. I gradually just ignored her and went anyway. [The way he ignores Eileen?] I spent a lot of time in my room, doing my homework. When I went to college, I was so happy to escape. They didn't take me there or anything. I just packed my suitcase and got a bus ticket. I wouldn't discuss anything with my parents. They didn't even know where I had applied to college. [In fact, Jack had won a scholarship to an Ivy League school.] My mother, I just avoided her as much as I could.

JMD: When Eileen has problems, it must seem like the same old thing. What can I possibly do? Nothing will work. I'm getting out of here.

Jack: I guess that's about it. I try to listen, but I just feel helpless.

JMD: Your mother had no inner resources, or she didn't use the ones she had. Eileen has a lot of resources. She's a different person from your mother, but you have to feel that to make this different. [Triangle of focus interpretation.]

Jack: I know you're right. I'm working on that.

Eileen's father was a critical alcoholic, her mother apparently passive. Her one brother, probably the victim of his father's projections, has survived alcohol and drug addiction but now has angrily withdrawn to a marginal adjustment in the rural Midwest. He rarely communicates with the family. Eileen makes little mention of her younger sister. She, like Jack, appears the lone real survivor of her family.

A survivor, but not one unscathed, as we'll now recognize. In the early sessions of the group, several times Eileen alluded to, but did not recount in any detail, a childhood sexual attack. In session 13 she said she had written a poem about the incident and wanted to share it with the group at our next meeting. In session 14 she read us the piece, which described her rape at age 12, and explained how this trauma had affected her at each life stage thereafter. The group members and the therapists fell silent after the reading, most of us fighting back tears. (Eileen's offer of the poem to the group signified that she was beginning to suspend her defense of noninvolvement.)

Eileen told us that her attacker was a "family friend," who assaulted her in a neighborhood attic, menacing her with a screwdriver. He threatened that if she told anyone about the rape, he would kill her family. Eileen, terrified, did not reveal the incident to her mother until some years later. The mother reacted by warning her not to discuss it with anyone, because people would look down on her and her family. She offered no empathy to Eileen at this critical moment. Eileen felt raped twice. The group members responded in strong support for Eileen and sympathized with her impossible frightened position as a child holding a terrible secret.

After their marriage, Jack accompanied Eileen back to her hometown and to the attic of her attack. I pointed out to Eileen that her mother had abandoned her in many small ways and this one big way, but that Jack had joined her at the scene and had listened to her story. I wondered with her whether her intense reaction to Jack's recurrent withdrawals and her subsequent sadness had also to do with desertions by her family.

(Group Session 14)

JMD: Given this history, it's very hard for you to deal with Jack without getting extremely angry when he moves away, which inevitably drives him further away and then makes you sad. You know, until you read the poem, you seemed very involved in the group, but perhaps you had trouble speaking up about yourself. I wonder if Jack knows when you really want to talk to him.

Jack: You know, that's a good point. I often don't know.

JMD: So you rob yourself of what you want most. Perhaps, Eileen, if you say, "I feel vulnerable when you're far away," rather than snapping at him, then maybe you'll have an intimate discussion instead of a fight.

Eileen: Yes, I hold back, too.

JMD: Sometimes you rob yourself of what you want most. You just assume abandonment.

Jack: When I find out more about her feelings about her past, I can understand more. Sometimes she seems angry with me so quickly that I don't know what to do.

We can see that Jack and Eileen, by group session 14, have entered into some valuable triangle of focus work, connecting early objects from the family of origin to important character features, his tendency to withdraw and her conviction of abandonment, character features that usher in the recurrent battle. She seeks him out for intimacy. He flees. She descends into first anger and then depression. Both have begun to acknowledge responsibility for their roles. Jack sees that he must tolerate his helplessness in order to listen to Eileen, and Eileen experiences how she pushes Jack away. Any astute therapist could sketch out the rough outlines of the triangle of focus for each member of this pair in the first two or three meetings of the group. But only after some dramatic working-through sessions, such as here in meeting 14, which included Eileen's description of her rape, could the partners begin to acknowledge, cognitively and affectively, their triangles of focus.

We can sense from the excerpt that Jack and Eileen have just started to work through their fight. Because both are, in fact, victims of trauma, we've had to invest two evaluation and 14 group sessions to support these partners to reach, albeit tentatively, a grounded starting place to begin to unravel their conflict.

Since the group ended a year ago, Eileen has returned to see me once for advice about her younger daughter, toward whom she acts somewhat overprotectively—understandable given her history of having received so little protection. She reported that the marriage was working better. The couple has not returned, as yet, for further sessions, so I'm guardedly optimistic that the two have continued to use the group experience to support further communication. Also, during session 14, Jack reported to the group that he had applied for a major promotion at his company, an appropriate step that he had previously considered but never dared to undertake. Jack appears, then, to have started to embark on some important individual moves toward separating from his depressed, hopelessly dysfunctional, original family environment and toward some realistic assertiveness and risk taking.

Mark's Triangle of Focus at Group End

Mark now took center stage in session 14. Recall Mark from chapter 2, the brusque, burly man given to impulsive acts, who had lost family money in the stock market, and who waved off any advice from his underconfident wife, Joanne, or from a succession of previous therapists. My co-therapist and I included Mark in the three-couple group with trepidation, sensing that his provocative style might preoccupy the group and keep it from other important work. After the first session, we wished that we'd heeded our reservations more faithfully. Mark opened the group by accosting Jack with the criticism that he thought it disrespectful of Jack to wear sweatpants to the meeting. Mark, also an athlete, changed out of his uniforms when he attended social gatherings. Jack, rightly annoyed, told Mark he was off base—not the ideal interchange on which to build cohesion for this very short, very small group.

However, as our meetings came to a close, Mark, almost incredibly, began to reassess his previously idealized childhood and to realize that his parents had left him to fend for himself in the outside world. We'll pick up the group at the moment just before Mark's revelation. Now, in the second half of session 14, I noticed that Mark began to cry silently after Eileen had shared her poem. I asked him what he felt.

Mark: Yes, I was crying. I've always been sensitive to anything to do with children. *Now I understand why.* In high school, I missed a baseball practice because I was in the science fair. When I came back to practice the next day, the coach kicked me off the team. My father never went to talk to the coach. I realize that's a basic parent role. I guess my father never considered doing that. I worked it out with the coach, and it was okay, but I sure could have used his help there. If that had happened to one of my kids, I'd be there the next morning at 8:00 A.M. I was always down at the school. Like I said, I have a special sensitivity to children's issues. My father never saw me play baseball. I was the captain of the team.

I listen to radio talk shows all day long at work. This guy wrote a book about parents' effects on their children. He said parents' behaviors will always form a behavior in the child, but it's never what you would expect, not a straight line. I ordered the book, and I've been reading it the last 2 weeks. It's really a good book. It's been very liberating for me. I can track down what my parents did. Why I behave like this. I just didn't understand this.

JMD: What did you discover?

Mark: My parents didn't know anything about my life. They never saw me play sports, and I was a football and baseball star. They didn't know who my friends were or what we did. Some of the kids I hung around with turned out big-time criminals, I mean, really big time, very violent as kids. [Perhaps Mark's choice of friends expressed his anger at his parents.]

JMD: A major parental role is to maintain safety for the children. To ask you who your friends are, to meet them, to see if they want to come over to the house for a soda.

Mark: That's right. Joanne and I didn't intervene very much, but we always knew if a kid was being nasty to one of our kids at school. My parents didn't know my life. Didn't know anything about it. There was no way to get any feedback. That's why I'm the way I am, just go ahead and do things, because there's nobody over there anyway. That's why I continually get it wrong.

JMD: That's why you rush into things. It's very difficult to develop social judgment in a vacuum.

Mark: Yes, my father died when I was 18. He never said much, but when my mother started yelling at me, he said, "Leave him alone. You'll make him a sissy." That's something, I guess. When he died, my mother said, "You're all I've got." Take care of the adults. That's a very difficult position for a child. I couldn't really take care of myself. Now, how was I going to take care of her? That's not what you should say to children. Now I try to listen to people. It's hard. I try to be different every day.

JMD: Your behavior's totally different from the first few sessions of this group.

Mark: I realize now that it's not an assault on my ego identity if somebody disagrees with me. Everyone brings a special sensitivity from his past life. I realize how some of my characteristics are like my father's. Realize how powerful it is to grow up like that. [I should have pursued the identification with his father more, but I didn't want to interrupt Mark at this place.]

JMD: Joanne knows a lot of things.

Mark: Yes, she knows how to do stuff. I didn't realize that.

Joanne: We have a better relationship.

JMD: He's making a big effort.

Joanne: Yes, he is, and I'm thrilled.

JMD: Did you tell him you're thrilled?

Joanne: I think he knows. [Joanne still can't find a strong voice.]

JMD: If you're thrilled, tell people that you're thrilled. Let him know.

Joanne: Yes, well, Mark, I'm thrilled.

Mark: Thank you.

Joanne: Your mother was a good grandmother to our kids. I could never see the problem that you had with this lovely, little old lady, but now I can integrate that. This is very helpful to see.

Mark: My parents loved me, but maybe that's not the love you need. You need something different, a different kind of love. I never figured that out.

Joanne begins to talk about visiting her family in the Midwest. Both parents are in their late 80s, and her mother suffers from severe Alzheimer's. Her father apparently keeps her mother alive with his meticulous 24-hour-a-day care. One sister looks after the parents but never asks Joanne for her advice or opinion.

Joanne: They cut me out of it, because I left. I have no influence on my sisters or on my parents' life. It's very upsetting. It's an awful thing.

JMD: In your marriage, it's been an awful thing that you felt you had no influence on your husband.

Joanne: Yes, I was very frustrated and very scared.

JMD: Was like being back in your family again.

Joanne: Yes, I guess it was.

This group session sparked intense, affective insights in several of the members, connecting: (1) their present, individual adjustment, that is, Mark's provocativeness and Jack's withdrawal, with (2) childhood themes and with (3) their recurrent marital fight—the three apexes of the triangle of focus. The material makes it clear that for several members of the group, repression has begun to lift, and affect has burst forth. In this state of openness, real learning can now take place. By session 14 we're no longer dealing with intellectualized hypotheticals but with emotional insight. We continue to explore the triangle of focus we groped for at the beginning but now in new depth. In Mark's case, at least, that insight has led to dramatic behavior change in his marriage and in his everyday interactions.

To summarize the signs of individual growth in session 14, Eileen realizes more of the complexity of her dilemma with Jack. His silence plunges her into a fear of impending abandonment and into anger, just the way her mother's silence in response to her drunken, ranting father and to her childhood rape also toppled her into depths of vulnerability, covered over by fury. Notice that in each of these crucial interactions lived through by Eileen, we can discover an object (the rapist, the mother, Jack), an affect (terror, abandonment, fury), and an experience of self (a terrified self, a lost self, a vengeful self). These represent the central object relations around which Eileen's individual and marital problems revolve.

Jack has now, to some degree, connected his rage (affect) at dealing with his impossible parents, particularly his mother (the disappointing libidinal object), to his straitjacket of helplessness (his experience of self) when Eileen wants to talk intimately. We cannot yet know how deeply Jack has allowed these insights into his psyche or whether he can reliably use them to support later behavior change.

Mark's transformation—little short of remarkable, even to the eye of an experienced therapist—follows the same pattern of de-repression. Mark realizes that as a child, his developmentally needy, lonely self required feedback and interest. The parental objects treated him with indifference, which, in turn, provoked affects (sadness and bewilderment) that he defended against with his characteristic helter-skelter bravado. These decidedly uninvolved parents represent the crucial internalized object relations with which Mark struggles and relives daily with whomever he meets, his interpersonal repetition compulsion.

Remembering Ogden (1982) and by studying Mark, we can see exactly how many of us do recreate our emotional life with every new person we encounter. In the past Mark has managed to annoy and alienate almost everyone in his world by ignoring their needs and particular emotional states, in exactly the fashion that his original objects overlooked him. Mark's insight into this pattern enables him to work toward changing it. He has now found a methodology to help him understand and refocus his emotional reactions. He studies his interactions and experiments with changes, where before he rotated in circles, like a whirling dervish, provoking the same exchanges over and over and living with bewildering confusion and frustration about what went wrong.

Joanne, too, experienced distant uninfluencable objects, her parents, sister, and husband, to whom she responded with a helpless self and with the affects of despair, frustration, and ultimately anger. Now, in tense situations, for a long time she doesn't speak up, and when she finally does demand a voice, she's so angry that she attacks, rather than constructively participates. Joanne has grasped her object relations problem with greater clarity now. She knows that she has to join in more actively and not assume that others will automatically overlook her. It remains too soon to tell whether she can or will use this insight to experiment with further behavioral change.

This group session excites us as therapists, because we can see the repression lift before our eyes. When the clients make these affective connections, a new set of options becomes available to them. We can accompany Mark, for example, as he actively finds himself in the midst of these choices and begins to alter his style.

Short-term object relations couple therapy starts with an exploration of the triangle of focus: (1) describe the fight in detail; (2) relate the affects embedded in the fight to problematic, individual character features; and (3) relate these to unsolved issues in the family of origin. The couple therapy may then range into any number of discussions of specific present conflicts—for instance, child-rearing problems or anger with in-laws, or into a confrontation with individual character problems, the triangle of conflict work, which we take up in the next chapter. But the treatment usually ends by returning to where it started, with the clients revisiting their triangle of focus, as Jack, Eileen, Mark, and Joanne have just done here in group session 14. This time, they confront their original triangles with less repression and more affective insight because of what they've learned in the intervening sessions about their triangles of conflict.

Recall Dicks's earlier statement that the major themes of the couple treatment appear early, and the bulk of the therapy consists of working through these themes. Dicks has misled us, though, if he implied that the working through followed a relatively straightforward process. In just the little we've already observed from these few cases, this stage hardly appears uncomplicated. A number of specific disagreements, standoffs, and resistances within the couple and between the couple and the therapist can intervene, any of which may throw the threesome off track. For the first half of the group, resistant Mark appeared pointedly to ignore suggestions by the therapist and the other members, as if we had no understanding whatever of emotional matters, but then, suddenly, he transformed himself and his entire interpersonal approach. Clearly, working through still holds many mysteries for us to unlock. The capacity of each member of the couple to de-repress and affectively approach his or her inner objects appears to be the most important variable, and the one that we therapists have the least capacity to control or to predict. I'll pursue this important topic, in depth, in chapters 6 and 7.

However, Dicks does point us clearly toward the idea that the couple therapy returns at the end to where it began. Our triangle of focus work illustrates this progression and indicates that the five-step model already requires revision. After exploring the fight, we start in pursuit of the triangle of focus, as I've shown here, but in the final stages of treatment we *revisit* the triangle of focus as the couple, ideally, breaks through into new insight about this old material. In fact, we emphasize the triangle of focus throughout the treatment, because here lies the heart of the content of the work: relate the old objects to the fight and to the character problems of each partner. But the triangle of focus usually looms more prominently at the beginning and then at the later stages of the therapy. The middle phases of the treatment often concentrate on the triangle of conflict work, but that, too, in some cases can come very early in the therapy as well. So the stages do not unfold in exactly the same sequence for each couple treatment. The five-step model actually represents an overlapping spiral of activity, rather than a linear progression. The model revised:

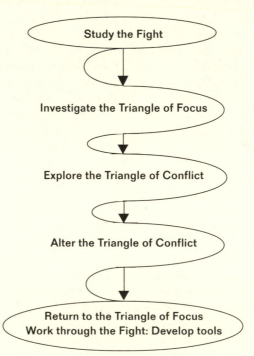

FIGURE 3.2

This diagram implies that because of resistance, the therapy might become short-circuited at any point. Each phase could continue briefly or for an extremely long time. Paul and Maria seem stuck in the middle of the triangle-of-focus stage. They've developed some insight about the connections between the fight and the family of origin. They show some improvement, but they continue to battle bitterly. Ted and Esther have just entered the triangle-of-focus phase, and we do not know how they will fare within it. But Jack and Eileen have done some solid work in revisiting their triangles. We begin to see shifts in their behavior toward each other, based on these new insights. Mark and Joanne have moved through the triangle of focus and have completed a good deal of triangle of conflict work, studying their own interpersonal dynamics. Then they've returned to the triangle of focus with new knowledge. They can discuss their fight openly now, to good effect, and Mark has developed tools to forestall the fight. Reevaluating the five-step model in this fashion lends us hints that when progress halts at a particular phase, the couple might retrogress back along the spiral. We see this backward movement with Paul and Maria. They begin to develop insights about the triangle of focus. They then encounter frustration or additional stress, such as the repeated disappointment of the fertility trials, and they retrogress back into their fight.

The five-step model allows us to define the place of any couple along the spiral, at any given time, regardless of the specific content or the particular style of their fight. This is a helpful feature when pairs revolve in and out of therapy, as so often occurs in today's managed-care settings. When the partners return, we can ascertain where they're presently situated on the spiral, which tells us what task needs to come next. We can also help the couple and ourselves account for any regressions back to the original fight.

In this chapter, I have tried to illustrate how, in the opening phases of short-term object relations treatment, the therapist attempts to uncover and organize the basic themes that underlie the couple fight. The best conceptual instrument that I know to drive this process is the triangle of focus. Here we begin to link the unresolved issues in the family of origin with the character problems of each partner and with the fight. In this fashion we can use the triangle of focus to outline the data our treatment will need to face. In the working-through phase, which represents the balance of the therapy, the therapist and the clients must address the unconscious resistances that keep the three parts of the triangle of focus psychologically separate. The group excerpts that we studied in the second half of this chapter illustrate, to paraphrase Semrad, that when the clients stop saying "no" about the connections linking the apexes of the triangle of focus, the treatment may be nearly over. However, first we also need to face the prominent intrapsychic conflicts that each member of the pair brings to the fight. We use the triangle of conflict as a starting place to investigate these.

In chapter 4, I'll illustrate a method to explore that triangle of conflict, a concept that explains what leads each member of the pair to engage in the fight in his or her repetitive, self-defeating fashion.

Step 3: Explore the Triangle of Conflict

Each couple represents a *system*, albeit a small one, and two separate *individuals*, the conceptual puzzle that renders couple treatment fascinating but also confusing. In every minute of every session, the therapist must ponder at which level to understand the difficulty and, quickly following that assessment, at what level to intervene. In a time-limited format, this decision becomes more crucial, and the therapist can rapidly feel pressured and tempted to become hasty in his or her approach. Many therapists, particularly systemic theorists, argue against an emphasis on individual intrapsychic functioning within a couple therapy. I strongly disagree. I'll quickly demonstrate both the necessity and the pitfalls of my position.

Chapter 4 concentrates on the triangle of conflict, individual character dynamics. However, I emphasize that in most cases, we need to postpone a thorough investigation of that triangle for each member until we've grasped the couple as a system first. For this reason the exploration of the connections in the triangle of focus—the fight, the family of origin of each member, and important character features of each—usually precedes attention to the triangle of conflict. But psychotherapy never unfolds with the precision of a geometric proof. The data and the affects swirl through the session, so we deal with the triangle of focus, then the triangle of conflict, then back to the triangle of focus at different times in different meetings.

THE TRIANGLE OF CONFLICT: EARLIER FORMULATIONS

Now I'll discuss the triangle of conflict as a metapsychological construct and trace a bit of its history, summarizing the contributions of prior authors. First, a few words about the practical utility of conceptual models such as the triangle of focus and the triangle of conflict. Couple treatment deluges the therapist with a plethora of material. Without conceptual schematics like the two triangles, the therapist could easily become overwhelmed by the torrent of detail. These triangles help us order the data and direct our interventions. Without these or parallel conceptual guides, we could proceed directed only by our intuition at any given moment—not remotely an option in time-managed work.

Leigh McCullough-Vaillant (1994, 1997), a student in brief dynamic therapy of both Malan (1976, 1979; Malan & Osimo, 1992) and Davanloo (1978), offers us the most sophisticated understanding of the triangle of conflict. She first reviews Malan's work based on an older rendition of this triangle.

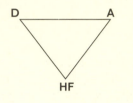

A = Anxiety
D = Defense
HF = Hidden Feeling

FIGURE 4.1

Malan used his triangle of conflict to describe the central process of short-term individual dynamic therapy. "Put the patient in touch with as much of his true feeling as he can stand at any given moment" (Malan, 1976, p. 84)—a succinct, one-sentence description of the goal of affect-defense psychoanalysis. The therapist softens the connections between anxiety and defense, which allows the impulse or "true feeling" into consciousness. This generic model of therapy, "make the unconscious conscious," has structured any number of crucial insights about human beings and about how to offer them psychotherapy, but McCullough, the self psychologists, and the modern object relations school have proposed important alterations in this basic model.

What if the affect defended against, and uncovered through interpretation, itself represents a neurotic or incomplete aim? For example, if the husband becomes anxious (A) in the presence of his wife and defends against this through timidity (D), which covers rage at a controlling mother (HF), we cannot represent the goal of individual, and particularly of couple, therapy as simply to uncover this rage. The husband expresses extreme anger at the wife; she retaliates or dissolves in tears. Wither the therapy? We require another step to promote intimacy in the couple. So far, the old model just helps us contact the husband's fury at his mother and, by transference, at his wife.

McCullough shows that the repressed hidden feeling or impulse pole fundamentally applies to growth-promoting feelings, such as the desire for closeness or understanding, not impulses per se. Intense affects—in other words, anger at the mother or the wife—although important, do not necessarily represent the primary underlying feelings we therapists seek. We must see these affects, such as this rage, as real but also as defenses against more important motivations such as the desire for acceptance and understanding. We can recast the Malan triangle for the husband thusly:

A = Fear of wife's judgments
D = Timidity, but also rage at women
HF = The wish for closeness

Susan Johnson (1999) eschews psychoanalytic concepts and does not push very deeply into the psychodynamics of her clients, but she makes the same point. Please recall her earlier case of the retired couple, in which the wife had recently recovered from cancer. The husband, Len, may scream at his wife, Clara, an obvious expression of feeling, but this affect may cover his hidden wish for her loving response. Since her cancer diagnosis, he feels terrified that she will leave him, either voluntarily or through death.

The modern object relations theorists, such as Christopher Bollas (1987) and the Scharffs, take a similar tact to the problem of repressed material. The goal of their therapy is not simply to uncover affect but to bring forward and reshape repressed senses of self in relation to another. So, using the triangle of conflict, we need to search for each member's characteristic manner of defending (D) against specific anxieties (A), in order to keep repressed certain primary wishes (HF) for self-care and for intimacy.

Projective identification and the triangle of conflict exist in an interlocking relationship. We can't fully understand one without a good grasp of the other. Projective identification represents a central, complicated, mutually agreed-upon defensive maneuver that keeps the partners involved with each other and with old objects but protects them from the real interaction they flee. Time and again, we observe that from within his or her triangle of conflict, one member of the pair projects a self or object image onto the other that the other, from within his or her triangle of conflict, modifies and accepts. Mark projects his intrusive mother onto Joanne, for example. She then becomes the more controlling, validating his triangle.

The triangle of conflict, therefore, represents a rigid defensive system that depends on projective identification to maintain itself. If I, Mark, can make Joanne into my bossy mother, then my anxiety/defense reflex toward her seems justified, and I need not reassess. If Joanne, in fact, frequently acts in a controlling fashion on her own, all the better for maintaining my triangle. Therefore, altering the triangle of conflict and suspending projective identification represent synonymous actions.

As I work with the triangle of conflict, I'm on the lookout to identify specific defenses, to show the individual and the couple the maladaptive nature of these defenses. Then I try to help each individual to name and to begin to tolerate his or her particular anxieties and to show both of them

how projective identification fits their defensive program. Using this terminology, we can appreciate that the triangle of conflict may also lie at the
core of Dicks's and the Scharffs' approach to therapy. They employ different words, but each of their interpretations seems aimed at supporting the
client toward a deeper understanding of his or her automatic anxiety →
defensive reactions, which contribute so forcefully to the marital standoff.

As we ponder methods for intervening within the triangle of conflict,
we can begin to see that character change in the individual members of the
pair has now become a major part of couple therapy, a substantial challenge, to say the least, particularly within a brief format. This challenge,
though, becomes somewhat delimited. We're attempting character change
but only in the areas that fall centrally within the triangle of focus. In other
words, we're interested in usually one or two character features that play a
central role in the recurrent fight. Also, we're not always trying to *alter*
character, as Leigh McCullough-Vaillant does in her form of extended brief
individual treatment (1997). We endeavor to render the participants aware
of difficult character features that they bring to the marital interaction. If
one member can *acknowledge* his controllingness and gain perspective on
it, this can introduce a new productive dimension into the relationship.
We'll see that the individuals do not have to work through deep character
change to improve their relationship, but they do have to understand, and
affectively accept, the character issues that they import into the fight.

Now I'll introduce three couples; in one, I failed to help the individuals
work out adequate character recognition, and in the others, I succeeded at
least temporarily. But both couples effectively illustrate the usefulness of
the triangle of conflict as a therapeutic guide.

THE UPTONS

I summarize this case at length because it offers us an excellent example of
the close interaction between the triangle of conflict and projective identification. I also include it because it demonstrates, admittedly in an extreme
form, the central role in marital discord played by rigidity in the triangle of
conflict.

> *Thirty-eight-year-old Robert Upton appeared alone at my office. Well
> over 6 feet tall and 300 pounds of muscle, he remains perhaps the
> largest person whom I've ever met and, with his shaved head, resembles
> a black Mr. Clean. Although perhaps initially an unlikely individual to
> express fear, Robert quickly shared his anxiety that his wife, Rachel,
> the mother of their three girls, ages 6 to 10, might leave him, now that
> she had begun activities outside of the home by returning to technical*

school. He described his wife's attractiveness and competence with near awe, but he did admit his anger at her for suspecting his unfaithfulness.

Robert acknowledged his outgoing, flirtatious nature but assured me of his fidelity to Rachel. She had recently discovered a woman's phone number in his pants pocket. He explained that women find him friendly and frequently press their numbers on him, though he never calls them. After this first meeting, I suggested that Robert invite Rachel into the treatment, so that we could try to understand the issues between them. He agreed, and she accompanied him to the next session. Her story revealed a far more serious and, in fact, more dangerous conflict between them than Robert had implied.

I found Rachel true to his description; 36 years old, also black, tall, blade slender, stylish, poised, and articulate. At subsequent meetings, one or more of their daughters accompanied them and sat in the outer office. Also as Robert described, the girls appeared well dressed and well groomed and behaved more maturely in the waiting room than many children I have observed of a similar age. The Uptons certainly appeared effective parents.

It immediately became clear that Robert feared that Rachel's emergence into the world, after raising small children, posed a threat that she might leave him for another man. He questioned her movements outside the house and suggested that she welcomed the attentions of men. She flatly denied this. Indeed, his detailed attention to her behavior and the vehemence of his accusations alerted me—accurately, as it turned out—to the possibility of Robert's pathological jealousy.

Rachel, in her turn, accused Robert of infidelity. The number in the trousers pocket represented the latest in a string of discoveries by her, strongly suggesting that her husband might have involvements with other women. He protested the innocent nature of each item of evidence. I soon realized that this pattern of mutual accusation of infidelity had undercut their 14-year relationship from the start. Moreover, this theme extended back into their families of origin. Apparently, both Robert's and Rachel's fathers frequently became involved in extramarital affairs. Although I never learned the actual truth of fidelity or infidelity for the Uptons themselves, it appeared that Robert had little objective data to suspect Rachel and she considerably more to distrust him.

Consistent with my experience in these cases, the actual facts usually become quickly lost in the charges and countercharges. The only chance to unravel the puzzle lies in unwinding the projective identifications that fly both ways and create a confusing context for all the participants. A close investigation of this case allows me to illustrate the interlocking individual dynamics in the couple, which the triangle of conflict can make clear for us. In particular, I will explore Robert's triangle of conflict, in depth, to exemplify the importance of this concept. The exchange between the Uptons followed a characteristic pattern.

(Fourth Session)

Robert: Here's the deal, Rachel. This is very, very simple. This is easy. If you can be above reproach and do everything you want, and I have no right to question, and you can question every single thing I do because of what happened in the past. . . .

Rachel: I don't question anything you do anymore.

Robert: So you can take the attitude that you don't care. Then I don't even know why we're here.

Rachel: Well, I just think we need to realize that we're two separate people. I don't want to be one. I want to be two *separate people* [Rachel trying to differentiate from Robert and escape the projective system].

Robert: You can be as separate as you want to be.

Rachel: I'm not saying I want to separate from you. I'm just saying that we are not the same person. I don't have to have the same views that you have. I don't have to want to do the same things that you want to do. I haven't hurt you. The issues that you have with me are stupid, and they're minor. They're so minor. I got home from school a half hour later than usual.

Robert: I have no idea where you were.

Rachel: What do you think took me so long?

Robert: I have no clue whatsoever.

Rachel: What has ever taken me so long to come home? Nothing. Ten years I haven't done anything to make you suspect anything of me, and I still get questioned.

JMD: It's much more likely that she stopped at the grocery store. [Countering projection with reality.]

Robert: She has a class. Her last class gets out at 10:05. Come 10:40, where is she? I want to know where she is. It's 10:40 P.M.

Rachel: I told you. I got my paper back. There was no letter grade on it. I stood in line to ask this man why there was no letter grade on my paper. I worked hard. I want to know why. I'm supposed to grab my bags and run out the door?

Robert: Well, at 10:05, yeah.

Rachel: Well, that's just the nature of this class. It's just how it is. But the first thing you would think is I'm doing something in the street. My God! Jesus Christ! Robert!

Robert: Why do you think that I think that?

Rachel: I'm tired of that.

JMD: What time did she get home?

Robert: Ten of eleven. I don't know if you even went to the class. I've got to believe that. [Robert's mistrust begins to reach paranoid levels.]

Rachel: You see, 10 years I've been going through this same bull.

JMD: Why would she deceive you?

Robert: She's done that before.

Rachel: Done what?

Robert: Said she was going some place and go someplace else.

JMD: Go meet some guy?

Robert: I don't believe she's meeting a guy.

Rachel: Yes, he does. He thinks I'm after my ex-boyfriend. That's what he thinks.

Robert: Oh, well, that's a given.

JMD: Is it a given that she's after her ex-boyfriend?

Robert: Yeah.

Rachel: That's what he thinks.

JMD: I don't think she's that drawn to her ex-boyfriend. [Counter projection.]

Robert: He's a wonderful guy. He's a complete wonderment. Hell, I want to date him.

JMD: Why would anybody want to cheat on you? [Moving into the triangle of conflict. What view of self sparks his anxiety?]

Robert: I have no idea. I seem to be the kind of guy people get tired of. That's all.

Rachel: No! You started out with that attitude. I think you just wanted that to happen. I really am starting to believe that. [Self-fulfilling prophecy of projective identification.]

Robert: So, Rachel, it's 14 years later. You're tired of me?

JMD: Can you expand on that, Robert?

Robert: I don't know what it is.

JMD: Did the Asian girl [former girlfriend] get tired of you?

Robert: We just split up very quickly. I come on pretty strong. I can be pretty impressive. Then when people realize it's not magic, I got more demons than most people. Everybody wants the good side of you, and then nobody wants the bad side. [Robert tells us he's a self split between good and bad?]

Rachel: That's what it is. You just test. It's like a 14-year-long test. [Robert tests whether Rachel will conform to his projection.]

JMD: You know, that's very interesting. Robert, what do you think about what she said? [Attempting to involve Robert in an exploration of the projective process.]

Robert: I don't buy that.

JMD: Let's play with this for a minute. Why would you want to test her?

Robert: That's interesting. I don't know. I think that most people quit. I think if you put enough pressure on people, they quit. I'd like to think she'd never quit. [Robert pressures Rachel with his projection.]

JMD: Right.

Robert: Well, that's not the case. After so much, anybody would quit.

JMD: But it's boot camp for Rachel.

Robert: I'll buy that.

JMD: Why would people quit on you? Did your parents quit? [Introducing the triangle of focus.]

Robert: Not really.

JMD: Your father didn't?

Robert: I find most people just quitters. [Projection of his impulse to quit?]

JMD: It just struck me. The way I feel about you is that you're an only child, but I know that's not right. You never mention your brothers and sisters.

Robert: I mean, I had them, but they weren't there. I never hung out with my brother, ever. I never did anything with my brothers or my sisters. [Robert's triangle of conflict keeps him self-involved.]

JMD: Why?

Robert: He's 2 years older than me. You'd imagine you're close. Totally different interests; he's a good guy though.

JMD: He's a good guy?

Robert: In his own weird way.

JMD: Is he married?

Robert: Yeah and he's dirtier than me. Everybody's dirtier than me, but I'm the one with all the dirt.

Rachel: I don't care about anybody else and their problems. I'm sorry. They have nothing to do with ours.

Robert: I'm not a real trusting guy. She says I don't trust her. I don't trust situations.

JMD: No, you're not a trusting guy in general.

Robert: Maybe I try to pay too much attention, created scenarios that really weren't there. [Beginning insight into his projection.]

JMD: Yes, you do, and you've been testing Rachel because you think people quit on other people.

Robert: I don't quit.

JMD: Another thing I've noticed is that I haven't heard you say this person, be it your brother, your friend, your mother, this is a really good person. I don't think I've ever heard you say that. [Everyone seems tainted by the projection.]

Robert: There are some people I like. I imagine people do this with me. You find their flaw, and you accept them for it, and you know how far you can go with this person. What this person's good for, and what they're not good for.

JMD: Okay, but now, Robert. I don't want to get in your face, but I think that we need to think, Do you trust anybody? [Confrontation of paranoid anxiety within triangle of conflict.]

Robert: Wow! This is Rachel, circa 1986, '87, '88, '89.

JMD: So I'm behind the times.

Robert: She says that all the time, and I say, "Rachel, I trust you more than I trust anybody."

JMD: But you don't trust her.

Robert: I do trust her.

JMD: No, you don't. [Counterprojection.]

Robert: You know who I trust more than anybody in the world? Robert. 'Cause I won't fail me.

JMD: Right

Rachel: Have I failed you?

Robert: No.

JMD: But you don't trust Rachel. I mean, she's 20 minutes late from her class. You're not actually thinking that she's having sex with somebody in the park, but sometimes things like that cross your mind.

Robert: And I'll tell you why. Maybe, lackadaisically, I took her for granted, and she has awoken, and now she has all these interests that don't include me. She filters what she tells me. She filters how she behaves around me. That scares me, so, yeah, I'm watching.

JMD: Okay, but to be honest, Robert, you didn't trust her before, and that's what those fights were about.

Robert: It's not that I didn't trust her; I didn't trust the scenario.

JMD: You don't trust that. She says, I love you, Robert, and you say, Oh, yeah, for today.

Robert: She kind of fed into that, too, because when we had arguments, I'd be the bad guy.

JMD: Do you think that when your father said, "I'm not true blue".... [Father implying that he is not a faithful husband.] Do you think that was really tough for you? [Triangle of focus—has Robert based his worldview on his father's betrayals of his mother?]

Robert: No, that never bothered me a bit. [Denial of triangle of focus connection.] I learned something in the military that's kind of stupid, I guess. But I always kind of admired it. You can't judge other people by yourself. If he wants to be foul, he can be foul. That's his life. Is my mother going to let him get away with it? I think it's terrible, but it ain't my life. [Denial of pain over parents' marriage.]

JMD: Okay, but to be honest with you, I think that you do judge everybody by you.

Robert: Rachel judges everybody by her.

Rachel: No, I don't.

JMD: But if a guy wants to believe in his dad, and his dad is saying or implying that you, his son, will stray, that he will take up with a woman here or there, then that's awful hard to take. [Back to the triangle of focus—how does family of origin influence his character and his fight?]

Robert: I was more upset this weekend, when I had to convince my mother that I don't cheat on my wife. My father does, my brother does. My father will make the foolish comment that "I know your bloodlines." Come on.

JMD: Your father's saying that to you?

Robert: My ego was too big for that.

JMD: But your father is saying to you that you're going to go out and do the same thing he does.

Robert: Yeah and he's wrong.

JMD: He's wrong.

Robert: He's absolutely wrong.

JMD: But I think that how can you really trust him, if he's not playing fair with your mother? [Triangle of focus.]

Robert: I don't trust him.

JMD: No, you don't.

Robert: I give him enough rope that I want him to have. I let people get as close to me as I feel comfortable them getting. But Rachel, on the other hand, is a little too close for comfort. [The core of the problem.]

JMD: And you push her away. [Defense pole of triangle of conflict.]

Robert: If I did trust her, I really gave my all, and I really fell into this, and I say this is bliss, and it betrays me, I'd be really hurt.

JMD: I'd be really hurt.

Robert: I'll be more hurt than I can think.

JMD: Than you can stand. [Robert's anxiety is that everyone will betray him. He projects this onto Rachel and tests her faithfulness. He cannot bear to suspend his triangle because of how deeply he would hurt if his genuine trust were dashed.]

Robert: Right.

Rachel: It's really funny 'cause that's kind of how I feel now. [Robert has projected his dilemma into Rachel, and she has accepted it, but she can't stand it.]

JMD: Now, Robert, by not trusting her, you're creating the problems that are screwing you. [Projective identification has created a self-fulfilling prophecy. Now Rachel does want more distance from his accusations and from him.]

Robert: I'm trusting her more every day.

JMD: But many of the fights you've been into are really jealous rages.

Robert: I think Rachel has a deep-seated hate. I think she hates me. [Projection.]

JMD: You think?

Robert: Yeah. Rachel's got a, she's mad at herself for loving me.

JMD: How do you feel about him, Rachel?

Rachel: I love him.

JMD: Yeah.

Robert: It's scary, though.

JMD: 'Cause she could snatch it from you.

Robert: Yeah, yeah, absolutely.

JMD: You don't want her to have that control over you. What about just letting her love you? [Counterprojection.]

Robert: I want that. I just don't know if she wants to love me.

JMD: Do you see Robert trying more?

Rachel: Yes, I do. And I'm a little upset with myself that I can't reciprocate on that. I know he's trying, and I know he's changed a lot of things, and I'm not really sure why I have a hard time accepting some of the things. [Now she's caught in the projective identification system. She can't reciprocate because she's identified with the mistrust projected into her.]

JMD: She thinks you're really trying, but she's worried that you won't keep it up.

Rachel: I don't think he understands how serious I feel about this. If there are any more physical altercations at all, that's it.

Robert: I can understand what you're saying.

Rachel: I don't know if I should say this, but I really, I could really hurt you. That's how angry I am about that. It could turn into something really bad. I know you don't think I can hurt you because you're big and mean, and all that, but I could really hurt you.

Robert: I never thought that.

Rachel: I could hurt you. I will probably try my best to kill you. [Explosive power of projective identification trap.] I probably would, and that scares me more than anything else. That scares me to death. I couldn't take that.

JMD: I think you mean that we should split up, before we end up killing each other.

Rachel: That's how I feel. He'll say something and maybe accuse me or insinuate that I did something. There's something in my mind that snaps, and I just blow up at him, and I start yelling and screaming, 'cause I just want it to end. I want him to hear me the first time I say it and end the conversation and go on to something else. I don't want him to pick and prod. "So what do you mean by that question?" He'll keep going. So now when he says something I disagree with or something I think is wrong about me, I blow up. That's the end of it. But that's ridiculous. [Rachel feels sucked into projective identification cycle, and she can't stand it any more.]

Robert: I'm pretty good at picking and poking and prodding. [Robert achieves momentary insight that he creates the rejection he requires.]

JMD: Don't do it. Just don't do it. [This marital fight has reached lethal proportions in the past and may soon again. I, perhaps too forcefully, try to coach Robert to begin to alter his triangle of conflict and to suspend his projective identification.]

This look inside the relationship of the Uptons allows us to observe Robert's triangle of conflict in action, and it also provides us with the unusual opportunity of watching projective identification unfold before our eyes.

I can illustrate Robert's triangle:

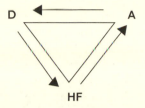

A = Mistrust of others (and maybe of himself)
D = Vigilant guarding against betrayal, projection of mistrust, "picking and prodding" testing
HF = Wish to feel others won't quit on him

FIGURE 4.2

Robert's anxiety over trust dominates his life. Although a bright, attractive, successful man, he cannot believe his wife or anyone else will not betray him. In the next session I learned that when his jealousy sparked in the past, he grabbed Rachel, threw her down, punched, kicked, and strangled her. It is this violence to which she has just alluded. Rachel now feels murderous hatred for him when he threatens her. In his rage Robert becomes paranoid and must annihilate the object who "makes" him so vulnerable. Rachel, formerly imprisoned by the projective identification, used to attempt to reassure Robert; now she fights back to gain her freedom. Perhaps similar dynamics underlie much domestic violence.

Robert endures a split in his ego. In his central ego he loves his wife and believes in her, but when he fears she's deceived him, his repressed ego takes over, and he wants to kill her and sometimes almost has. The betrayals in Robert's family have left him unable to trust anyone. He recreates his family life with each new person and assumes that this person will "quit" on him as well. In this way Robert's untrustworthy repressed objects underlie the anxiety/defense connection in his triangle of conflict. When he fears betrayal, these objects take over and activate that connection. Soon he is overwhelmed with jealous rage.

Robert's defense against his mistrust is to project his fears onto Rachel and to believe that she means him harm and has committed, or plans, infidelity. He knows realistically that she could not be stopping off for a liaison on her way home after class, but, at the moment, he doubts her and projects his own insecurity onto her. He's the type of guy people quit on, so she will quit on him. His anger can boil to lethal proportions.

Some evidence suggests that the origin of Robert's mistrust extends back at least one generation. Robert described his father as a gigantic, handsome, jovial man, like himself, but although Robert denied womanizing, his father made no secret of his own infidelities—saying, apparently in front of Robert, his siblings, and his mother, "I'm not true blue," later implying that neither was Robert, because of his "bloodlines." Extreme violence also marked the relationship between Robert's parents. Some 15 years ago, his mother confronted his father in a bar with another woman and stabbed him in the abdomen with a carving knife, leading to an emergency hospitalization. Robert's mother tried to kill her husband, and Rachel now fears she will do the same. The process of projective identification has reproduced the same murderous conflict in the next generation.

Here ends my hard data about Robert's family of origin. The picture Robert paints of his father communicates a narcissistic man so unsure of his masculinity that he must regularly pursue women outside his marriage. That he would boast of his infidelities in front of his wife and children perhaps implies sociopathy, as well as narcissism. I hypothesize that Robert identified with this powerful, authoritative, attractive object and now has a dangerously split self. In his central ego Robert lives as a successful worker and a caring family man. But Robert's identification with this swashbuckling, omnipotent father object may have created inside Robert a split-off self, a tyrannical, violent man. He cannot stand this self and projects it onto the other. "I'm not untrustworthy; she is." Despite his protestations, Robert doesn't trust himself, nor, obviously, because of his projection, does he trust anyone else. His partial identification with his father object has corkscrewed Robert's inner, and then his outer, life into a shambles.

Robert's dialogue with Rachel demonstrates projective identification in a pure state. Robert wrestles with a wrenching internal conflict. Has he become the omnipotent entitled tyrant? He expels that conflict outward. He's not tempted by infidelity; Rachel is. He's convinced she'll quit on him, push him out of his house, and quickly invite other men in, probably the ex-boyfriend. Rachel resists the projection, but Robert "picks and prods" and continually accuses, and he also beats her. He regularly provides her, in addition, with possible evidence of infidelity. Under this extreme pressure and despite his obviously genuine recent efforts to change, she has now lost faith in him. She succumbs to the projection and to Robert's efforts to make it come true. Rachel begins to quit on Robert, just as he imagined. Tragically, he has created the "scenario" he most fears. His repressive split, his basic fault, in Balint's terms (1968), betrays him at the exact place where he must trust someone not to desert him, but he can't cross that barrier.

Clearly, if I hope to help this troubled couple, I will need to enter

Robert's triangle of conflict at its core to help him soften the immediate link between his anxiety and his defensive projection. I must explore with Robert why he mistrusts others. Does this relate to his manifestly untrustworthy father? How does he experience his identification with his father? Why must he automatically project this worldview onto his intimates, particularly Rachel, apparently a mature, loyal woman in whom he has objective reason to have faith.

The reader can see my attempts to initiate this investigation, but Robert, unfortunately, remains defensive. He tells us that he's not like his father and has distanced himself from both his father and his brother. He admits Rachel's propriety and trustworthiness, at one moment, but the next, begins all over again to needle her and insinuate her lack of support and fidelity. We can observe how his defensive reflex snaps back into place, no matter how directly, but respectfully, I challenge him. The unconscious identification with the seductive object of his father evidently remains too intact and the projective need too ingrained.

I met this couple in the midst of crisis. I felt that I had to confront Robert quickly with the destructiveness of his projections. If I had more time with Robert and Rachel, I would have switched away from my interpretive, counterprojective approach and attempted even more of a relationship intervention to connect with Robert's vulnerability. I'd counter-offer, "It's hard to love someone so much and feel that they're slipping away, particularly when you observe so much disloyalty in your own family. It seems like no one remains true to anybody, I guess." If Robert senses the vulnerable feelings in my empathy, perhaps he will talk about his own.

At this point I had met Rachel only twice, and I had learned little about her. She did report her father's promiscuity and her disillusionment with him. Perhaps she tried to master this trauma by marrying a more open, loving man than her father and proving to herself that she could make the match work by offering him enough patience, loyalty, and realistic feedback. But the marriage became a Hypothesis (1A) proposition. Robert acted out her father's part, and she her mother's, after all. She felt trapped in the familiar unfaithful man–angry woman battle. Rachel's triangle of conflict probably resembles:

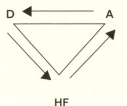

A = The primary object will deceive and abandon me.

D = I'll behave so perfectly that the object will be faithful, love me, and stay.

HF = I can act my independent self but also have love and acceptance.

FIGURE 4.3

In our few meetings, Rachel did recognize Robert's efforts toward change, but then she could see him retrogress into his old self, although he did keep his pledge against violence. Perhaps Rachel felt captured in her fear that her HF could never come true with Robert, or perhaps now that it might come to pass, she lost her courage to go forward. We'll never know.

I was unable to pursue constructively the triangle-of-conflict work with Robert or with Rachel. At the end of our fourth conjoint session, Robert returned to provoking Rachel over her lack of belief in him. She burst into anger and stamped from the office. I couldn't convince her to return, and neither Robert nor Rachel responded to my follow-up phone calls. I wish I had the opportunity to work with them more. I was afraid that this likable, industrious couple may have separated after our final stormy meeting. I had no way of knowing. Robert promised during our sessions that he would not engage in further violence. If physical altercations returned, then the separation represented a better outcome than remaining together. Robert's ability to alter his triangle of conflict and Rachel's capacity to fend off his projections and believe in her HF will probably determine the eventual fate of this match. Three years after their very brief treatment, I accidentally encountered Robert in the hallway of the clinic. He greeted me warmly and told me he and Rachel were still together but needed more therapy. He promised to arrange another visit but, as yet, has not.

THE TANWORTHS

The treatment for the Uptons ended sadly. Fortunately, I could use work with the triangle of conflict to help the Tanworths more successfully in a brief therapy.

Sharon and John Tanworth, both 56, a successful college teacher and a nurse, respectively, married for 30 years and the parents of two adult sons, appeared at my office, mired in their subtle, intermittent, but prolonged standoff. The Tanworths seemed desperate over their recurrent conflict, a fight with few words. Slightly built, diffident John apparently let equally petite, more expressive Sharon direct nearly all aspects of their personal lives. She handled the money, orchestrated their social interactions, and planned their vacation trips to the last detail.

Sharon occasionally delegated household tasks to John—for example, to mail in the taxes. Often John forgot his errand and then lied to her when she checked up on him. Sharon then became enraged, screaming at him that the relationship had no trust. He would either sheepishly apologize or attack her as a critical bitch. The partners would withdraw from each other for two or three days and then resume their relationship without discussing the incident further. Sharon had become so exasperated by this destructive cycle that she suggested a separation, which made the terrified John break into tears. The unmailed tax return, which Sharon discovered in John's car, precipitated their latest confrontation.

I learned that John came from a blue-collar family, his father a policeman, his mother a secretary. His father rarely mentioned his dangerous job, but John watched reports on television of the major crimes and fires that involved his father and held him in awe, all the while terrified for his father's safety. Although more than qualified, John's father delayed taking the captain's exam for years.

John's mother, apparently the emotional power in the family, applied her high standards to the father, whom she refused to allow to drink, and to her sons' comportment and scholarship. Both John and his 5-years-older brother amassed outstanding academic records and attended the same renowned university some 500 miles from home.

As an adolescent, to his memory, John never rebelled against his parents and experienced great difficulty making personal decisions, such as selecting a college major or which summer activities to pursue. He apparently allowed his mother's opinion to shape his choices and his view of himself. He idealized both parents and still becomes tearful when he mentions their deaths in recent years. John also idealized his older brother, participating in the same sports and selecting the same college and the same ROTC service branch as his brother.

I quickly guessed that John projected his controlling mother object onto his wife, Sharon. Well-organized and assertive, Sharon superficially fits the projection, and then the projective identification cycle sweeps them both away. As John meekly complies, Sharon becomes more shrill and John even less assertive. During their crises, she screams that he's babyish and a liar. John has fully participated, through projective identification, in creating the monster mother-wife, whom he needs, of whom he's terrified, but whom he also hates. He passive-aggressively rebels by sniping at her, by refusing to answer any of her questions, and by "forgetting" the household tasks he's agreed to complete. The partners sink deeper and deeper into their morass, reliving the old object relationships.

I learned less about Sharon's family, but she, the eldest child, apparently had one dysfunctional, depressed brother (the precursor to John in Sharon's unconscious?). She had a demanding father, who never completed his PhD but expected much achievement from her and her brother. Sharon experienced her mother as more realistic and approachable but as interpersonally somewhat insincere and reaction-formatted.

Beginning in the second session, I started to explore the parallel between John's mother and his wife, as internal objects. Although John continued to idealize his mother, he admitted that her controllingness "grated" on him, that he never felt like his own person around her, even as a middle-aged, married man and father. He felt that both his wife and his mother were critical of him, but he was too intimidated by either to speak up. He remembered lying to his mother as a teenager, telling her he was off to the library to study and then going out with his friends. He acknowledged, with chagrin, that he could not admit to his wife that he forgot an errand and sometimes lied about this to her as well. During the fourth and fifth sessions, John, who skillfully directed a large department, rarely botching details, began to consider whether his forgetfulness at home represented an indirect attack on his wife.

I supported John as he struggled with connecting the objects of wife and mother. Meanwhile, I became aware of my frequent overenthusiasm. I caught myself trying to speed up the work by doing too much of it for John. Using my countertransference, I now understood more about the trap that snared Sharon when she tried to force John toward behavior change. Feeling the impulse to nag, I backed away a little, leaving him to ponder his inner state aloud. I also had to fend off Sharon, who predictably became frustrated and prone to impatience with John, as he stumbled toward self-awareness. She apparently identified with her critical father and so, in reality, conformed to some of John's projections. Through the first six meetings, the partners reported improvement in their interactions at home but almost as many setbacks as gains.

In session 7, a turning point arrived unexpectedly, as, in my experience, abrupt shifts in couple treatment often do. John reported that he had taken an action. He had become enraged with Sharon for ostensibly criticizing his wardrobe and had retired for 4 days to his furnished basement, eating and sleeping below ground. However, when he emerged, he felt like a different person.

John: I had a major meltdown. I felt that everything she said to me had connotations. I said, I decided to buy another pair of loafers. She said, You already have three pairs. I said, Those aren't loafers. She said they were, and we argued.

Sharon: It seems so ridiculous, saying they weren't really loafers but a little different style.

John: When I came out of the basement, I had an attitude transplant. I realized I loved Sharon and was pushing anger onto her. I felt hateful toward her like my mother [Triangle of focus.] I'm just coming around on anger at my mother. Denied it for years. I feel guilty about what I haven't done and project the anger onto her [Sharon] then I don't have to feel guilty. [This represents an example of projective identification. John feels guilty and self-critical. He projects that feeling into Sharon and then reidentifies with it and becomes convinced that Sharon looks down on him, which, by the time this process takes hold, she sometimes does.] I make assumptions about what she's saying. Everything she says is cutting, out to get me.

What brought me up out of the basement was an attitude transplant. I felt good about myself, able to listen and absorb and talk back and feel heard. The last week things were great around here. [Altering his triangle of conflict, John stops projecting his anger and self-criticism. In other words, for the moment, he ceases recreating his mother.]

Sharon: Things have been spectacular. The best we've ever done. [Triangle of conflict suspended, marriage flourishes.]

John: I remember my father avoided the captain's exam for so many years. My mother orchestrated; my father followed. I felt I'm incompetent; someone will rescue me, never created a life, just along for the ride. I was comfortable being taken care of. [Mother controls him but also protects him. He looks for same from wife.]

We can diagram John's triangle of conflict like this:

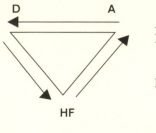

A = I'm inept, indecisive, babyish.
D = Projection of self-criticism. She devalues me. I'm furious with her, but I must comply.
HF = I've a right to self-esteem and self-expression.

FIGURE 4.4

John and Sharon presented me with a complicated, chronic marital problem, but the triangle of conflict made some sense of John's dilemma and directed my work with him and with her. I grasped that his conscious, inept, indecisive self, around which his anxiety circulated, represented only part of the whole story. His self-defeating defenses of compliance, passive-aggressiveness, and projection of anger kept this self in place, and here I confronted his defenses. Did he, who had published a successful training manual and headed a major academic department, really have so little self-confidence? Didn't his diffidence and indecisiveness cover his anger at the other—at present, his wife, but more fundamentally, his mother? By interpreting these defenses, I hoped to bring John into more touch with his hidden feeling—a wish to contact his self-esteem and to speak his true voice. I began this exchange with John in the office, but he finished it in his basement.

With these interesting clients, we can see that as John questioned his defensive assumptions under the pressure of a crisis with Sharon and disappeared into the basement, he did capture his true self, with immediate positive effects for himself and for his marriage. For a period of a month after his emergence from the depths, John altered his triangle of conflict, stopped regressing into self-defeat, and ceased projecting his anger and fury onto his wife. "I devalue myself. She doesn't do it." He could start living his hidden feeling. "I have a right to self-esteem and to make choices." Sharon reported, "This is the best month we've ever had in our marriage." When changes come in couple treatment, it often takes the form of one individual making a breakthrough into his or her triangle of conflict, as with John here. I'll discuss this central finding more in subsequent chapters.

Our observations of John begin to teach us about two important features of the triangle of conflict. The first of these I've noted already, but it stands as so fundamental that I'll draw attention to it again. Projective identification and the triangle of conflict exist hand in hand. John's conviction of a devalued, inhibited, unformed self (A) represents the key to his triangle. He can't stand this feeling so he projects it onto Sharon. He does not look down on himself; she sneers at him and orders him around like a puppy dog. Notice that John has created a complete, mostly fictional, object relationship with Sharon in his characteristic fashion—a cowering self, a demeaning object, and his affect of humiliation covering over rage. Sharon actually is a somewhat impatient, judgmental woman, although basically a constructive one. She accepts the projection and becomes scathing toward John. (Shortly, I'll need to draw attention to her triangle of conflict as well, lest I unbalance the treatment.) The fight commences.

But, after our seventh session, a fascinating development rearranges the picture. John spontaneously reverses the direction of energy in his triangle. He retires into the cellar. When he emerges, he has curtailed his conviction of rejection (D); has dismissed his inferior, tentative self (A); and has contacted his hidden feeling (HF). He feels self-acceptance and self-confidence. As amazed as any of the three of us, John cannot account for what has transpired inside, down below in the basement. I couldn't get him to describe the process in much understandable detail, but John has helped us stumble across one of the major curative elements in couple therapy:

suspend the action of the triangle of conflict, help the client meaningfully touch the hidden feeling. John completed this action for himself. Clearly, if we could understand the specific steps to take in supporting and leading our clients toward this kind of breakthrough, it would represent a great advantage to us therapists. We can already begin to see that clients remain quite inarticulate about this process, certainly a clue that much of it remains unconscious to them. In chapters 6 and 7, I'll pursue the topic of how therapists can stimulate these important, but complicated, shifts within the triangle of conflict.

I do not think this treatment complete, and I predict that John will spend more nights in the basement, chasing his attitude transplant. In fact, this has happened once already. John has suffered one relapse and has withdrawn downstairs again for a day or two. I'm convinced that the first time remains the most important, even though relapse almost inevitably occurs. Choosing freedom from his triangle of conflict once increases the likelihood that John will make the same choice again. His expression "attitude transplant" implies that John, thus far, feels the transformation a phenomenon that befell him from the outside, as if induced by an unseen hand. When pressed, John admits that no one external accompanied him to the basement and rearranged his psyche, once he got there. He must have done it, but he remains vague about the process.

Can we piece together more about what happened in John's cellar? John encountered affect in the basement, the affect tied to early primary objects. He acknowledged anger toward those objects. He appears to have put it into perspective and no longer has to project it, at least for the moment. Now another affect, self-esteem, emerges. John, like most clients, has not become articulate about this process. John, as yet, does not cognitively know the specific facts about his object relations that I think I know, but his affective realizations about those objects feel valid for him. He's become convinced that he's angry at his mother and that he has projected that onto his wife. John needs to initiate this kind of new experience for himself, living with the triangle of conflict suspended. He does not have to grasp consciously each aspect of the triangle and explain in detail to himself what relationship or which objects carry responsibility for his inner conflicts. But he does need to stop projecting his anger onto Sharon. This last represents our second insight about the triangle of conflict. Working through the triangle does not happen all at once, but partial insights do sometimes result in crucial behavioral change.

What was my role in John's shift in his triangle? I grasped John's need to comply to an authority and then to resent that figure. In my relationship counter offer to him, I supported his independence and made sure not to direct or control him. I offered interpretations connecting his behavior toward his wife with that toward his mother. None led to a breakthrough at the time, but John clearly could suspend his triangle of conflict, at least for a while, once he got to his basement. The causative chain of events remains unclear, but for the moment, the outcome seems quite plain. He, Sharon, and I immediately recognized the dramatic shift in him and in the relationship.

Sharon's triangle of conflict plays a more ambiguous part in the drama. I diagram this with less confidence.

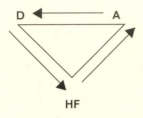

A = My loved one doesn't trust me.
D = I scathingly attack.
HF = I'm lovable and trustworthy.

FIGURE 4.5

Notice that each pole in Sharon's triangle corresponds to a repressed object relationship. Some loved one, apparently, didn't trust her. She attacks that object defensively, but in her hidden feeling, she wishes trust from an important person. At this point, however, we know little about what specific past object relations come into play for Sharon, but her anxiety over trust did not begin when she met John. I guess that she needed to master this trauma and chose the ambivalent John to help her with the task. Her aggressive, attacking self likely represents identification with a split-off aspect of one parent. I hypothesize her father here, but I lack the data to confirm this tentative notion.

I have observed, though, that Sharon's hidden wish for trustful interaction can become readily accessible in a productive way. When John struggles toward more openness, she can respond constructively, again probably the mark of a positive object bond with at least one parent. Sharon's hidden wish apparently has not become overly entangled with paranoid drives toward vengeance, the need to prove absolutely that the partner, and thus she herself, does not merit trust.

Regrettably, we encountered an inability to shake loose of the triangle of conflict when we studied the Uptons. Mrs. Upton's father, as well as her father-in-law, engaged in serial infidelity, so the unconscious relationship with both sets of parental objects smacked of mistrust. Robert Upton couldn't believe that he or his partner could maintain fidelity, and Rachel Upton, too, apparently had trouble imagining a faithful partner in her unconscious.

When we think about a rigid connection between anxiety and defense and about problematic identifications with early objects, we quickly can reflect, unfortunately, that both sets of these conditions obtained for the

Uptons, particularly for Robert. He recurrently suspected betrayal (A). He then automatically began to question Rachel, prod her, and insinuate that she might leave (D). I tried repeatedly to interrupt the cycle, to push his projections back on him, but he could not suspend his mistrust for long and rapidly reverted back to it. His identification with his demonstrably un-trustworthy father probably lay at the base of this pernicious cycle. Finally, his wife, Rachel, could stand his pressure no longer and stomped out the session and out of the therapy.

When one, or both, of the pair cannot shift his or her triangle of con-flict even a few degrees, the therapist finds himself and the treatment in deep trouble. The projections become locked within an immovable triangle of conflict and continue to seem real to the imprisoned couple. Under such distorted circumstances, suspicion, withdrawal, and flight from the mar-riage seem the only sensible strategies. Projection, which in the Uptons' case ushered in extreme jealousy and violence, has created a loss of hope for the relationship.

In practical, clinical terms, what does "shifting a few degrees" mean? Perhaps Robert could reconsider the proposition that sooner or later Rachel would inevitably betray him. Perhaps he could review the data of their lives and ponder whether she had ever quit on him. Perhaps he could wonder with himself why he automatically distrusted the other. Perhaps he could tolerate his vulnerability long enough to entertain, genuinely, the thought that some of the problem might reside within him and in his original fam-ily. But Robert could move in these directions for only a moment or two, and then he would dive back into the self-fulfilling conviction of his tri-angle of conflict.

Because Robert failed repeatedly at altering his triangle even slightly, we must conclude that this likable, attractive, hardworking man may have a personality disorder of a mixed paranoid and narcissistic nature. A marked inability to shift the triangle of conflict, coupled with rigid, dysfunctional, interpersonal responses, implies, in operational terms, a personality disor-der. Both sets of these conditions existed in Robert. Robert's personality disorder, in interaction with Rachel's hesitancy to trust him—an under-standable reluctance, given his past violence—sank the therapy.

Back to John and Sharon. As we study their triangles of conflict, we can observe once again that, in couple treatment, although we deal with two separate psyches, illustrated by the two triangles of conflict, the *inter-actional*, interdependent nature of the fight and of its resolution clearly emerges as well. Sharon cannot feel confident until John deals with his ambivalence, but if John allows his real self to peek out, he, and it, will quickly scamper away unless Sharon drops her attack. Their triangles col-lide to produce their fight:

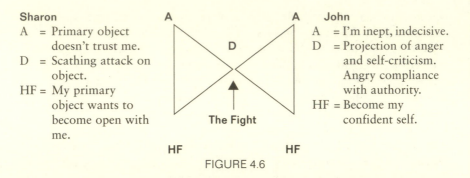

Sharon
A = Primary object
    doesn't trust me.
D = Scathing attack on
    object.
HF = My primary
     object wants to
     become open with
     me.

John
A = I'm inept, indecisive.
D = Projection of anger
    and self-criticism.
    Angry compliance
    with authority.
HF = Become my
     confident self.

FIGURE 4.6

So far in this treatment I've investigated Sharon's triangle of conflict only tentatively, because both Sharon and John present his emotional state as more central to their fight. However, I cannot temporize her more full entrance into the therapy much longer, or I will lose an evenhanded emphasis. I need to go back with her to the place where she learned the mistrust of her primary object and her attacking response. On the other hand, Sharon speaks very clearly about her hidden feeling. She wishes that John wanted to be open and trusting with her. She reports that when he is, their relationship feels deeply satisfying to her.

We do not need to help Sharon to transform her triangle of conflict in some fundamental fashion so that she understands the origin of each point on the triangle and can readily tolerate the sense that her primary object might withdraw from her (A), without her needing immediately to snap back in anger at that object (D). Sharon needs to undergo a small, but still significant, shift in the functioning of her triangle so that she can more productively engage with John about their central conflict, without the moment-to-moment risk of exploding at him. We can already observe that when John offers a little more openness and Sharon a little more forbearance, they relate in a more helpful way for both. The triangle of conflict points us to the site for the necessary work, the A–D connection for each partner, but the necessary changes in that reflex action seem delimited enough that a brief therapy of 20 sessions or less could carry a reasonable chance of success.

Now we find ourselves in the middle innings of a couple treatment with a pair like John and Sharon. The meetings oscillate back and forth between emphasis on the triangle of focus and then on the triangle of conflict, between the interactional and the individual. But we must place the stress on the interplay, on the triangle of focus first in most cases, or else we'll embark on an individual versus a couple therapy, probably with an unfortunate outcome.

This discussion of the necessary sequence of the treatment lends us some more hints about the reasonable length of short-term couple therapy, a tenure dictated by clinical reality, not by assigning an arbitrary number of sessions to the enterprise. Step 1, exploring the fight, involves perhaps 2 meetings, and Step 2, investigating the triangle of focus, 2 more meetings at a minimum. I cannot reasonably anticipate investing less than a total of 4 to 6 meetings in the triangle of conflict work for both members of the pair. We stand at 10 to 12 sessions, before we can expect the partners to begin relaxing defenses and finally working through their fight themselves, which will, in turn, lead to their devising "tools" to forestall its destructive impact. I expect, then, meaningful change usually to take 14 to 16 meetings in this model, not coincidentally the length of the couple group that I will describe in the next chapter. Many of Dicks's therapies lasted about 20 or 30 sessions, and like mine, these sometimes spread over many months or a year or two.

The rate at which people change varies a great deal from couple to couple, but we can see that the speed of that change depends heavily on the structure and functioning of the triangle of conflict for each character in the drama. If the anxiety–defense connection smacks of great rigidity in one or both members of the pair, and if the hidden feeling for one or both remains out of reach due to problematic identification with early objects or to trauma, the treatment will take much longer and will carry more uncertain promise. Personality disorder of varying severity—that is, the marked incapacity to soften the triangle of conflict—represents, then, the central limiting factor in couple treatment (and in most psychotherapies, probably regardless of their theoretical persuasion or technical approach).

However, clients surprise us all the time in their ability to alter—at least, along certain dimensions—their triangle of conflict. Recall that Ming, a rigid man with major traumas in his history, could somehow shift his triangle sufficiently to engage in real discussions with his wife, Cathy, about how to manage Jerry, their disorganized teenage son. Ming, a controlling, mistrustful man, did not bring so severe a personality disorder into his marriage that it prevented constructive work for the couple. I find it hard, often impossible, at the outset to gauge the rigidity of the participants, but using Ming as an interesting example, we can see that even quite constricted people can productively engage, at some level, with their triangles of conflict and therefore in the couple therapy process.

As a further illustration of this complicated matter, I'll offer a new pair in which rigidity in the triangle also poses a major problem.

DAVID AND LATISHA

My psychiatrist colleague referred 61-year-old David and 51-year-old Latisha, because Latisha presented with major depression and also complained of serious marital problems. This small, soft-spoken, Irish American Catholic couple owned a travel agency, where they worked together. Married 20 years, they had one child, their high school senior daughter.

David's two previous marriages had ended in divorce. In the first, his wife appeared to suffer from major depression and in the second, from severe bipolar disease. Unfortunately, after their divorce, his second wife committed suicide. In both instances David had accompanied his wives to couple counseling, only to have the marriages soon end. Suffice it to say, his heart sank when Latisha, his third wife, strongly suggested that they seek therapy.

I've seen this pair only four times so far. Both partners talk a great deal in the session to present their side of the conflict. Only infrequently do they address each other directly. Careful, precise, duty-bound David expresses his anxiety that Latisha will likely tell unnamed confidants and relatives about their attendance in the therapy and about his upcoming medical tests to investigate a prostate problem. Latisha has begun menopause, and although she's clearly depressed, often feeling tearful and despondent, David has decided that she should probably not take antidepressant medicine, because her mood disorder may represent a hormonal imbalance. His first two wives were prescribed antidepressants, and both deteriorated further thereafter. Latisha, against David's wishes, has begun the medicine and to good effect.

Latisha describes David badgering her with criticism, monitoring her movements, and trying to influence who she speaks to. She reports that if she tells a friend or relative something that David wishes kept secret, he becomes angrily withdrawn and uncommunicative. She feels very controlled by her husband, much more so since she's become depressed and started the medicine. He now sees her as ill and in need of more supervision and protection. Latisha appears quite desperate now about her marriage and says she does not know how much longer she can stand David's surveillance of her and his apparent attempts to manipulate her behavior through guilt induction. David does not strike me as paranoid, because he can be joyful and empathic with his wife and with me, but he's certainly intrusive.

Working together in the same agency has exacerbated this marital conflict, because they spend nearly every moment together, day and evening. Latisha complains that David scrutinizes her interactions with other employees and interrupts her work to help him on complex projects. In the past year she's experimented with scheduling one day a week out of the office and not accompanying him on business trips. David seems to resent her absence and reportedly insinuates that she seems less committed, lately, to the business and, by implication, to him.

This standoff reminds Latisha of her recently deceased mother's behavior. The mother seemingly bound Latisha, her oldest child and only daughter, to her and demanded her constant attention when together. David and Latisha moved the mother into their home for the last year of her life, and even then the mother never seemed satisfied with Latisha's efforts to care for her. Latisha's serious depression began shortly after the mother's death. She reports that she now has a fear that with her mother gone, she has a new mother in David, who wishes to shape her life and her opinions, by tweaking her guilt whenever she starts to act with more independence. Both have recreated old familiar objects to love and to fight with. David needs to protect, but also to smother, a vulnerable other, and Latisha needs to make war with an enveloping parent.

From the opening minutes I, and almost any therapist, would sense that this treatment will focus on control and that David's triangle of conflict may represent a key variable in our therapy. Tentatively, I can diagram his triangle as follows:

A = Anxiety over the unpredictability of the primary object.
D = Surveillance and control of the object.
HF = I can find a stable love object whose behavior I can trust.

David has the feel to me of a hyperconscientious, parentified child. Because his immigrant uneducated parents struggled with the language and with the culture, David felt required to step in to stabilize the household. He can remember rising at 4:00 A.M. to help his sickly father with the father's maintenance and custodial work. He also recalls, early on, becoming the one in the family responsible to complete all legal and business papers. David was the first family member to complete high school, college, or graduate school. Now when he sees his previously vivacious, energetic Latisha sink into depression, he senses his world crumbling once again as it did when his other two wives became unhappy and ill, déjà vu all over again. David feels alone and responsible to right the ship. We can look back developmentally and see that David's repressive split took place at the time when he had to trust someone to have the capacity to act independently but not to desert him, as part of that freedom. David could not tolerate that crisis in his past, and he has great trouble managing it now.

David's parents, despite their limitations, acted lovingly and appreciatively toward him. He has grown into a warmhearted, generous, loyal, and extremely conscientious man. The problem comes with his rigidity. He apparently does sometimes monitor Latisha's movements and cross-examine her about conversations. David has attempted to institute a gag order about the therapy and to extract a promise from Latisha that she will not mention the treatment to any third parties. Latisha has reluctantly agreed, but she feels rebellious toward David, as she did toward her suffocating mother. David's vigilance does represent an objectively problematic behavior, as does his sulking withdrawal when Latisha opposes him. David appears to have an unconscious need to protect but also to envelope a helpless object, witness his first two marriages. If I cannot help him with this lockstep triangle of conflict, I fear limited gains for the therapy.

On the other hand, I can't unbalance the treatment by concentrating on David exclusively. If he senses that the therapy has become a project, jointly arranged by Latisha and myself, to remedy his shortcomings, he will become angry and demoralized, and he will withdraw from genuine participation. Tipping the scale in this fashion will also encourage Latisha to experience David as even more incorrigible than she originally thought and may lead her to overlook any signs of constructive shifts in his outlook. I will need to work with Latisha's triangle of focus and triangle of conflict to maintain an even emphasis in treatment. This requires self-discipline on my part, but inattention here will probably sabotage this or most similar couple therapies.

In a curious way David is like a Caucasian version of Ming. Both are industrious, responsible oldest brothers, the leaders of their generations in their immigrant families of origin. But both also seem controlling, fixed in their ideas and strongly disinclined to negotiation. Both also demonstrate stigmata of ADHD and seem disorganized in their daily habits. Both present with something like obsessive characters. They're cautious, careful, not affectively expressive, and overly concerned with what appears fair, right, and just. In my experience such men rarely seek psychotherapy on their own and only appear at the determined behest of their wives. Predictably, I have found that dynamic interpretations usually carom off these heavily armored males. Prone to feel shamed if I press insight on them, they feel criticized and recoil.

Any therapist needs to pass a test with these men (see Joseph Weiss, 1993, on control mastery theory). They fear that the therapist will prove that they have made mistakes or have become derelict in their duty. Focal relationship interventions versus focal interpretations work best. I call attention to David's loyalty and concern, first, to allay his fear and open him to influence. Then, perhaps in a humorous off-hand tone, I will suggest that he might relax, just a little, his vigilance toward his wife. If he can exchange with me on this plane, I can begin to tentatively script write and speak out some of his fears about loss of control over the relationship.

Change with these men comes slowly and rarely seems dramatic. The rigidity of the triangle of conflict lessens only somewhat, but, luckily, couple therapy does not require radical shifts in character functioning. With these cases, I sense, although I certainly cannot prove, that a key development comes with the man's capacity to identify with the therapist as an understanding, but slightly more open, colleague, working with him toward a shared goal. Positive self-objects in the client, in other words, need to connect with the therapist as a positive object. To facilitate this process, we need to present ourselves in a friendly, nonthreatening fashion. If we want to reach the client's positive inner objects, we'd better act like a warm accepting object ourselves. In my experience a more remote blank-screen therapist, particularly a male with those characteristics, would have little chance of engaging clients like David or Ming.

This process of connection now seems underway with David. I praise his industriousness and multiple skills, which include not only professional capabilities but carpentry and remodeling abilities. I laugh at his jokes, and he at mine. He reports that there seems less tension in his home, and his wife appears brighter. But he's going to have to alter the controlling behavior wrapped within his triangle of conflict, and this has happened only a little so far. This shift need not occur in complete fashion or with conscious insight, but David will need to link his need to protect and control Latisha with the more realistic obligations he felt to watch over his parents and his sister, all objectively more vulnerable people than competent Latisha. She's a capable mother and an experienced and well-organized businesswoman, not fragile like his original family members, whom he really did need to protect. In other words, with his triangle of conflict relaxed somewhat, David can return to his triangle of focus in a more open state, psychologically, and begin to make the crucial affective connections between past and present that will allow him to shift his behavior toward Latisha a little, but a little may be enough.

I've also begun to enlist Latisha's aid in supporting David to suspend his triangle. I'll need to work with her to offer positive feedback to David when he relaxes his grip somewhat and to reassure him that she's safe and capable on her own. We'll study Latisha's triangle of conflict in a moment. We'll observe that in her characteristic defensive mode, she bristles and snaps at David when he begins to intrude. Then, having attacked the object, she feels guilty and withdraws into hopelessness about him and about her marriage. An exacerbation of her depression soon follows.

Latisha brings her own triangle of conflict to the match. Designated the lifelong nurse and social worker for her depressed mother, she feels anxiously responsible for the primary object, but, inevitably, she's ambivalent about that object. Faced with envelopment, she becomes angry and starts fighting to maintain her boundaries. Sometimes a client's hidden feeling remains hidden and difficult to define, but for Latisha this pole of the triangle appears clear: find an object who will love you but will allow you individuation.

Latisha's triangle of conflict:

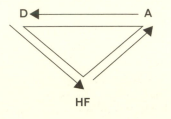

A = Anxious, guilty responsibility for the object.

D = Dutifully comply but then attack the object to maintain boundaries, then become depressed to control anger.

HF = Find an object to love me but to permit me freedom.

FIGURE 4.7

I need to intervene with Latisha not to growl at David and deride him when he intrudes but to oppose him in a more gentle fashion. Latisha's character allows her more openness to interpretation than does David's, but I'll rely some on relationship interventions with her as well. The test I must pass with her is to support her independence and *never* to aggravate her guilt over her wish for more freedom. Latisha's depression, now thankfully somewhat lifted with the help of therapy and medications, can sink her into dangerous waters. If she senses any disapproval of her need for individuation, trouble awaits all three of us. I need to offer her genuine acceptance for her drive toward independence but also a realistic correction for her view of David as relentless, ruthless intruder. In other words, Latisha needs to experiment with suspending her triangle of conflict, to experience David as a man trying to suspend his as well. We can see that the outcome of this therapy will turn on how constructively David and Latisha can introduce seemingly small, but quite specific and quite necessary, alterations in their triangles of conflict. They do not have to change their basic object relations assumptions or interchange radically differently with all parties in their lives, but they do need to suspend their triangles long enough to relate in a more open way with each other, particularly at the important times when the fight approaches.

Couple therapy alternates between an interactional and an individual focus. We can't overstress or deemphasize either, so we walk a tightrope. The concept of the triangle of conflict allows us to introduce the intrapsychic level of analysis in the treatment. The case reports in this chapter demonstrate the explanatory potential and the clinical utility of that concept. We can also see that we can't really understand the inner workings of the triangle of conflict without a prior grasp of the object relations phenomena, particularly repression and projective identification, that we first encountered in chapter 2. Next, in chapter 5, I'll describe short-term couple object relations *group* therapy, as an alternative format to work with both the triangle of focus and the triangle of conflict.

Short-Term Couple Group Psychotherapy

A Tale of Four Fights

Peter: (Group Session 15) Eureka this past week! I suddenly saw a lot of anger I have felt toward Ellen wasn't really about her. [It's a] black cloud, projection of my own psyche, all the anger I grew up with in my home, particularly from my mother. I confused it with Ellen. All my insecurities, a lot of what Ellen says to me, gets filtered through that, more to do with myself [than her]. I felt anger dissipate. I have felt different and more serene about things. Something has moved over last couple of days.

This chapter describes a 15-session, four-couple psychotherapy group offered within an HMO setting and led by co-therapists, myself and a postdoctoral fellow. This format allows us to work with the triangles of focus and of conflict in a new context, one that brings to bear the powerful influence of group cohesion as an additional therapeutic support. The five-step treatment model underlies the therapeutic mechanisms of this modality, just as it did with solo pairs. However, when we study couples as they move through the phases of the time-limited group, we can observe the sequential steps of the model particularly clearly. Object relations theory, once more, will help us make sense of the clinical phenomena that unfolds before us.

I have described the organization process and group phases of this powerful intervention elsewhere (1995). Budman and Gurman (1988); Budman, Simeone, Reilly, and Denby (1994); Framo (1973); MacKenzie (1990); Sander (1998); Burlingame, Fuhriman, and Johnson (2001); and particularly the Cochés (1990) have described short-term couple group and generic short-term group treatment in helpful ways. Unfortunately, space

157

does not permit reviewing all this work here, but any therapist planning to begin a short-term couple group should review these references carefully before starting.

CURATIVE ACTION OF THE GROUP: APPLICATION OF THE FIVE-STEP MODEL THROUGH GROUP PHASES

I have co-led some 25 short-term couple groups, and all follow the same sequence (Coché & Coché, 1990; Donovan, 1995). After a pregroup evaluation workshop (Donovan, 1995), the group enters (1) a getting-acquainted initial stage, then (2) a phase of early engagement, followed by (3) group crisis, (4) passionate engagement, and (5) termination. Excerpts from different phases demonstrate the shifts in object relations that take place from beginning to end and illustrate the considerable curative power of the group. We use the five-step model to guide the therapeutic action here, just as for the solo couple work: (1) explore the fight, (2) pursue the triangle of focus, (3) investigate the triangle of conflict, (4) soften the triangle of conflict, and (5) develop tools to work through the fight.

The opening group sessions contain many reports of the fight. These almost invariably conform to the triangle of focus diagram. For instance, Beatrice and Ken describe their prototypical frustrating interaction in session 3. The characterologic and family-of-origin connections to the fight readily present themselves.

Triangle of Focus Work Within the Short-Term Group

Ken and Beatrice

> *Ken is a 40-year-old consultant, and Beatrice a 42-year-old stay-at-home mom who cares for their 5-year-old adopted daughter. They unfortunately bicker almost constantly. In this excerpt, Ken once again ignores Beatrice's need for help in leaving the house. She becomes furious. Round one of their fight has begun. The therapists, working on the triangle of focus, discover that Ken's mother regularly burdened the family with her somatic ills (family-of-origin focal point) and that Ken taught himself to ignore these and most complaints from outside persons (character trait involving past and current others).*

(Group Session 3)

Beatrice:	When we get ready to leave the house, I'm always rushing around to clean up and he says, "I'm ready. Let's go." *No matter how many times I complain about this pattern, you don't seem to care. I'm just furious.* [The fight]
Ken:	Well, there's two sides of it. *You're never ready.* [The fight]
JMD:	Does this remind you of anyone in your family who is kind of daffy, always complaining? [Family of origin]
Ken:	No one like that. My mother always pushed on and got it done. She was a hypochondriac, though. [Family of origin]
JMD:	Oh?
Ken:	She always had some ache or pain.
JMD:	Oh, always complaining about something?
Ken:	Wife's always complaining, similar pattern I guess.
Co-therapist:	What does it feel like when your mother is like that?
Ken:	Frustrating, you don't listen.
JMD:	You can kind of make a pattern of that. Problems come by, from whatever source, and you kind of turn away. Can't stop the music, whatever you do. Does that happen in other parts of your life as well? [Character clarification involving other current persons.]
Ken:	Well, I guess. [Patient unconvinced of link between family-of-origin issue, character trait, and current fight. Should this continue, group may have minimal impact.]
Beatrice:	*It's very hard not to be heard.* [The fight]
Ken:	It always seems as if *it's one more thing, one more thing, when will it stop?* [Defense remains intact.]

How should we make sense of the details from this case, applying what we know about the triangle of focus and about object relations theory?

Ken's mother apparently burdened her son and her family with her psychosomatic complaints. Ken projects this repressed, frustrating mother object onto Beatrice, because he perhaps feels in his marriage that he can at last stand up for himself and oppose the manipulative woman. Predictably, he soon becomes exasperated, "Wife's always complaining." As he ignores Beatrice, she protests in still shriller tones. He has recreated his never-satisfied mother. The repetition compulsion enters the picture. We can also see that projective identification now has begun to operate within the couple. Beatrice feels Ken's projection that she's the unrelenting complainer. She identifies with this role, and her natural inclinations in this direction augment.

At this point the therapists had little data about Beatrice's family of origin, but soon we learned that her alcoholic parents ignored her needs and left her in charge of her younger siblings. Her drug-addicted sister was murdered by another addict some 15 years before our group, sealing Beatrice's repressed image of her destroyed family. Finding her family of origin so bruising, she never intended to marry and have children. Until her mid-30s, Beatrice maintained the life of a counterdependent career woman. Now, finally deciding to marry Ken, she finds herself once again alone, overwhelmed, and responsible for a chaotic family. As an adult, she has regularly had to fight the inclination to sink into despair and hopelessness. Beatrice has recently begun treatment with antidepressant medicines.

Clearly, to unlock the almost nonstop conflict between Ken and Beatrice, the therapists must help both free themselves from the repressed objects of their childhoods and to support them to come to terms with how they abortively attempt to master these old traumas in their present marital relationship. (Some direct coaching about how to compromise respectfully with each other won't hurt, either.) So, as we learned in the previous chapters, the first step in helping individual pairs is to explore the details of the fight, and the second is to begin to construct a triangle of focus for each, hypothesizing about the crucial role of repressed object relations wound into their fight and into their characterologic issues.

The therapists now play two roles. First, they try to fill in the triangle of focus as completely as they can by sifting the data for more and more connections with the family of origin. But second, they attempt to introduce a neutral investigative tone into the discussion and to salve the blame and move the interaction toward deeper mutual understanding versus accusation. In what fashion did Ken's mother complain about her physical maladies? How did this make him feel? Did he experience this as a manipulation on her part? In what way did his father react to the mother's entreaties? Does Ken respond to his wife as his father apparently did to his? We try to move the couple away from the hot stove of accusation and toward the cooler activity of psychological exploration. To do so, we attempt to introduce more mutual empathy into the equation. Ken lived with a mother who frequently made him feel guilty. He becomes furious with Beatrice's complaints, but we hypothesize out loud that Ken's reaction means that he's pinioned with guilt and helplessness, not that he's indifferent to Beatrice and to her suffering. We'll also explore Beatrice's terror and anger when her parents handed over the family for her to raise and how her marriage resonates with the same theme of abandonment.

The triangle of focus work soon slides into an examination of the triangle of conflict for each group participant, Step 3 of the model. Ken fears control at the hands of a woman (A). He projects manipulativeness onto Beatrice and so he disregards her pain and snaps impatiently at her (D). In the group we'll explore with Ken his automatic anxiety/defense reflex action and attempt to help him forestall it. We also guess that Ken has a repressed hidden feeling and the attendant object relations, in which he can remember and longs for happy cooperation with a woman. We'll try to help Ken de-repress these memories and tolerate his wishes to repeat these positive interactions. We'll support him to struggle with the idea that he might approach Beatrice in a new way, in an attempt to help him experience his growth-promoting hidden feelings in an actual, present-time intimate situation. We'll undertake parallel work with Beatrice on her triangle of conflict and help her tolerate her fear of a family once again disintegrating before her eyes into complete lack of cooperation and bitter alienation. Applying the five-step model to Ken and Beatrice's dilemma makes the plan for their treatment quite clear.

Unfortunately, in the group and in some 10 postgroup couple sessions, we proved unable to bring either Ken or Beatrice to accept, meaningfully, these crucial connections linking the fight to their pasts. The early object relations, particularly Beatrice's, were repressed in the face of too much pain. Even coaching this couple toward more polite cooperative behavior failed. In the unconscious, both members probably still saw, and felt, the other as the old exploiter. Determined not to give one inch, they continued to snap and hiss their way through their marriage. Ken and Beatrice eventually dropped from treatment. In chapters 6 and 7, I'll discuss alternative approaches to precontemplative couples like this one.

Triangle of Focus and Triangle of Conflict Work in the Short-Term Group: Bill's Dilemma

Now we reencounter Bill, age 52, a somber, bearded, highly intellectual, self-employed business consultant, whom we first met in chapter 1. We'll see that Bill, the son of an authoritarian, sometimes brutal father, becomes enraged and withdraws, his prototypical defensive solution, when he senses that others wish to control or intrude upon him. He needs to maintain his freedom, but he also wishes to work closely with a few others, particularly his 52-year-old wife, Andrea. Bill must realize, cognitively and emotionally, that he needs and wants some intimacy in his life and not just isolation. This is the hidden feeling, deeply repressed, with which we need to help Bill come into contact. His anger serves a defensive function because it quickly leads Bill to his unvarying long-term maneuver: Sever all ties and disengage completely, psychologically annihilate the enemy.

As we now join his treatment, Bill contemplates one more such scenario. This time, business partners have become the foe. Unfortunately, Bill also frequently projects the intruder-controller role onto Andrea. Periodically, he angrily spurns her as well, as we'll see. Guilt-wracked, frustrated, and now angry herself, Andrea feels caught in the snare of her husband's projection, with no idea of how to free herself. True to projective identification, she begins to act the unempathic, invasive nonpartner whom Bill fears but has ironically, fatalistically just recreated.

(Group Session 11)

Bill: Isolate myself. [Defensive solution] It's the way I work, not just an issue with my wife. I've had a feeling like this my whole life. [Character issue]

JMD: Really, honest to God, it isn't all her fault. [Counterprojection] Andrea feels very blamed right now. [The fight]

Andrea: A lot. [The jaws of projective identification have closed on Andrea.]

JMD: Some variant of this would happen with any woman. [Character conflict → the fight.]

Bill: It's the major component of my work world right now. [Current relationship] Historically, always ended up leaving the work group. [Defensive solution] I'm beginning to separate from them now. [Character issue with current persons]

Martha (group member): What is the problem? Is it procedure oriented?

JMD: Yes, exactly what does the problem appear to be with your work associates? [Anxiety = ?; hidden feeling = ?]

Bill: Chemistry thing, inability to communicate. My invention is my technology. They're setting up a distribution system that will force me to abandon my technology. [Anxiety = fear of being controlled and destroyed.]

Dick (group member): What exactly is the problem?

Bill: They don't understand how to market it. This work group can only do so much damage to my core. [Anxiety pole of triangle of conflict] My dilemma, I have to think very carefully. [Cognitive attempt to construct solution to control anxiety and bind anger.]

JMD: Can you recall any important relationship from your childhood that had exactly this configuration? [Movement on triangle of focus from current character issue to family of origin.]

Bill: Not exactly this configuration. Hurting relationships, though.

JMD: Your father? What exactly went on with him?

Bill: Very limited communication, authoritarian type, didn't allow a lot of free expression. [Father controlled Bill, damaged his core?]

JMD: You wanted much more. He was very limited in what he could offer. [As in current business relationships]

Bill: I grew to accept this with him. [Foreclosed solution]

JMD: But not thereafter! [Confrontation of foreclosed solution]

Bill: No, not forever! [Expression of partial hidden feeling = wish for autonomy. Bill also longs for relatedness, although this aspect of the conflict remains more deeply hidden.]

JMD: Do you suppose that when you look at your work associates and your wife, the negative features of the partner stand out in bold type? [Bill emphasizes the limitations of others to avoid getting too close and risking destruction of core = defensive apex of his triangle of conflict.]

Bill: Marriage is different. I'm not trying to separate from Andrea. [Denies repetition of the defensive solution.]

JMD: But you are! [Therapist confronts Bill's repetitive defensive solution of withdrawal.] I think you're turning passive into active. Instead of a helpless child who craves communication, you hold yourself apart, as if you didn't need communication. Then Andrea becomes you as a child. [The interpretation includes both the triangle of focus and the triangle of conflict. It links the fight with Bill's childhood dilemma, and it confronts and starts to explicate his characteristic defensive solution.]

Bill: Wow! I'll have to think about that. [Defense lifts momentarily—possible affective breakthrough within triangle of conflict and triangle of focus.]

This glimpse into our interaction with Bill captures the manner in which the therapists work with the couples in the middle and later stages of the group. We roam around the triangle of focus, descending into important triangles of conflict at each major stopping point; that is, every couple's fight, Bill's relationship with his father, Ken's with his mother. We then link the defenses, affects, and object relationships we find at one focal point to those discovered at another; for example, Bill's fight with his partners and with Andrea connects to his original conflict with his father. This repetitive journey represents "working through" in short-term couple group psychotherapy. (See Malan and Osimo, 1992, p. 36, for a description of the similar process in short-term individual psychotherapy.)

By the close of the group, several of the couples have sufficiently explored their triangles of conflict at enough focal points to have gained a constructive cognitive and emotional grasp of the meaning of the fight and some new understanding of the object relationships involved in that conflict. Then, and, it seems, usually only then, can the partners find themselves free to experiment effectively with reasonable and affectively genuine alternative behaviors to master the irrational dispute that so familiarly beckons. We meet William and Barbara just at the point where they have devised "tools" to defuse their fight, before it boils over—Step 5 of the model.

William and Barbara: Fashioning Tools

(Group Session 15)

William (40-year-old attorney): Tools we learned. Tools beginning to practice. [New solution] Occasional slippage. Now recognize problem I have. Why it bothers Barbara. My parents are closest to the old stereotype—Ozzie and Harriet. What surprises me is that I'm focusing on how my father communicates with my mother. [Triangle of focus: family-of-origin pole.] What surprises me is that it's the exact problem that I have in communicating with Barbara. It does help to see the connection and to understand where I developed the habit. [Cognitive and affective breakthrough connecting fight with family of origin within the triangle of focus.]

JMD: How does he communicate with your mother?

William: When he disagrees, he doesn't acknowledge a legitimacy to her arguments. He attempts to win the argument by being louder, attempts to assert total authority. He ends discussion. "Let's drop it" is a phrase he uses. [Triangle of focus: William has identified with his father's domineering character trait.] Mother usually just defers. [William has been waiting in vain for Barbara to defer.] Understanding where habit develops is helpful. Earlier, I would deny I was using an offensive tone of voice to Barbara [Defense pole of triangle of conflict]. Now when she points it out, I usually acknowledge it. [Anxiety = loss of control of interaction, defense = condescension. William lifts defense, alters triangle of conflict. Hidden feeling emerges = wish to communicate genuinely.] I think about it [cognitive realization] and acknowledge [affective realization] what I do, which I really didn't do before. [Argumentative defense relaxed, true cooperation takes place.]

     I used to anticipate remarks Barbara would say in the past, lead me to dismiss her point. [Barbara probably played into this dismissal by accepting William's projections and offering predictable rejoinders; projective identification is afoot = old solution.] Catch myself right there. [Projective identification broken.]

> *I change my response* [Behavioral tool of self-observation used to anticipate and avoid fight]. "[Not] will you please call Doctor ____ about the baby's cold!"

Barbara (37-year-old social worker): When he spoke to me this way, *it made me feel I'm not doing my job as a mother*. [The fight] Now he'll say that's not what I meant. Could you do this tomorrow, because I can't? [New tool, nondefensive solution]. We're at this point, not at the point where we started the group.

This excerpt teaches us much about the optimal outcome for short-term object relations couple group therapy. Notice that William begins to experience his parents, himself, and his wife as new objects, as the group sequence unfolds. He's lifted his repression and now sees his father as a more problematic object. The father whom William previous pictured as easy-going begins to sound quite overbearing and controlling toward William's mother. William also grasps a new sense of himself, that he has identified with a controlling father. Barbara, too, has become a new object for him, one of equal value with whom to cooperate, rather than one to coerce with a loud, condescending voice. William also looks different to Barbara. He now seems like a person who treats her with respect and with whom she looks forward to interaction. She no longer just walks away, frustrated.

William achieved this fresh experience of himself and of his objects through insight into his triangle of focus, linking the discoveries there to his triangle of conflict. He observed and acknowledged his identification with his controlling father—connecting a character trait from his family of origin with the fight. Notice that at the close of his treatment, William, like Mark earlier, has returned to reconsider his triangle of focus in light of new learning. Then he related that observation about his father to condescension, his defensive style within his triangle of conflict. This insight about the interaction between the two triangles allows William to take a historical perspective and to choose whether he needs to behave in the same way as his father. He realizes that he no longer must rush to control his anxiety by manipulating his wife. William does not articulate his hidden feeling (HF), but he does enact it when he becomes more egalitarian and open with his wife.

Apparently, only when the triangle of focus work and the triangle of conflict work seem well underway can the couple develop effective "tools" to forestall the fight. William's attempt to monitor his tone and acknowledge his vulnerability to act superior represents an important new strategy in this couple's struggle toward a cooperative exchange. Barbara's courage in confronting William about his condescending attitude represents another tool that she uses effectively. Triangle of conflict work means acknowledging maladaptive defenses that the self brings to the marriage. We can see that William has completed some of this task. Barbara's defenses evidently do not impede genuine interchange, so once William changes his tone, the partners can move more smoothly ahead together.

If a pair can fashion tools that function effectively, then this implies a rearrangement of unconscious past and present object relations. William, for example, no longer seems unambivalently identified with his father. Notice that William has not transformed himself, but the attention to a particular character feature, in this case, his coercive tone, represents a small but significant alteration in his conscious and unconscious self. Note, too, that William's change includes all three dimensions of an object relationship. He perceives the objects, here his father and his wife, in a different way. His affect of defensive condescension shifts into one of more trusting mutuality, and his experience of himself moves from a controlling, defended self toward a more cooperative self.

We can see that these behavioral "tools" to curtail the fight don't usually embody precise stratagems as much as they do general communication skills. The word *tool* makes them sound more concrete than they usually are. But this is the term coined originally by William, and I continue to use it. The appearance of these tools in the closing sessions represents the single best informal outcome measure for the group. If Ken, from earlier in the chapter, could only recognize, bear, and work through his anger at his mother and his wife, he could sincerely cooperate with Beatrice by asking, "How can I help get us out of the house more quickly?" Beatrice then would no longer feel so blamed and vengeful and would not need to cuff Ken in return. The couple would have forged a tool to hold the fight at bay. Unfortunately, neither Ken or Beatrice ever made the crucial connections to their conflicted object relations from the past, so they couldn't question their own defensiveness and develop a solution to their fight. They felt compelled to keep battling on.

If the tools work reliably over time, it demonstrates that the couple wishes to communicate, rather than to continue as thralls to the projective identification. William stops seeing Barbara as an inferior, and she stops resentfully identifying with this role. Furthermore, both parties have modified their triangles of conflict at important focal points. Realistic problem solving has, to some meaningful extent, replaced the rigid anxiety → defense reflex. The partners now have more access to their hidden growth-promoting feelings, which allows them continued improvement in their intimacy. In Dicks's and the Scharffs' language, repression of past objects has lifted somewhat, and the partners can pursue their adult development together.

At least two intriguing questions remain unanswered. First, we can readily grasp once again that the fight represents, above all, a complex, shared defensive maneuver and that the key to the treatment turns on couples and individuals relaxing those defenses. The couples need to alter their triangles of conflict somewhere on their perimeter; that is, William must no longer express his fear of loss of control through his automatic argumentativeness and condescension. But why do clients choose to suspend their triangles voluntarily? Second, the group excerpts report on the interaction within one couple or between one or both therapists and an individual client. Why do we need a group at all?

Group cohesion represents a key variable in the curative thrust of the group. As that cohesion increases, greater intimacy can take place, creating an almost-ideal atmosphere in which individuals may lift defenses and encounter in a different, more helpful fashion the conflict with repressed objects. Cohesion carries a contagious effect. Genuine communication in one pair stimulates openness in others. The members can then face themselves and their triangles of conflict in greater depth than ever before, as Bill probably does in session 11, and William certainly does in meeting 15.

When the group bursts into passionate engagement, usually beginning in meeting 9, this dramatic shift in atmosphere means that high cohesiveness has supported the members to take on the psychological work of suspending defenses and lifting repression surrounding old objects. When repression suddenly dissipates, affective intensity markedly increases. We consistently observe this phenomenon in the second half of the short-term group. So we've answered the first question, at least in part. Many couples voluntarily lift defenses, supported and stimulated by the cohesive atmosphere of the group. They choose to do so because they're encouraged by the therapists and other group members in this direction and because they see instructive examples of other pairs becoming less rigid and feeling more happy and satisfied in their relationships.

However, every member of every couple does not seem ready to suspend a defense at the same time or at the same rate. What do couples do before they embark on this kind of psychological change? One thing they do is gaze into the mirror provided by the other members of the group, and there they recognize their fight, illustrated with real actors.

(Session 15)

Elizabeth (50-year-old manager): Couple group is extremely valuable because *you listen to other people the way you don't listen to your spouse or to yourself.* [Or to your therapist?] It sounds different, but you hear the similarities, incredibly useful way to enter the dialogue on your own—much more valuable than single couple's therapy.

Sometimes, grasping the triangle of focus and softening the triangle of conflict clearly occurs step by step in a particular couple. This progress seems public and obvious to the group, session by session. However, William and Barbara's case does not conform to this pattern. He and she certainly have entered the dialogue, although they waited until the very end to do so. Did the therapists and other group members, meeting by meeting, patiently help William to confront defenses and uncover hidden affect concerning his family of origin? No!

Actually, we felt pleasantly shocked by William's session 15 statement, because the group had dealt minimally with his childhood, although a great deal with those of other members. William has evidently worked quietly on his issues, listening and learning from others who entered the dialogue earlier. Little by little, he apparently reassured himself that it seemed safe to relax his own defenses and dare an action by beginning to experiment with newfound openness at home with Barbara. Apparently, change occurred for William, mostly absent direct intervention by the therapists, and mostly outside the group's awareness. But by session 15, William participates nondefensively, with an attitude of openness and cooperativeness, matched by Barbara's constructive stance.

How can we understand this kind of sub-rosa change? Confronting the triangle of conflict (and the triangle of focus) seems central to the therapeutic action of the group. But mounting a frontal assault on the defenses within that triangle represents a high-risk tactic, susceptible to backfiring. The real importance of the group format may not be its economy, treating multiple clients simultaneously, but rather its capacity to encourage the participants to suspend defenses at their own initiative and at their own rate before any therapist feels tempted to try radical surgery. Cohesion, in other words, is important when patients speak, but also when they are silent. Now we've answered our second question. The advantage of the group format seems clear. Cohesiveness supports the lifting of defenses, and cohesiveness holds clients while they contemplate a shift in of those defenses.

FOLLOW-UP AND OUTCOME (SESSION 16)

As termination approaches, the group often clamors for either an extension of weekly meetings or a future reunion. I have experimented with adding 5 to 10 sessions to the group at this point. This strategy usually fails. The extra meetings often seem anticlimactic, but partly in response to requests for more meetings, I've begun to schedule a follow-up session 3 to 6 months after termination. This additional meeting allows us to gauge the sustained effectiveness of the group and to reevaluate each couple's need for further treatment. It also provides a key maintenance-of-change support for the couples; more on this in chapters 6 and 7.

(A 3-Month Follow-Up)

In the waiting room, before the session began, several of the members embraced each other. [Cohesion continues.] Then our meeting started.

John (51-year-old professor): We've had two bad arguments [in the last 2 months]. Pretty quickly resolved them, a day or two, used to take a week. Used the things we learned here, get over it, put it behind us.

Joanne (59-year-old business manager, Mark's wife, from chapters 2 and 3): Things going well for us. Spring difficult historically, baseball, remodeling the house. Things pretty good now. Something really nice has happened.

Co-Therapist: What made the difference?

Joanne: Mark committed to knowing more about himself. Feel like we're really talking to each other.

Mark (59-year-old businessman): A lot of times I don't have a clue, but I've learned to ask. At least, knowing I don't understand helps. Temper my highs and lows, understanding what caused my behaviors.

Handle things differently. A parent came up to me at softball and told me how to teach his kid to pitch. I've done this for 30 years. I handled it. It bothered me, but I let it go. Didn't take his face off. In the past I wondered, why does someone think so little of me that they will tell me how to teach pitching? I would forget about it, but I wouldn't know I was mad about that event, but I would be in a bad mood. Fights a lot less intense. I understand stuff now. Last 53 years, what a waste!

John: I had the same feeling. We could have had a really good relationship. We struggled for so many years.

(Group discusses another member, Eileen, now deciding to enter PhD program.)

Jane (47-year-old former business manager, John's wife): In 1988 got up to my last semester of undergrad, psychology major, loved it. I broke my arm; I dropped out. I thought my husband [John] had impossible expectations for me. If I got a BA, you'd want an MS, then you'll want me to get a PhD.

Mark: Who did you get even with by dropping out? Husband? Mother? Father? [Note the remarkable gain in Mark's capacity for insight.]

Jane: My mother—never satisfied.

JMD: Could you say to John, "I feel expectations from my mother and from you"? Put it out on the table.

Jane: Seems obvious. Wasn't obvious for a long time. I saw my individual therapist last week. She said go home and tell him. I did, and he was very reasonable.

JMD: When you start a fight and go in his face, you've given up already.

Eileen (45-year-old teacher): Reacting against your mother. Not being who you are. This group continues to be a valuable experience.

John: Surprised I got so much out of this [group]. Thought I would learn a lot, but I got much more than I ever imagined.

Although, as yet, I lack formal outcome data for any of the groups, in these follow-up sessions I've observed that often one or two couples out of the four has retreated toward their status at initial interview. We usually suggest further treatment for one or both members of these couples. We can see from this excerpt that two or three of the couples seem to have internalized a psychological understanding of their fight and can continue to use the methods developed in the group to unravel their conflict-laden issues, before they reach incendiary levels. Despite the improvements, members of these pairs may wish or need some additional therapy, which we arrange. Often the short-term couple group does not represent a definitive, once-and-for-all treatment, but instead a key episode of therapy, bracketed by solo couple or individual short-term treatments—or both.

My impression is that the woman's level of functioning usually sets the tone for the postgroup adjustment of the couple. If the wife suffers sustained personal impairment—for example, a fragile sense of trust, due to trauma or to major dysfunction in the family of origin, she remains hampered in her capacity to support the couple in maintaining the psychological focus learned in the group. The men appear less likely to take the lead in preserving this perspective, but if the wife seems free to do so, they will usually join her.

The clients themselves often arrange their own follow-up by continuing to meet after termination as a leaderless group. These sessions usually occur monthly or bimonthly at members' homes over dinner and may continue a very long time. Several of our couple groups still meet regularly, years after the clinical termination. If we reencounter one of the couples from these extended groups, the partners usually communicate few details of these meetings, although they often attend religiously and seem to find them valuable. Cohesion evidently does not stop with session 15, nor does the group collapse without the therapists. Because we are never present, we cannot report on the group process or on what further benefits the members gain from these meetings.

CONCLUSIONS

The couple group encourages the participants to dare a crucial shift in their interaction, to stop fighting the fight and to begin working it through. This reorientation, to my eye, represents the key to all couple treatment, regardless of the therapist's theoretical orientation. Wile (1981) illustrates this point in his version of "nontraditional" couples therapy. He encourages the partners to view the fight not as a pitched battle, but rather as a comment on their relationship. Both members of the couple feel trapped, deprived, and powerless at different points in their relationship, and they need to begin to experience the fight as a healthy attempt to draw attention to this fact and to alter it.

For example, William and Barbara became frustrated with, and isolated from, each other in their control struggle. Both wanted to become closer and more cooperative. The fight expresses and comments on this need. Exploring all their feelings about the fight and its historical antecedents with the group, and with themselves, ultimately helped William and Barbara to grasp it as a struggle toward the positive goal of mutuality and not as an antagonistic melee.

The short-term couple group serves almost as a demonstration project, in which we can observe the five steps of the model particularly clearly. Indeed, I developed the model mostly from my group work at first. In the initial meetings the couples describe the fight in detail; then we all investigate the triangles of focus and of conflict; next, the pairs struggle to alter those triangles of conflict; and finally, they begin to work through the fight and to fashion tools to unravel it. Because the group has a distinct beginning, middle, and termination and because four couples progress through it in the same phases, we can see the five steps of the model unfold more plainly here than in solo couple work. The fact that the same conceptual strategy underlies both formats offers the clinician a great advantage, because he or she can treat couples sequentially in the two modalities and can gain therapeutic leverage from the advantages of both.

The short-term couple group, like the vast majority of psychotherapy interventions, does not represent a once-and-for-all treatment. When they feel the need, people return intermittently for more therapy throughout their lives (Budman & Gurman, 1988), and many of the couple group participants certainly have. Long-term treatment may realistically remain available to relatively few potential clients, but if we sequence our therapies with interruptions in between episodes, we can cast our net over a potentially wider population of patients (see Stadter, 1996). Other practitioners have developed similar strategies to treat client groups with common problems, such as adult children of alcoholics (Linda Camlin, PhD, personal communication).

Because the five-step model fits the group so well and because many couples seem to gain so significantly from this experience, we could easily wonder if we should encourage almost every pair to join such a group. However, many couples lack sufficient motivation to enter the group, and others remain unsuitable because of their personality style, rigidity, and so on. Because of the demands the group imposes on the clients to expose themselves at fairly deep psychological levels, in front of and with the participation of strangers, not every pair can manage this kind of challenge. I pursue these issues more deeply in chapters 6 and 7.

Change in the group probably occurs at four levels or phases of activity, which occur very roughly in sequence. At the first level the members try to make *cognitive* sense of their fight and to put the pieces of the triangle of focus together intellectually. In the second phase the couples work with the *object relations* and the *affects* contained in the triangle of conflict. In the third phase they wrestle with *self* or *existential* questions: What is my responsibility to initiate change in my marriage? How will this shift support a different life experience for me and my spouse? How will this outlook differ from how I grew up in my original family? The fourth phase, usually emphasized at the end of the group, represents seeking *behavioral change* and fashioning *new tools* to process the fight (Vicky Putz, PsyD, personal communication). These four levels of movement run parallel with Prochaska's stages of change, an important connection that becomes the focus of the next chapter. Furthermore, as Gustafson (1984) and Pine (1990) note, psychiatry needs to engage clients with the theories and techniques of more than one school (i.e., dynamic object relations or interpersonal and self psychology approaches), because people function on many and not just on one of these planes.

Mysteries about the short-term group still remain for me. William and Barbara apparently gained so much, but until the very last meeting this couple rarely spoke in the group. Mark, a truculent and troubled man, appeared to undergo almost a transformation in his therapy group. How did these shifts unfold so quickly and so much to the surprise of the therapists? Obviously, we still don't understand a lot about change in couple treatment. The triangles of focus and of conflict represent helpful, maybe even crucial, schematics to help therapists order our observations. But the triangles comprise abstractions. Clients certainly don't think and feel in anything like the terms of the triangles, as they stumble toward altering their behavior. In chapters 6 and 7 I'll try to pursue the change process more from the client's viewpoint and closer to its subjective center.

CHAPTER 6

Steps 4 and 5:
How Do Couples
Change in Brief Therapy?

Since graduate school in the late '60s, I've been struck by an odd asymmetry in the study of psychotherapy. We teach and learn much about evaluating clients: What are the presenting symptoms? Biological, psychological, or both, in cause? Core relationship themes? Contributing family history? Most mental health professionals also seem skilled in crisis intervention and medication referral (at last count, over 50% of the clients in our large HMO psychiatry system used psychotropic medicine as part of their treatment). So we know a lot about how to start with our treatments.

In addition, Leigh McCullough-Vaillant (1994, 1997), James Gustafson (1984), David Malan (1976, 1979; Malan & Osimo, 1992), Henry Dicks (1967), and many others have helped us to understand how to constructively begin and continue time-managed therapy with individuals or couples. They stand as experts in the middle innings of dynamic, or object relations, brief therapy. Gustafson (1995) has also carefully studied when long versus brief treatment seems required.

However, we appear less informed, and publish much less, about *how* and *when* people actually change—that is, about the end state of successful psychotherapy. A related, and equally important, matter now also breaks into the discussion. Inevitably, we write our books and articles from the viewpoint of therapist activity. We don't concentrate much on the clients' moves to alter their own behavior. In this chapter and the next, I'll examine the underpinnings of successful change in brief couple therapy, sitting, as much as possible, on the clients' side of the room, in an attempt to understand growth in psychotherapy through their eyes and hearts.

When do clients actually change, and how do they do it? Since the early '70s, I've wondered: Shouldn't we study the change process in successful therapies and then work backward to attempt to construct, from the start, in our new treatments, the circumstances that best support positive development? If we study the desired outcome, can't we structure our activity throughout therapy to create the eventual result the clients need? Perplexed, in the past, I couldn't find books, papers, or teachers who operated according to that general strategy. For the most part, I still can't.

I don't intend to overstate this point. I realize that when Leigh McCullough, David Malan, and Henry Dicks ask us to accompany them studying a successful case, they indirectly point out signs along the way that the patient has begun to demonstrate some change, and they spell out the actions of the therapists and of the client that have presumably promoted those shifts. Watching a sequence of Leigh McCullough's videotapes, for example, we can observe her clients become less defensive and express gradually deeper affects, as she pushes them to do. For us and for her clients, Dr. McCullough directly relates these gains within the therapy to parallel ones in the clients' lives. She points out to her clients that they feel less defeated at work and more able to stand up to spouses or family members, for instance. Still, I'm strongly convinced that we need to study, with much more care, what happens toward the end of therapy, how people actually change their feelings and their behavior. I'll undertake this project by investigating, from the client's viewpoint, how clients begin to work through their fight and devise tools to forestall it, Step 5 of the model.

THE PROCHASKA STAGES OF CHANGE RESEARCH

James Prochaska and his colleagues (Prochaska, DiClemente, & Norcross, 1992; Prochaska & Norcross, 2001) offer us a unique body of research, studying when and how people change. I'll use their work as a point of departure in attempting to examine positive shifts in time-managed object relations couple treatment.

The Prochaska findings represent a valuable resource in pursuing the change question. I will summarize them at length. Prochaska and his co-investigators studied the widest imaginable spectrum of clients across an equally broad arc of therapies. They've reviewed treatments of people attempting to control their smoking, their weight, and their alcohol addiction, as well as general psychotherapy clients. The researchers studied those in cognitive-behavioral programs, in insight-oriented therapies, and in self-help formats. They discovered that all those attempting alterations in personal behavior appear to move through five stages of change—precontemplation, contemplation, preparation, action, and maintenance—regardless of the specific nature of the problem, the theory of change involved, or the participation of a professional helper.

Prochaska describes those in the precontemplation state as demonstrating no realistic intention to alter behavior in the foreseeable future. "As far as I'm concerned, I don't have any problems that need changing" (Prochaska et al., 1992, p. 1103).

Contemplation, however, represents a stage in which the person acknowledges a problem and has started seriously thinking about overcoming it but has not, as yet, made a commitment to take action. Serious consideration of problem resolution represents the core element of contemplation.

In preparation the client, or self-changer, combines intention and behavioral moves. He or she intends to take action in the next month and has unsuccessfully done so in the previous year. Although these people may have altered their problem behavior somewhat, they have not yet met a criterion for effective action. For example, some have reduced their smoking or switched to low-tar cigarettes, but they have not attempted to stop the habit altogether.

However, in the action stage people decisively change their behavior, their environment, or both. "Modification of the target behavior to an acceptable criterion and significant, overt efforts to change are the hallmarks of the action phase" (p. 1104).

In maintenance, individuals strive to prevent relapse and to fortify the gains of the action stage. Those within maintenance endorse statements such as, "I'm here to prevent myself from having a relapse of my problem" (p. 1104).

This research establishes and describes the five stages of change, but it offers us more. Prochaska and colleagues go on to examine the sequential movement that takes place from stage to stage. Evidently, this represents no straight-line affair. In weight loss and in addictions, and, one suspects, in general psychotherapy, relapse represents the rule rather than the exception. Smoking self-changers complete a mean of three or four action steps before they achieve abstinence, for example (p. 1104). So, rather than passing through the five stages in a neat linear progression, during relapse, changers, when they fail at the action stage, return to earlier phases, recycling back to preparation or contemplation. The model, then, describes a spiral path suggesting a cycle of attempts at action, then relapse, next regression back to earlier stages, and then more successful drives toward change.

These findings seem interesting so far, but now they become even more intriguing, because the *pretreatment* stage of change appears highly predictive of outcome for any presenting problem, for any client, in any treatment approach. For instance, among those attempting smoking cessation, 22% of precontemplators, 43% of contemplators, but 76% of those in action or in preparation, at the start of the study, had stopped smoking 6 months later (p. 1106). The researchers replicated these findings for psychotherapy patients. They suggest that programs need to move clients to the next phase, one stage at a time, that is, contemplators toward preparation and preparation people toward action, regardless of the target symptoms or the theoretical orientation of the treatment. Apparently, many therapies, across all theories and all problems, fail because they overlook the change stage of the participant. For example, some programs, such as psychodynamic ones, assume that insight and preparation lead to change, skipping the action stage.

Prochaska and colleagues make several points that we need to ponder in some depth and then apply to our observations about successful short-term couple therapy. First, apparently, we must try to advance the motivational stage of the participants as forcefully as possible. We should probably start by excluding precontemplators from many of the couple treatment models I've reviewed here, because all call for considerable motivation and activity on the part of the participants. The five-step model certainly does. A group educational intervention appears more appropriate for precontemplators. Such a program might help the participants decide if a serious problem exists in their marriage. Once we identify precontemplators and offer them a less rigorous intervention, then we need to approach the contemplators and move them toward preparation as quickly as we can, and so on.

Second, contemplation and preparation stand as necessary preludes to change, but to change, the individual (or couple, presumably) must *do* something, form a plan to stop smoking or to end pointless fighting, *and* follow it. If we want to help couples change, it seems we must include an *action* phase in our therapy. Grasping the specifics of that action phase and devising a realistic means of introducing it into our insight-mediated couple therapy become major challenges, which I take up later in the chapter.

Third, couple therapists apparently must pay careful attention to the issues of relapse and relapse prevention, whatever their change model, because the Prochaska findings suggest the pragmatic truth that most couples will probably relapse and return to earlier stages before they initiate productive therapeutic actions for themselves. Moreover, change does not represent a once-and-for-all event; well after successful actions, couples can still retrogress. So we must build maintenance capabilities into our treatment programs.

Fourth, Prochaska and his colleagues demonstrate that the motivation and activity of the client account for much of the variance in outcome for all manner of treatments. The fact that self-changers progress through the same motivational stages as do psychotherapy clients, for example, lends even more conviction to the idea that the locus for change resides within the client, not inside the psychologist or the weight-loss counselor.

To cite one example of this complex change process to which Prochaska introduces us, I report on a former career. In the past I specialized in the psychotherapy of alcoholism and treated, or supervised, the treatment of hundreds of alcoholics. With a few exceptions, I cannot recall ever convincing a patient not to drink—initially a distressing realization, because the objective of my work was to curtail the alcoholism. Many, probably most, patients arrived at my office in the precontemplation state, sent by exasperated spouses, children, or primary care physicians. Some, not independently motivated to stop drinking, left almost as quickly as they came. Others either entered the contemplation stage after a few sessions of therapy or arrived within that stage at the start. After a good deal of reflection, I began to feel that at some point, the clients who remained wished to curb their alcoholism, and they began to use me as a consultant to support the project.

In one dramatic case, I "cured" the alcoholism without ever seeing the patient. He called, never gave his name, but did recount his history. "I drink eight beers a day. I think this is a problem. My doctor says he drinks the same amount and not to worry about it, but I think he's wrong. Tell me to stop drinking." I said, "Fine, stop drinking." He said, "Okay, I will." I instructed the patient to reduce his intake by one beer a day, in order to counter the risk of withdrawal, until he became alcohol-free in 8 days' time, and then to call me 1 week after that for follow-up. Two weeks later he phoned, sober, and thanked me for all my help. I do not present this unusual case, though surely a cost-effective one, as a model of optimal treatment, but it does illustrate the power of the preparation and action stages. This man had clearly invested serious thought to his alcoholism before his phone call. He stood prepared for change, but he needed an authority figure to direct him toward decisive action. He skillfully scripted my lines for me.

I hold the impression that most successful treatment of alcoholism follows something like this same form, although, of course, in a more complicated, protracted fashion. The client decides to stop drinking, begins to do so, in small steps (the preparation stage), we hope with medical supervision, and then engages with the practitioner about the guilt, anxiety, loneliness, and symptoms of personality disorder, which precipitated and continue to prolong the addiction (Donovan, 1986). The "practitioner" need not have a professional license. AA sponsors, ministers, and probation officers successfully treat more alcoholics than do professional therapists (Valliant, 1983). However, the latter do seem particularly helpful in working with ambivalence, investigating past and present family problems, including family members in the treatment, and advising patients about employment and social relationships. Therapists potentially provide these valuable resources, but, in my experience at least, either the clients reached for these tools, or they didn't. It appears that therapists do not often cure alcoholism and perhaps, by extension, marital problems. As we continue through this chapter, we'll watch how the therapist may help couples through the contemplative and preparation stages and push them toward the action phase, but it turns out that, ultimately, the couples may make the crucial moves somewhat independently.

My alcoholic patient, whom I never met, clearly had passed through contemplation and preparation. The decision to call me, consult a professional, represented entering the action stage for him. The resolve to follow my advice clearly placed that action into motion. I do not know how this gentleman, whom I never heard from subsequently, fared within his maintenance stage. I do know that he remained sober for at least 1 week.

The stages of change represent a transtheoretical model that helps us understand *when* important alterations in attitude, initiative, and behavior unfold and in what sequence. But Prochaska and colleagues tell us still more. They have isolated a matrix of generic change *processes* that teach us *how* the shift from stage to stage may unfold. This research group has identified 12 different general processes that clients, counselors, and therapists all seem to use to guide their behavior. In other words, clients and health providers employ the same change processes to grapple with a wide spectrum of problem behaviors: weight loss, smoking cessation, and psychological distress. For instance, consciousness raising, that is, learning more about the problem; helping relationships, that is, forming a helpful alliance with a counselor; and self-liberation, committing to act on a problem, represent the most frequently used change processes across problems.

The stages and processes of change interact to predict strongly the outcome of all therapies. Clients apparently must use the *appropriate* change process at the *correct* point in their motivational cycle. Among smokers, the stage and process variables carry more predictive outcome value than do demographics, health history, or even severity of the problem (p. 1105). The researchers found that premature psychotherapy terminators most often fell in the precontemplation stage and reported that these people, inappropriately, relied more on will power and stimulus control than did clients who continued in therapy or terminated satisfactorily.

To clarify, the change *process* must match the change *stage*. In moving from contemplation into preparation, clients need to use change methods such as environmental reevaluation, that is, "When I drink, my family environment deteriorates"; and self-evaluation, that is, "I disgust myself when I smoke three packs a day." In the action stage, clients use "self-liberation" and "willpower" effectively. They employ affirmations suggesting personal autonomy and undertake definite, willful actions to change behaviors and to reach their goal. For example, they throw all the liquor out of the house. Will power apparently works in the action stage but not earlier in the precontemplation phase, for example.

Prochaska concludes,

> From our perspective, the underlying structure of change is neither technique nor problem specific. The evidence supports a trans-theoretical model entailing (a) a cyclical pattern of movement through specific stages of change, (b) a common set of processes of change and (c) a systematic integration of the stages and processes of change. . . .
>
> Probably the most obvious and direct implication of our research is the need to assess the stage of a client's readiness for change and to tailor interventions accordingly. . . .
>
> We have determined that efficient self-change depends on doing the right things (processes) at the right time (stages). We have observed two frequent mismatches. First, some self-changers appear to rely primarily on change processes most indicated for the contemplation stage—consciousness raising, self-reevaluation, while they are moving onto the action stage. They try to modify behaviors by becoming more aware, a common criticism of classical psychoanalysis: insight alone does not necessarily bring about behavior change. Second, self changers often primarily rely on change processes associated with the action stage—reinforcement management, stimulus control, counter conditioning—without the requisite awareness, decision making and readiness provided in the contemplation and preparation stages. They try to modify behavior without awareness, a common criticism of radical behaviorism: overt action without insight is likely to lead to temporary change. (pp. 1110–1111)

Prochaska presents his findings in abstemiously atheoretical fashion, but we can observe that he and his colleagues have described the phenomenology of mastery in detail. How does an individual confront, wrestle with, and resolve a personal problem? Prochaska has therefore made a major contribution to a general psychology of human adaptation with his research findings.

WORKING THROUGH THE FIGHT: STEP 5 OF THE MODEL

We can guess the next turn in the discussion. We'll try to apply Prochaska's findings to the five-step model of couple treatment, to observe if this new perspective, offered by Prochaska, helps us more deeply understand the change process in object relations couple therapy. Although I had no such intent when I first constructed the model, we can see fairly quickly that the first four phases of couple treatment—(1) investigate the fight, (2) map the triangle of focus, (3) explore the triangle of conflict, and (4) alter the triangle

of conflict—roughly correspond to Prochaska's contemplation and preparation stages. We introduce phase-appropriate change processes in these
four steps that match the client's motivational state, particularly consciousness raising, that is, developing more insight into the problem and forming
a helping relationship with the therapist. This treatment sequence prepares
the way for the members of a couple to work through their fight, the action
stage of the model.

Most of the issues in the fight will never disappear from the couple's
life. Any pair of people will have genuine differences of temperament, of
opinion, of preferred activities, and of valued commitments that clash, as
well as contrasting family backgrounds. Gottman (1994) and Wile (1999)
suggest that the difference between most successful marriages and most
unsuccessful ones resides in how the couple deals with those continuing
conflicts. They do not erase the issues. In the final stage of the model, working
through the fight and devising tools to unravel it, the partners need to take
actions to develop for themselves a methodology to resolve the fight in a
new satisfactory fashion. No matter how much insight or historical perspective the couple gains, treatment fails unless the partners can rework
their fight. Although neither I nor many of my colleagues, whose writing
I've mentioned earlier, use Prochaska's terminology, we all seem to agree
that the clients need to take actions to change the fight. Depending on the
theory involved, the pair may need to solidify a boundary, soften an affect,
or suspend a defense. Partners do need to take new definitive moves to have
any chance of altering their recurrent conflict.

In our discussions so far, we imply that in the first four stages of the
model the therapist assumes the lead, making relationship counter-offers,
coaching, or contributing interpretations or clarifications. But Prochaska
marshals research data to prove that toward the end of the treatment, the
clients need to take more responsibility through their actions. The leader-
ship of the therapy shifts somewhat. I'll spend the balance of this chapter
describing how and when clients assume more of this initiative and begin
their actions. This review of change in couple therapy inevitably will point
us toward therapist behaviors that either contribute to or impede client
preparation for, and the taking of, action. I'll identify these along the way.

Nancy and Tom: Taking Action

Nancy and Tom offer an example of partners who learned to work through
their fight. We have not met them yet. I'll introduce you to them in a second. They provide a particularly apt illustration of undertaking a curative
action in couple therapy, because both represent wounded, awkward people,
who grew up in disturbed families. If a couple treatment helps 45-year-old

Nancy and 49-year-old Tom, we can realistically hope for efficacy across a wide range of marriages.

> *Tom's aged, distant father rarely spoke with him, and his mother inter-acted not much more. Nancy's alcoholic family abandoned her psy-chologically, again and again. Tom, a gangly, shy, fidgety man, worked as a contractor, rehabilitating and reselling dilapidated housing, per-haps a concrete metaphor for his equally dilapidated family of origin. Tom, although devoted to his wife and two teenaged children, rarely addressed personal topics with anyone in his life and felt at a loss for how to begin with Nancy.*
>
> *For her part, energetic, anxious Nancy, although proactive in her teaching job and in her community involvements, seemed too over-committed to work and too personally uncomfortable ever to sit and talk with Tom. Obviously, this couple rarely exchanged conversation about intimate matters and predictably enjoyed no sexual life. At the beginning of the group, Nancy projected the responsibility for the couple's almost total lack of communication onto Tom. "You always choose the wrong time to talk, when I'm busy with something else. You end up chasing me around the house."*
>
> *In the group, we explored the underpinnings of the anxiety both felt over personal closeness. We learned that Tom's distant family of-fered him virtually no training whatsoever in communication, and that Nancy's anger and mistrust toward her unreliable father led her to-ward a counterdependent stance in which she expected little, and gave little, of a personal nature, particularly to men. In contrast, toward her junior high school students, Nancy appeared remarkably available and supportive. Clearly, she identified with the students and offered them what she had most wanted at their age and probably still wished for now as an adult.*
>
> *Two crises from external life, then, by chance, befell the couple, which strained their relationship mightily. But these events ultimately forced them toward the interaction from which they habitually physi-cally and emotionally fled. The couple's 13-year-old son required a spinal operation to correct a congenital defect, a procedure that neces-sitated that he remain in a body cast for 2 months. Tom and Nancy needed to talk and cooperate, nearly constantly, to coordinate and pro-vide his care. The other parents in the group offered this stressed couple heartfelt support and advice about how to manage this wrenching family medical emergency.*
>
> *Just after their son's situation stabilized, a legal matter intruded that Tom and Nancy found even more trying. Tom's sometime real estate partner had apparently engaged in numerous questionable*

financial schemes and had come under investigation by the state authorities. Tom, although innocent of wrongdoing, received subpoenas to testify. Official envelopes streamed into the house by registered mail. Nancy felt terrified that her husband had fallen under legal scrutiny and would lose his professional license. She feared that he might go to jail, the near fate of her apparently feckless father. She blurted out her concern in the group. But paralyzed by anxiety and, once again, fearful of total abandonment by a man, Nancy could not bring herself to ask Tom directly about the meaning of the ominous mail.

In session 13, we introduced an enactment into Tom and Nancy's treatment. In enactments, the therapist pushes the couple hard to interact directly around an important emotional topic and does not let the partners evade or stonewall (Nichols & Minuchin, 1999). Nancy mentioned the frightening envelopes in passing during session 12 but quickly tried to drop the subject. By now, though, the therapists and the group members had become aware of her proclivity to speak out on an issue and then scamper away from it. So when the matter came up in the next meeting, we all teamed up to block the escape route. We insisted that she describe her anxiety at length. It turned out that she feared that Tom would be prosecuted, lose his work permits, and go bankrupt. We clarified with her that she couldn't deny her anxiety but had to pursue the matter directly with Tom. We asked her how she would introduce the topic. Then we turned to Tom and questioned whether he knew the extent of his wife's concern. He also had learned the coping skills of evasiveness long ago, and he tried to minimize the danger. We interpreted this defense and reiterated that in the near future, he had to discuss the issue with Nancy in depth.

An interesting aspect of these exchanges was just how adept the group members had become at spotting and clarifying defensive behaviors. Tom and Nancy left the group that evening with the homework assignment to discuss the mail. During the meeting, they did commit to having the conversation on an upcoming car trip to Maine. Now the couple felt accountable to the group to initiate this important action. In the last session they reported on how their confrontation evolved.

(Session 15)

Tom: Yes, the group sort of forced us to be in the same place, too, you know . . . just being together. And it makes other times we're together easier. If we go to a movie, we don't argue about being late to the movie or early to the movie so much.

	We just go with the flow. And in the house, or going out to dinner, it's just easier. It makes life easier. It's improved our relationship.
Nancy:	I think we've learned how to give each other space. We learned how to listen to each other, but also how to respect each other's space, too, to the point where I was able to listen to Tom about the legal stuff. Of course, it was in a moving vehicle, and I couldn't walk out. But I think having that agreement up front that we were going to discuss it in the car on the way to Maine really helped. And Tom is also respecting my space in the mornings, when I'm rushing off. You've been pretty good about that.
Co-therapist:	So you did talk on the way to Maine?
Tom:	Yeah, we did.
Nancy:	Yeah.
Tom:	The kids were in the back, and they couldn't hear us. Yeah, all it took was 5 minutes. *I just said it.* [Action step] She says, "Is that all there is? Is that it?" That was it. And we were just talking about our lives. [Taking cooperative action about the crisis increases intimacy.]
Nancy:	Yeah, we just talked.
Co-therapist:	What was the conversation about?
Tom:	Just my responsibilities, my involvement in these lawsuits. In fact, I got phone calls today from the Board of Overseers about my friend. I didn't return the call. I know it's about him. He may lose his license, 'cause he's being investigated. I have nothing to lose. I have a broker's license, but I'm not being investigated. He is. I just had to convey that to Nancy, that I'm not liable. [Action step]
Co-therapist:	But that conversation was only 5 minutes. Try not having it and see what happens. [Change probably cannot take place without an action.]
Tom:	Yeah. It took us months to get to that. [Many relapses before the action.]
Nancy:	Well, it was the buildup, just trying to have it, resisting having it. [Preparation stage]
Co-therapist:	Then it wasn't quite as painful, when you got into it, as you thought it was going to be.
Nancy:	No, I'm not sure how much detail we went into.

Female group member: But you heard enough to make you feel better.

Tom: She felt comfortable that that was all there was.

Nancy: So I think that's helped. And it's helped to see each other in
a noncompetitive kind of atmosphere and to see each other
as vulnerable people, instead of two people always compet-
ing in some way. That has helped a lot. I think Tom is seeing
me as a more vulnerable person, and I see him as one also.
It's disarming. [Mutual blaming ceases, both people equally
vulnerable, the problem reconceptualized as an externalized
one with which both of the pair need to struggle as equals.]

JMD: Tom, how was that 5 minutes for you? Did it seem like that's
something you could repeat?

Tom: I rehearsed it. [Group laughs.] I just streamlined it down to
5 minutes. She knows the details of most of what had been
happening. She sees the registered mail and all of that.

Co-therapist: God, you must have been scared.

Tom: Yeah, she was scared.

Co-therapist: To see all this official-looking paper coming into the house.

Nancy: Yeah, but I just go into this instant denial. It's easy for me.
[Defensive apex of triangle of conflict.]

JMD: Though that defensive move is easy for you, it's very costly.
[Confrontation of defensive pole of triangle of conflict.] It
would really be better for you if you didn't do it, even though
you feel like you're going to throw up. It would be really
better for you, if you say, "Okay, I'm really nervous. What
am I really nervous about?" And then try to get a little bit
of perspective. Ask him about it. [Coaching toward externalizing the triangle of conflict, making it a topic of couple
conversation and cooperation.]

Nancy: I would feel more like an adult if I did that and not like a
child. [Tentative move toward more mature object relations.]
I mean, I instantly go into my child mode and say, "Okay, I
don't need to know this. This is his thing. I'm not dealing
with it." But then I get angry if he treats me like a child.
[Projective identification and defensive pole of triangle of
conflict: Nancy projects her childlike self-concept onto Tom.
Now she believes that he thinks she's infantile. Then she
reidentifies with the projected material and blames Tom for
dismissing her, which sparks their recurrent fight.]

JMD: You would in fact be acting like an adult if you . . .

Nancy: Yeah, I know. I know.

Co-therapist:	That's what adults do, and it isn't easy. I bet talking about your feelings will greatly help your relationship. [More coaching[
Tom:	Just having talked like that makes it easier now to deal with the next thing that comes along. [Maintenance]
JMD:	Now you can't tell yourself that you don't know. Right, you know that you know what to do, and if you don't do it, it's your responsibility. [Exhortation toward mature action]
Nancy:	Another thing I've decided to take some responsibility for, I think, is to get involved in a group for adult children of alcoholics [ACOA], because I've never done that. I've read everything I can get my hands on. I've tried to understand what's working inside of my head, and what my reactions are all about. What my fears and anxieties are about. [Contemplation stage] Now I have kids, and I'm transferring all that *stuff* to them. I'm trying not to, but I know it's going to happen, if I don't take care of it. [Reevaluation of family environment.] Tom has always encouraged me to deal with it and try to get some help, so I think that's probably the next step I may take. [Preparation step for a second decisive action.]
Co-therapist:	Sounds like a real constructive step. [A possible action]
Group member:	That's good.
Nancy:	'Cause then I can deal with all those things aside from our relationship and then come back to the relationship healthier.

This excerpt allows us to observe a compromised couple struggling to take action by the partners' working through their fight. Of course, Tom and Nancy rarely fought overtly. They became exasperated with each other and withdrew into their separate rooms. This time both acted on their unwillingness to endure the same unsatisfying outcome. This time, after relapses and false starts, Tom and Nancy, confronted by the group's enactment, took decisive action and moved to Stage 5 of the model. They suspended their defenses, at least for the moment, and rather than fighting the fight, they devised tools to pick their way through the conflict.

Tools

We observed in chapter 5 that *tools*, the term couples often use when they describe how they work through their fight, do not represent concrete procedures, as the word might imply. Tools rather appear the general guidelines of communication with which the couples, supported by the therapy, experiment to unravel their conflict. We can now grasp that the development and use of these tools correspond to the action stage of the therapy and, if the pairs keep reaching for their tools, to the maintenance stage of the treatment.

Tom and Nancy have developed several of these. First, they have set tacitly agreed-upon limits to their availability to one another. If the assumption reigns that no boundary exists between them, then communication comes to mean complete, endless, and frightening mutual vulnerability, particularly for this skittish pair. Couples like Tom and Nancy then back off, rigidly protect themselves, and routinely use projective identification to blame the other one for the standoff. But now Nancy tells us that they have agreed to "give each other space." She needs to rush to school in the morning, and Tom does not interfere with this. Setting and respecting boundaries seems to function well for this couple.

Tom and Nancy have also agreed that they *will* discuss important topics and take action, but at mutually agreed-upon times and places—for instance, on the much-anticipated car ride to Maine. We can see, once again that "tools" do not represent sophisticated, complicated stratagems for communication, but rather simple, commonsense guides for interaction to which both of the pair remain faithful. So, explicit agreements to communicate represent another important new tool for Tom and Nancy.

William, the 40-year-old attorney, originally introduced me to the word *tools*, referring to the behaviors that couples develop for themselves to work through their fight. We have already met William and his 37-year-old wife, Barbara, in chapter 5, where I described their career in the couple group. If we look carefully at their dialogue again, as we will in a moment, we can see more clearly the relationship between working through the fight and developing tools to confront the troubling issues.

Nancy and Tom and William and Barbara—in fact, all couples—must find a method to talk about emotionally charged matters without activating their triangles of focus and their triangles of conflict to such an intensity that the triangles become the topic. Then the couple starts the fight, rather than engaging with the original issue. To work through the fight, the couple first needs to make a commitment to tolerate the affects wound into the partners' triangles. They need to maintain this stance steadfastly throughout their interaction, however tempted they might become to give in to their anxiety and their defenses. For example, Nancy tends to withdraw, as she so often has in the past. Both Tom and Nancy project responsibility for the conflict onto the partner. William uses a ploy learned from his father in defensive fashion. He attempts to yell louder than Barbara. Time-managed couple therapy will probably not transform character, but each member of the pair needs to learn to *suspend* or *move around*, or at least *acknowledge*, their defensive pole within the triangle of conflict, at the key moments. This represents a required action for them to work through their fight, perhaps the crucial lesson of the five-step model. Naturally, the introduction of the tools quickly follows.

Once the couples commit to stop fighting and start working, a primary task of the first six to eight sessions of the therapy, they begin to soften the automaticity of their triangles and to practice studying, versus battling through, the fight. Then they have completed the contemplation and preparation stages in Prochaska's model. When they actively choose to behave differently during the fight, they've begun the action stage. But they must rehearse this phase of change, often multiple times, as Tom and Nancy have, before they can complete the action of negotiating the central conflict. Let's study William and Barbara again and try to observe how they develop and continue to use their tools.

WILLIAM AND BARBARA: THE ACTION AND MAINTENANCE STAGES

Returning to William and Barbara from chapter 5, we can recontact them in the midst of committing to work through their fight and deriving their own particular tools to help themselves through that struggle. I'll repeat some of the earlier dialogue, because it illustrates the stages of change unfolding in front of us.

(Group Session 15)

Barbara: We were very unhappy with each other. And part of that was he was doing his thing, and I was doing my thing. We were trying to run a family, but we weren't together on it. I felt very alone. I don't know if that was your sense, too, William? But our communication was really difficult. It seemed like we couldn't even have a simple conversation without it being very tiresome. It was like it wasn't even worth it, and I got to the point where I was just kind of walking away, not really staying there. [Dysfunctional conflict resolution] And now I don't feel that way. When we don't understand, we work it out. [Working through the fight—constructive conflict resolution.]

William: Something else, just by coming here for 15 weeks, it becomes a habit, sort of a routine. Hopefully, that's what's happening. We're getting into the habit. [Maintenance] I think the group has been very helpful. I agree with everything Barbara said. It's definitely helped our relationship by helping our communication, and I think the *tools* that we learned are *tools* that we're beginning to practice and use.

Occasionally, there is some slippage. But now I'm recognizing problems that I have in the tone of voice I use with Barbara sometimes. I understand now why that bothers her, and I understand it's a legitimate perception on her part. I expected the group to help us out. I've been in a group a few years ago about relationships also, and that helped me out. I'm glad we finally agreed to come, and I think it's helped us a lot.

My biggest surprise, I think, is that based on what I've heard of everyone's parents, my parents are probably the closest to the Ozzie and Harriet stereotype. I had basically a loving, supportive family and childhood, except for some rocky times in the teens, like all of us had. What surprised me is that I'm focusing on how my father communicates with my mother, and it's the exact problem that I have communicating with Barbara. I guess it does help to see that connection and understand where I developed the habit. [Consciousness raising, discovering more about the fight.]

Co-therapist: How does your father communicate with your mother?

William: When he disagrees with her, he doesn't acknowledge any legitimacy to her arguments. He attempts to win the arguments by being louder and using a tone of voice that asserts total authority and ends discussion, so that she can't rebut what he's saying. There's a phrase he uses, "Let's drop it."

Co-therapist: After he's had his say.

William: Yeah. And my mother, who often has a more legitimate point, usually just defers to him. So, I guess getting me to understand where the habit developed is helpful, and I think I'm making progress.

Earlier, I used to deny that I was using an offensive tone of voice with Barbara. And now when she points it out, I usually acknowledge it. [Change process of self-reevaluation]. Even if I don't acknowledge it, I recognize it, and so I think we're definitely improving, and we are certainly going to make an effort to spend more time together. We are really going to make a commitment to get babysitters more often and spend more time out. [An action, it is hoped, leading to maintenance.] We never went out before. We hardly ever went out, once or twice a month, maybe.

Now, as I think about responding to a point she makes, often I catch myself right there. [An action using change process of self-liberation, choosing a new behavior.] I hesitate for a second and then change my response. In other circumstances, where I don't catch myself, Barbara immediately reminds me that I'm using that tone of voice again. Most of the time I back off and then try to communicate. [A further behavioral commitment to action.] Sometimes I deny having used that tone, like I always used to do. But if Barbara insists that I was, then I have to wonder about it and reconsider. [Change process of helping relationship.]

I feel encouraged. I don't feel anxiety about the group ending now, because I think we have a lot of things we can continue to work on. [Maintenance] We can continue to improve our relationship, based not only on what we've discussed about ourselves, but also what we've learned from everybody's situation. [Group cohesion abets the preparation and action steps.]

Female group member: Yeah, I agree, it's helpful just listening.

William has devised tools to work constructively with Barbara. In this exciting excerpt, already analyzed from a different viewpoint in chapter 5, we can observe William taking an action by deciding to resist the defensive pole of his triangle of conflict, fighting back his need to defend through controlling behavior, a maneuver learned from his father.

The tool William has developed for himself represents his willingness to question his tone of voice (change process of self-reevaluation), sometimes on his own initiative and sometimes with Barbara's intervention. He alters his approach toward a more egalitarian, cooperative one (change process of self-liberation, experimenting with a new behavior). Because he recognizes the benefit to his marriage, he's highly motivated to continue in this new direction (change process of reinforcement management, i.e., receiving reward for his behavioral shift). Not just William, but Barbara has also learned a number of new tools: She can now offer William positive feedback (change process of reinforcement management), and she can question his tone of voice when it seems offensive (change process of self-liberation, committing to a new behavior). Finally, we can observe these partners entering the maintenance phase of their recovery. They commit to continue to work through the fight, and they have decided to set aside regular times to talk and to go out.

I see at least three additional important lessons in studying these tools that Tom and Nancy and William and Barbara have described for us. First, the tools almost always reflect cooperative, two-person behaviors. Barbara points out William's tone; he then alters it. Tom and Nancy agree together to discuss the legal terror on the way to Maine. The fight represents the quintessence of a one-person solution or nonsolution. Each member of the pair fanatically prosecutes his or her position, dismissing the opponent. "It was like it wasn't even worth it, and I got to the point where I was just kind of walking away" (Barbara). The tools, then, represent the opposite psychological maneuver from the fight. Cooperation replaces the disrespectful trading of blame.

Second, after the clients have engaged in preparation and contemplation, therapists can and do effectively push them toward action, often through enactments. But the couples must take the decisive action at their own initiative. When we see couples fashion their own tools, as these two pairs have, we know that they have begun to direct the treatment and have fully joined the campaign to defuse the fight. They've taken constructive actions.

Third, the clients may move into the next motivational stage without the therapist's knowledge. In the earlier sessions of the group, the therapists and the group members, once or twice, pointed out to William that he behaved in a controlling manner toward Barbara. We never remarked specifically on his tone of voice, and we knew nothing of the parallel dysfunctional interaction between his parents. William pursued these topics on his own and then shared his discoveries with us at group end. "Agency" refers to real phenomena. William actively took charge of his treatment by session 18.

We also never suggested that Tom and Nancy identify a precise time to discuss their crisis, or that Tom rehearse his presentation, nor did we ever recommend an ACOA group to Nancy. Although in retrospect I must wonder why not, because it appears so obviously the next step for her. The development of tools, then, represents not only the action phase of time-managed couple treatment; it signifies a self-initiated move toward change by the couple. When the pair continues to use those tools, a successful maintenance phase begins. It makes sense that the strategies that couples devise on their own work best for two reasons. This evolution demonstrates that the couple is genuinely motivated to change and is not just complying with therapists' suggestions. Also, self-conceived techniques will fit the couple better than those that any therapist could choreograph.

Suspending defenses, working through the fight, and devising tools to do so represent profoundly cooperative actions on the part of each member of the couple and, in my experience, invariably lead to a successful outcome in terms of decreased fighting, greater feelings of closeness, and higher satisfaction with the marriage, outcomes that the couple can, we hope, arrange to maintain. If, in psychoanalysis, the treatment ends when the patient can truly free associate and stop saying "no" (Rako & Mazer, 1980, p. 117, quoting Semrad), then an episode of couple therapy terminates when we observe the partners, on their own, developing and testing realistic tools to work through the fight. I have not encountered a couple who devised the tools before session 8 or 9. Preparation precedes action. But neither have I observed partners who, once they had developed these strategies and continued to practice them, did not markedly improve in treatment. I haven't encountered the inverse either, positive outcome without the couple using new, less defensive modes of conflict resolution. The action phase of treatment, in other words, appears necessary to positive outcome. This paragraph has the ring of the obvious to it. Of course, people change who formulate new behaviors and cooperate in practicing those alternative approaches. However, something inside them permits or encourages that change, the real mystery of the piece. We'll continue to pursue that something in this chapter and the next.

If and when a pair returns for further therapy, the tools, by definition, have ceased their efficacy. Usually, a new stress has disturbed the system—for example, physical illness, increased job pressure, the death of a parent, or perhaps the problematic characterologic issues in either member of the pair have become exacerbated. The focus when the couple returns seems clear: we have to discover what undercut the maintenance phase and provoked the relapse in which the tools failed in their role.

UNILATERAL ACTION INITIATIVES

I've just emphasized the cooperative quality that is so important to working through the fight and finding the tools. But I've also observed important changes in brief couple therapy that apparently do not take place within a give-and-take, two-person format. Sometimes one member makes a responsible, individual choice and an accompanying action, to shift his or her attitude and behavior. This can occur independently of any parallel initiative by the partner.

Of course, the locus of change in couple treatment represents a complex and interesting question, because it remains so difficult for the observer to pinpoint the origin of any alteration in an interactive system. Systemic therapists have constructed their treatment models based on the core assumption that we cannot conceive of, or promote, couple or family change in any linear fashion. We can intervene in the system, but we can never prove where the conflict or its resolution started. Shifts in the system remain circular in movement and explication.

Even if we carefully examine bilateral change in couples, as we have so far in this chapter, can we really assert that the partners have chosen to change together? Or does the "togetherness" represent two separate individuals deciding to cooperate at approximately the same time? Here we come face-to-face with an important epistemological debate, and as our solution-focused and systemic colleagues have convincingly argued, a debate that carries considerable influence over how we conceptualize and conduct our therapy. William perhaps couldn't alter his stance if Barbara did not first voice her complaints and then positively reinforce his behavioral shift. Change has obviously occurred, but who can say who initiated the transformation? Can the therapist helpfully intervene at the individual level, then, or should he or she only interpret systemically? The debate carries on and on.

Nevertheless, my observations of couple change lead me to the provisional conclusion that although pairs shift their behavior for many reasons and within many different patterns; in some cases, at least, we can identify where the process begins. Most positive shifts do appear interactional and systemic. Tom and Nancy agreed to meet at a particular time and place to work on their legal crisis; both participated cooperatively in that meeting, and they moved closer together. I, however, feel struck by the crucial role sometimes played by a unilateral shift in other couples, when one individual assumes the bulk of the responsibility. I'll offer two examples.

Joe and Mary: The Gift

Joe and Mary, ages 44 and 38, an accountant and a business school teacher, respectively, presented physical and psychological contrasts to each other: Joe was tall, bony, intense, and assertive; Mary was short, round, self-effacing, and apparently dependent. The couple had a boy and a girl, ages 6 and 8. Their fight began when Joe became critical of Mary's unstructured mothering and housekeeping style. He frequently demanded more of her and of his children, with whom he often became exasperated and whom he considered spoiled and poorly organized. Mary experienced great difficulty defending herself from Joe's charges. Sometimes she snapped back at him. Usually, she lapsed into self-criticism and depression, which led her to keep a frustrated distance from Joe much of the time.

Joe and Mary had lived very different early lives. Mary's nuclear family remained intact and relatively functional, although Mary's mother damaged her by often comparing Mary unfavorably to her gifted older sister. But Joe began his life in poverty and tragically lost his mother to a heart attack at age 7. Joe's father could not care for the children and institutionalized Joe and his sisters at an orphanage. Joe did not experience this arrangement as traumatizing and did closely bond with his sisters there, but he never enjoyed any family life after the second grade. Understandably, Joe grew up a competent, serious, laconic, strongly counterdependent man with few close relationships.

Mary had repressed the significance of the vastly different object relations history between her and her husband, but just before the 11th session of our couple group, she made a startling internal discovery. Her defenses lifted, and, as she now tells us, she used her new insight about Joe's childhood to move unilaterally toward him with great warmth.

(Group Session 11)

Mary: I've got some positive things to talk about. I was just thinking, trying to bring it all back. It was on the ride home last week. It was almost like a revelation sort of thing. I came to the conclusion that I'm a *gift* to Joe and his life. It kind of just hit me.

JMD: That's absolutely true.

Mary: My family wasn't perfect, by any means, but we had no crises. We weren't torn apart by tragic things. There were three kids, and my father came home every night. It was a very regular sort of family in that way. I'm giving that to Joe now, a very regular sort of family. It hit me on the way home. It was like "Whoa!" Joe has a cousin who's a nun. When we were getting married, she said to me, she said I was like a gift. I thought that was a nice comment, but I didn't really know what she meant.

JMD: That's what she meant.

Mary: And so that kind of *opened me* up, because I can be very closed. [Repression lifts.] We can get in a mood, both of us, sometimes, where we're both kind of closed off from each other. It happened last night, because the two of us were tired. We were trying to pay bills, and we were both . . .

Tom (group member): Fun!

Mary: Yeah. You could have just put a match in there, and it would have gone whoosh. (pause) But when we were going home, it just occurred to me for the first time, about being a gift. We kind of lived on that for a few days. I mean, I was trying to talk to Joe, basically, "What do you need from me? What else do you need from me? I will give it to you. You just have to ask, and I'm going to give it to you." I felt that way. It was like, "Wow, *it's there.*" 'Cause I was just thinking of him as that poor little kid without a mother, and *you can have it.* It's as easy as that. [Here Mary initiates an action and uses the change processes of self-reevaluation and self-liberation. She changes her view of herself and commits to a different behavior.]

Joe: It was a nice week.

Mary: But there was a point where I got kind of aggravated. Joe was being critical about something. But something just clicked in my head and I thought, "Oh, he's just nervous." [Here Mary grasps Joe's triangle of conflict. He gets anxious (A) and becomes critical (D).]

JMD: Were you aware of that, Joe?

Joe: Was I?

Mary: Critical and nervous.

Joe: If I open my eyes, I am. [Momentarily suspending triangle of conflict.] In the past I really wasn't. It would turn into an argument where we would drag back all the old dirt.

JMD: I think you become critical when you're anxious. [Interpretation of triangle of conflict.]

Joe: That could be true. Like, if we have a dinner party at home, something like that, I'll get critical. I'll take over in the kitchen. [Partial insight into triangle of conflict.]

Mary: Yeah.

Joe: And Mary feels left out.

Mary: He gets critical, but he's in control. I was amazed. Here is this guy organizing this and doing that, and I was . . .

JMD: But these things come from somewhere. I think that when you're having a dinner party, everyone's nervous, worried if it will work out. So a person feels nervous, then they feel critical, then they feel if only I were totally in charge. [Therapist makes empathic relationship offer to Joe.]

Mary: People deal with it in different ways. I deal with it by going numb and not being able to do anything. Joe deals with it by being authoritative and being in control. [Mary's remarkable summary of both their triangles of conflict.]

Co-therapist: (to Joe) What if you tried to slow down and figure out how you feel? It's likely to be more helpful if you tell your wife, "Honey, I'm nervous. What if the fondue turns solid?" Share your feelings with her and allow the two of you to become a team. [Suggesting an action, a tool.]

Mary: It's almost like you can't admit that, because you'd lose control.

Co-therapist: People in your family didn't say, "I'm anxious." As little kids, you never learned to talk about feelings. Even when your mother died, no one talked about how sad or scared they felt. There was only a "This is what we got to do to survive" attitude. You didn't talk about how you felt. [Coaching Joe toward self-reevaluation.]

Joe: Which would have been nice. We never talked about it.

Mary: Joe's sister is really the only one who gathered all the pictures that she could from aunts and cousins and tried to piece the history together.

JMD: What did your Mom look like, Joe? [Therapist guesses that Mary represents a replacement for Joe's lost object and that more insight about this connection will increase his openness to Mary and to himself.]

Joe: Short. It's hard to remember. She was so young at the time.

JMD: Short and rounded?

Joe: She came from a family of 12.

JMD: Did she look anything like Mary? Same build?

Joe: Dark hair.

Mary: I recently saw a picture of Joe's father and mother, and he was up here, and his mother was down there. I was very surprised by that.

Co-therapist: Just like you and Joe.

Joe: Yeah. [Defense may be lifting?]

Mary: I was surprised by that. I guess the struggle is in keeping that momentum going. [Maintenance] I knew I had to go away a little bit. I was just exhausted, and I knew that anything we said was just going to start a fight over nothing. It was like a broken connection. So then we have to reconnect somehow.

JMD: And you let it go. [An action can take the form of not implementing a behavior.]

Joe: Yeah, we just let it go. (long pause)

Mary: The other thing that I noticed was my feeling of independence. I try to be dependent on Joe when we're not connected. I try to make a connection; the connection is dependence. If there's a connection already, then I can be my own person. I can be decisive [an action], not relying on him to push me along. Or not let his criticism bother me as much [withstand his projective identification]. I guess it's basically feeling good about myself. [Mary suspends her triangle of conflict; her hidden feelings of self-esteem and self-confidence emerge, which, in turn, support her to avoid, further still, the projective identification trap. She begins a new interpersonal transaction with Joe. She starts to individuate.]

Co-therapist: Sounds remarkably different from some of the things you were saying a few weeks ago. [Change has taken place.]

Mary: In what way?

Co-therapist   Well, it seems to me you were just talking about getting needs met.

Mary: Yeah.

Joe: That's very important to me. The independence and the combination of independence and connection, a strong sense of self and a strong sense of connection go together. They're inseparable.

Barbara (group member): You two had a good weekend.

Mary has suspended her triangle of conflict in one important sector. Her hidden feelings of altruism, generosity, and self-esteem, closed off when she feels numb, have now blossomed. This important development did not take place until after the 10th group session and it occurred driving home from group, so we must provisionally conclude that the analysis of her defenses of retreat and low self-confidence, which preceded her insightful breakthrough, played an important role in this pivotal event. Mary used her new insight to alter her behavior toward Joe and to shift, dramatically, her own participation in the fight. Mary has discovered a tool to promote intimacy on her own. She can move lovingly toward Joe without her customary reticence and anxiety. Once Mary grabs the initiative, Joe apparently can respond cooperatively.

Mary has also learned to recognize the fight about to arrive, "Just throw a match in there." She constructively steps backward. Joe, too, grasped that this disconnection made sense. He dropped his familiar role as well. He did not aggressively pursue or criticize his wife. The partners have found a tool to circumvent their fight: judicious withdrawal. They have initiated another definitive action step.

Mary makes a further discovery as well. She realizes that her dependency on Joe, and her submission to his unreasonable dominance, may represent a defensive attempt to preserve a relationship with him. She does not consciously make this second connection, but she probably struck the same bargain to maintain her relationship with her undermining mother. Mary, like many of us, seems drawn to repeat self-defeating relationship patterns. Mary learns that when she curtails her regressive reliance on Joe, she feels more independent but also closer to him. Interrupting her defenses propels her toward more intimacy and toward a more mature level of object relationship to her husband. For Mary, differentiation begins to replace enmeshment, at least for the moment. She has discovered an alternative intimate stance. She doesn't use dependency as the vehicle to maintain connection to Joe (see Mitchell, 1988, p. 162).

From session 11 through session 15 of the group, Joe and Mary's relationship continued in its closeness, and they both participated in encouraging other couples in the group to begin interacting with more openness. In the next to the last session, Mary brought a poem about love to the group that reflected some of what she had learned and read it aloud to a warm response.

Joe's role in this couple's change remains indistinct for me. He somewhat passively accepted and reacted to Mary's powerful moves toward him, but, after the group ended, we could only guess to what extent he could maintain his character shift away from destructive criticism. The story of this couple's growth remains with me as a powerful example of a major interactional shift initiated mostly by only one member of the pair. Given its unilateral structure, I had doubts about the permanence of the change that Joe and Mary had started. Did Joe realize the implications of Mary's remarkable insight, and could he make a corresponding alteration in his defensive style? Could he suspend his criticism consistently enough to enjoy and return the gift?

Eight years after the termination of the group, this couple returned to me for help with their daughter's school difficulty. This child apparently suffered from ADHD and needed structural monitoring at home, a commitment the couple had just begun to make. Mary spontaneously recalled her "gift" speech and reported that this attitude had sustained the two of them fairly well over the intervening years, although, under pressure, Joe still became snappish and demanding. She also mentioned that she continued to struggle with depression as she had at the time of the group. She had started antidepressants. All in all, however, Mary felt the marriage more satisfying and closer than when they had originally come to the clinic. Unilateral change like Mary's can, then, lead to long-term constructive outcome. I must admit somewhat to my surprise. I do not know of maintenance measures that Joe and Mary may have developed to solidify their behavior changes.

Dick and Peggy: Saying Yes

With Dick and Peggy, we again observe a unilateral insight leading to a one-sided action, in this case on Dick's part, although Peggy seemed more able to reciprocate than did distant Joe. Fortuitously, I also have follow-up data about this case.

Dick, age 48, an energetic, loquacious, but disorganized man, whose school performance implied an ADHD diagnosis, grew up in a highly disturbed family. His parents divorced early, and his father abandoned the children, leaving his mother alone to raise Dick and his brother and sister. Dick's mother remarried a man who could provide materially, but whom she apparently did not love, and who seemed indifferent to his stepchildren. Dick's sister, like his mother, suffered from severe, lifelong depression and chronic medical problems. As a teenager and an adult, she made suicide attempts and was hospitalized several times. Dick's brother, possibly borderline psychotic in adolescence, regularly regressed into violent rages and still, as an adult, often becomes furious and wildly disinhibited. He threw computers and furniture out of windows on a number of occasions.

Dick, understandably craving normalcy and order, married steady, well-organized Peggy, age 47, who unfortunately came from a cold, depressed family. For much of her adult life, intropunitive, strong-willed Peggy had dysthymia but characteristically refused antidepressant medication.

Dick fared poorly in school, usually not finishing assignments, but later harnessed his energy to develop a successful sales career. Peggy also worked diligently and capably as a medical technologist. The partners focused their days and nights on their jobs and on their teenage sons. However, they both resented the perceived inattention of the other, and they lived a distant, somewhat spiteful relationship, with little affection and no sexuality. In an individual session with me, Dick confided that he strongly considered leaving Peggy. He often fantasized beginning an affair to enjoy the warmth he so badly needed. They had participated in a previous couple group with me, an intervention that apparently had changed little. When they joined their second group, they both realized that their marriage teetered on the edge of failure. In other words, this couple had contemplated action previously by seeking treatment but then had relapsed back into the precontemplative stage after the partners' first episode of therapy. Trying again in their second group, they reentered the change cycle once more, but, until the moment at which we're about to join them, they seemed stalled again.

On several occasions Dick shared with the group his fear of rejection by Peggy. We tried to relate these apparent snubs to his experience of alienation in his family of origin. He felt his family to be so strange that any outsider, including his wife, would probably find him odd as well. Dick repeated the complaint over and over, that he loved Peggy, but whenever he tried to approach her, she turned a cold shoulder. However, in session 9, he guessed out loud that perhaps he might act tentatively and ambiguously toward his wife, because he anticipated rebuff. Then he bitterly read rejection where Peggy intended none. Dick's pattern illustrates the repetition compulsion in vivo. "I'm sure you'll reject me, but if I make a perfunctory move toward you, I can tell myself I tried and that I'm the injured party. I'll prove my point about your coldness, and I can enjoy righteous indignation in the bargain."

I sensed that Dick might now find himself running out of defensive excuses, and he might be about to enter the preparation stage. I also felt some desperation for this couple because, should this second group fail, their marriage might slip away. I began an enactment between Dick and myself, challenging him to approach Peggy directly and announce his availability. "Stop saying, 'Maybe' to her; start saying, 'Yes, I want you.' Maybe she'll say 'Yes' back. Either she'll respond or she won't. If you say 'Maybe" much longer, you may lose her. Just do it." Dick bristled and said he had tried that. Now he'd become discouraged (relapse out of preparation stage). Why would it turn out any differently this time? Reticent Peggy responded in almost a whisper that she might say "Yes," if he acted more assertively.

Later that week at home, concrete, intense, nonpsychologically minded Dick faced himself and his anger and anxiety and initiated remarkably open action steps toward Peggy.

(Group Session 11)

JMD: So, what are the things that are going on in here?

Dick: I had a feeling of happiness tonight, and it was really unusual to be able to acknowledge that I was happy and know what the feeling was. It really was pretty terrific. I've been using the word *epiphany* a lot lately. Peggy and I had our epiphany several weeks ago, and it's like our whole lives just flipped over.

JMD: What happened?

Dick: It was you, Jim.

JMD: Oh? (Group laughs.)

Peggy: You were there.

Dick: Well, you weren't exactly there, although your advice to just go ahead and take the risk was really all that was necessary. [Therapist pushes client toward action.] Everything else that we've been doing over the years and the weeks that we've been here led up to when you said, "Just do it," and Peggy said, "Well, I say 'Yes.'" I don't know if she said it in those words. [Contemplation and preparation have led to action.]

JMD: She did here.

Dick: But she did say "yes." She said "yes" to a whole bunch of things, and I was thinking tonight, you know, we've been through a whole lot of this stuff that's been under discussion and had all kinds of advice [consciousness-raising change process]. But, suffice it to say that in the last several weeks, we've been real connected and having a good time being with each other. It's been pretty extraordinary, and I'm feeling great.

JMD: That's what it's all about.

Dick: Saying "yes," I guess. I guess that's true. But it's extraordinary; that it's simple, yet so complex. It's sort of too bad that it took all this time to find it, but I don't think it's something to lose.

JMD: Take it where you can get it.

Dick: I'm getting it everywhere.

JMD: Fine.

Dick: Like I've said, it's been extraordinary, and I'm happy about it, and other things seem to be falling into place very well. You know, making decisions about what things to do and things not to do.

Last week our son, Mike, was on vacation and, as is typical for him, he's not reaching out and trying to find things to do [like his father?], and I realized that I was going to be away for a couple of days. I said, "Why don't you come with me, Mike?" [Dick takes action toward other family members as well.] And he did. And we spent a couple of days together. He whined at me about this and that, but we had a real good time. We went to New York State. I don't think he'd ever been in New York before. I had several appointments there, and then the next day we went to Vermont.

I think we drove about 600 miles, which gave him an opportunity to see what my job was really like, and he got to sit in on three or four of the appointments I had, which was also good. What was interesting to me is how astute he is about what's going on, and how he was able to absorb things. It was really fun. We had a really good time.

JMD: So now we know two people who will never forget this trip for the rest of their lives.

Dick: Yup, that's true. But actually I think three people won't forget it, because Peggy was scrambling around, trying to figure out what to do with him while I was gone. So we talked about him going and the shortcomings of his going, 'cause it's a long, tedious drive. I bet Peggy persuaded him that it was a great idea, and it was good for all of us. That's what I mean about making good decisions about things. It wasn't just a decision for me and Mike. [Dick has found a new tool; a family-wide decision-making process works better than unilateral choices.] It was a decision for all four of us, because it was much better for us to be doing that, and for Mike and I to have a wonderful memory [change process of self-liberation, committing to a different behavior]. It's been a good time, and the best part, I think, is that I have every expectation that it will continue and get better. [The action breaks the repetition compulsion. A hopeful expectation replaces a pessimistic one.] That's what coming here was about; that was the intention.

JMD: Well, if you say "yes" . . .

Dick: I don't think I have a problem with that.

Peggy: It's just been great. We've just been doing everything for each other that we want. And he's doing all the things that I want him to do for me, and I've been doing the things he wants me to do for him. It's been easy. It's been nice. It's been great.

JMD: So, that's why the two of you originally got together.

Dick: That was a long time ago, but that's probably true. It probably is true that we got together to be with each other to make a life.

JMD: It's probably true.

Dick: And we're making a life.

Peggy: We have a great life.

Dick: We just have to keep that in mind.

JMD: What enabled you to take the risk? [Daring to take the action step.]

Dick: Acknowledging that that's what I had to do. I just had to do that. I couldn't not do it. [Self-reevaluation] You have to decide what it is that you want, and then you have to decide what you can do, and what you can't do. Then you have to make a decision [self-liberation change process in preparation stage]. And when you have a time limitation, as you do here, you have to compress that thinking. That's what was going on here. We're running out of time. [Short-term treatment focuses the action.]

Peggy was very clear before we started coming to this group that she was tired of going through the process over and over again [stuck in the relapse cycle, return to precontemplation and contemplation stages], which we've done over the years. I mean, we obviously care about our marriage, our relationship, but we never

had made so much effort over the years [no movement into preparation and action stages], and there were times when I really wanted
out, but I didn't want out. I was torn back and forth, and Peggy
was saying, "Hey, this is enough already. We spent the last 22 years
trying to make this work. It's not working. Let's get it right or
forget it." And as the group was getting closer and closer to ending,
something's got to give here, because I know this. It wasn't an ultimatum, but it was like an ultimatum, and I was treating it that way.

JMD: You treated it that way inside yourself. You didn't risk this thing
because your wife was beating on you. You wanted to risk it. [Clari-
fying client's self-liberation, change process of deciding on a new
behavior.]

Dick: Absolutely, this didn't have to do with Peggy. *This had to do with
me.* I mean, I'm certainly happy that Peggy is as happy as she is. I
can't tell you how good it makes me feel when I see Peggy glowing.
But that wasn't what motivated me. It was myself that motivated
me [self-reevaluation]. I'm not one to let this go. I think certainly
the *coaching* I got here helped. 'Cause I always say I'm coachable
or trainable. Someone gives me some directions, says this could
help you. I'll try it. I'll risk the potential failure, but I'll try it. If
someone that I respect says this could work for you, I'll try, and
that's what happened in this case. I was at a point where I needed
to do something. I felt compelled to do something. [Preparation
over; action required.] I was given some direction that seemed like
a valid thing to do, and I tried it. And the thing is that once I tried
it, it was just like it was so easy. It was just so easy.
        Last night we were home. Dave was at a class, and Mike was
off doing whatever he was doing, and I said to Peggy, "How about
going upstairs?" She says, "Well, I have something to do. How
about in a little while?" And the whole thing was natural. There
was no risk. I didn't feel like I was taking a risk. There was no
tension or pressure around it, and we did it. It was great. Peggy
commented last week that we were like newlyweds, and I said,
"Yeah, in some ways we are." Checking all this out, experimenting, having a good time and being real relaxed about everything,
and not just sex, but our whole relationship.

Female group member: I don't understand what risk you took. You took
the risk that you said, "I need you. I want you," and you acted on
it?

Dick: Yeah, I guess, but I think there's a lot more tied up in it than just
that it had to do with being sexually intimate. Because, I mean, we
had a whole history around that issue, but our behavior was filled

with roadblocks. I'd been anxious that I might be rejected, then I was rejected, and then I'd have more anxiety about it, and so it didn't stop just there. It was all throughout our marriage. Around any issue, there was a possibility that it could go off in the wrong direction. I would hesitate and be uncomfortable, even if I knew the right thing to ask. I'd be so distressed about asking that it wouldn't go well.

What has happened over the last several weeks is just the opposite. [Feedback loop reversed.] Everything is easy. We have a discussion about something we don't agree on, and even that's okay. Before if we had a disagreement, it was like a tug of war. [Defense lifted, couple can constructively resolve conflicts.]

[Here we can see one very human reason that couples cycle in and out of contemplation and preparation. A negative projective feedback loop develops. Anticipated rejection by the partner leads to anxiety and resentment. This, in turn, provokes the withdrawal of the other partner, who then actually becomes rejecting and unresponsive. Under these adverse conditions, action feels very difficult for either to initiate. The triangle of conflict dominates both partners individually, and they become excessively defensive, which freezes the system into a repetition compulsion. Creative moves then seem impossible.]

Peggy: See, it really started several weeks ago, when he started paying more attention to me. Not running out of the house. Acting like he really wanted to be with me. And so it just grew. [Dick suspends the defensive pole in his triangle of conflict. He stops his passive-aggressive nonparticipation.]

Suddenly, he was doing things for me. I said before I'd asked him to do the "guy" things around the house. He's been taking care of little things, put a new hose on the dryer, and it works now. I don't have to dry the clothes twice. It's a big thing. . . .

Dick: You know what the shift was? I don't know if it was the entire shift. But what I think the shift was when I understood that Peggy's love for me was unconditional [self-reevaluation]. That doesn't mean she doesn't get mad at me or disagree with me, but her love for me is unconditional, as is mine for her, and all the risk went away. All the tension went away, and all the reasons to hide went away. I'd go out of the house, what Peggy was talking about, my desire to escape in some form or fashion. When the risk goes away, and the tension and the apprehension go away, I stay. [Dick doesn't have to activate his triangle of conflict and regress into defensive withdrawal.]

JMD: Peggy's on your side. She's not your enemy. She's on your side. [Projective identification cycle has broken. Dick stops projecting his hostility onto Peggy, and she stops identifying with it and focusing it back on Dick.]

Dick: Right and I never should, in retrospect, I never should have believed that she was anything but that, but I made it up inside. [Projective identification within triangle of conflict.]

JMD: Yes, you did.

Dick: So what I needed to do is to get over it *inside* and say, well, this isn't how it is. [Note the rearrangement of inner object relationships. Dick realizes he doesn't resent Peggy. He hates the attributes he has projected onto her from inside himself. This represents important individual change in couple therapy.] How it is is that Peggy loves me. [Reevaluation of Peggy; she no longer seems a rejecting libidinal object.] That I love her, and we've been through this whole thing, with its ups and downs, but we're still together, because we want to be together. We add better quality to our lives together for the fact that we trust each other.

        (To JMD) By the way, I admired you quite a bit for being willing to push me like you did, because I was pretty hostile in return. I mean that sincerely. Peggy and I talked about that twice. You did that to me. And I'm not a happy camper when somebody pushes me like that. I respect you a lot for being willing to do that, that was really good. It can make a difference.

How to make sense of Dick's transformative move to action? Dick had a wretched early life. His first father abandoned him, and his second had little interest. His mother, burdened with responsibility and depression, could not begin to mirror his needs. The obvious psychopathology of his siblings left him further shamed and lonely, although he did, and does, feel close to his sister, despite her debilitating medical and psychiatric difficulties. Dick probably also suffers from undiagnosed ADHD and felt like a miserable failure through high school and the beginning of college. He could never finish his work. Given this troubled history, no wonder he would fear rejection from intimates.

Yet from somewhere, he summoned the courage to take a risk and pursue openness with Peggy. He began by unambivalently attending to the household tasks that he knew she wished him to take on but that he previously felt too angry to complete. He then dared to approach her sexually, and she responded. The couple moved into the cooperative, affectionate relationship that both partners longed for but that they both had so stubbornly defended against. (Here we see Dick and Peggy using the change process of reinforcement management, i.e., they reward themselves with satisfying joint activities. They also use the change process of helping relationships. They support each other to express feelings. Prochaska finds these mechanisms typically associated with the post-action stage.)

This treatment took place 5 years ago, but, luckily, I have encountered Peggy several times informally for a few minutes. She suggested that their closeness continues intact, for the most part. I cannot identify what relapse-prevention procedures these partners may have developed to solidify their action steps, though I'm guessing that if we pursued it carefully with them, we could specify some of their maintenance behaviors.

We can illustrate the change in both Dick and Peggy by mapping their triangles of conflict, both now softened.

Dick's Triangle of Conflict   Peggy's Triangle of Conflict

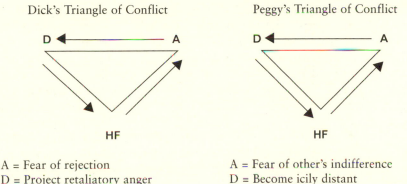

A = Fear of rejection   A = Fear of other's indifference
D = Project retaliatory anger   D = Become icily distant
HF = Need for love and cooperation   HF = Need to give and get affection

FIGURE 6.1

Viewing the triangles side by side, we can grasp, once again, the key role of past object relations and projective identification in the development of marital disharmony. Dick did meet real rejection in his disturbed family. As we listened to his story, it seemed as if he had no parents. Peggy had parents, but they, preoccupied by their own anger and depression, apparently showed her and her brother little warmth. From this blighted background, Peggy learned few skills to use in offering Dick the warmth and affection he craved. To me, Peggy seemed more rigid and constricted than rejecting, but Dick felt pushed away and projected his hostility over this onto Peggy. "She's cold and demanding on purpose." Used to the distance of a bleak home life, Peggy readily identified with Dick's projection and isolated herself still further. Now she did feel irritable and cold. The regressive spiral of their marriage circled downward. But Dick, with his courageous move, suspended his triangle of conflict and reversed the momentum of their destructive interaction, maybe just in time. Peggy responded to Dick, and the couple began a new psychological life. We can see that the function of the action stage for each couple is to break the repetition compulsion and to start a genuine exchange not soured by the negative preconceptions associated with old objects. At this point Dick, at least for a period of several weeks, stopped clinging to the destructive patterns in his family of origin and actively chose an alternative transaction with Peggy (see Mitchell, 1988, p. 162 for further discussion of this core change process).

I experienced Peggy as a competent, counterdependent, insular, insecure person with few, if any close friends—no surprise, given her frigid background. If Dick had not grasped individual responsibility and leaped forward, I doubt that Peggy could have, and the marriage might have dissolved.

Did Dick leap forward on his own or in response to external intervention? We can make a case for both scenarios. The group and the therapists engaged in much preparatory work with both Dick and Peggy, exploring the ravages of their disturbed families. In addition, the group cohesiveness encouraged experiments with change. Finally, in the group, I forcefully pushed Dick toward action. I said, "Say yes," meaning go ahead and dare to approach her. Despite the damage done by his earlier objects, Dick retained a capacity to use genuinely helpful present objects, possibly the warm relationship with his sister figures, in here. He could accept my good-hearted but firm challenge to change his approach to Peggy. I think Dick experienced my affection and respect for him, which he returned to me. Perhaps he used a partial identification with me, among other resources, to support himself in attempting his difficult initiatives. But at home alone with Peggy, Dick ultimately chose, on his own, to take action. I'll pursue the object relations underpinnings of changes like this one more in the next chapter.

THE STAGES OF CHANGE: IMPLICATIONS FOR THE FIVE-STEP MODEL

Let's try to clarify some of the lessons we've gained from these case reports. Perhaps the most important of these is that clients seem to follow a general path toward change that conforms to its own rules and to its own timetable, largely independent of the therapist's theoretical persuasion or technical input. Evidently, the treatment will not move any faster than the stages of change unfold for any given couple. Indeed, some of the vignettes we've studied here in chapters 5 and 6 reveal clients decisively moving toward changes that, somewhat embarrassingly, appear to proceed without direct crucial input by the therapist. Mary's gift to Joe and William's insight into his identification with his father serve as two examples.

In the next few pages I'll develop two themes that become intertwined. In the first, I'll enlarge on the idea that the five-step model—serendipitously, I admit—conforms to the principles Prochaska has outlined. This circumstance, in turn, explicates much of the change that we've observed in our case reports. I think that other successful approaches to brief couple treatment also coordinate with Prochaska's ideas, a topic I'll return to in chapter 7. Second, however unilateral it may sometimes appear, that change often occurs through the interaction of the client's natural momentum, described so well by Prochaska, with moves by the therapists. The latter appropriately react to and shape the stage of change stance of the clients. The analysis of this reciprocal exchange between client and therapist can afford us a deeper understanding of what really transpires in brief couple therapy. As we continue the discussion, it will point us toward a better grasp of the many dimensions of the therapist's optimal role in couple therapy.

Let's reexamine either a solo or a group therapy report to see how that treatment follows Prochaska's generic stages of change, and whether it also depends upon a series of interventions that the therapist coordinates with those phases. We'll take Dick's treatment as an example. In the early meetings of his group, we pursued triangle of focus and triangle of conflict work with him, exploring his trauma with his family of origin and linking that with his present-day expectation of rejection. Here we introduced the phase-specific change processes of (1) consciousness raising, that is, learning more about the problem; (2) dramatic relief, experiencing feelings about his marital conflict; and (3) environmental reevaluation, that is, studying how his issue affected important others, particularly his wife, Peggy.

Until session 9, we did not confront Dick to consider any major behavioral shift. By introducing suitable change processes in the appropriate sequence, we fortunately followed Prochaska's advice to "do the right things (processes) at the right time (stages)" (Prochaska, Norcross, & DiClemente, 1992, p. 1110). But in session 9, when the group members had recommitted to treatment, we preconsciously sensed that Dick was ready for serious preparation, and we challenged him to undertake self-reevaluation. Would he accept the distance in his marriage or would he take the risk to say "yes" to Peggy? Dick pondered his decision for a week or more but then engaged in self-liberation and committed to an act. The therapists, using reinforcement management, praised his resolve and his successful efforts toward change.

A number of tentative but important conclusions emerge from this reading of the data. First, Prochaska appears correct. Change apparently does not occur based on insight or action but on insight followed by action. Second, neither clients nor therapists produce change; rather, their roles usually, though not always, interact to support shifts in behavior. We pushed Dick to act, and he constructively responded. Third, couple therapy, and maybe all psychotherapy, needs to include a challenge toward action, either introduced by the therapist, self-imposed by the client, or the product of an interchange between the two. Recall my anonymous alcoholic patient who instructed me to tell him to stop drinking. I did, and he stopped. I challenged him, but he coached me how to do so. At the appropriate time, each member of the couple must use self-liberation to commit to new behaviors, but therapists can't let treatments drift, lacking some kind of confrontation toward action.

Fourth, an intervention like short-term couple group, which admits mostly contemplators and then propels them hard through that stage into preparation within the first few weeks of therapy, has great potential to produce constructive change. As Prochaska and colleagues have discovered, in those instances where clients move forward one motivational stage within the first month of treatment, the likelihood of successful outcome 6 months in the future becomes greatly enhanced (Prochaska & Norcross, 2001). However, fifth, the couple group, or some similar arrangement, does not represent an ideal treatment for any pair. Its success probably derives from the fact that the demanding pregroup evaluation assures us that most of the couples entering the group reside in contemplation. The pregroup workshop winnows out precontemplators. The more advanced the motivational stage of the clients, the greater the likely efficacy of the intervention. Probably only a minority of couples satisfies the rigorous entrance requirements for the group.

SHIFTS IN THE THERAPIST–CLIENT OBJECT RELATIONSHIP THROUGH THE STAGES OF CHANGE

We've wound through a complex discussion of applying Prochaska's stage of change findings to the therapeutic action within the five-step model, and presumably within other similar systems, but a piece seems missing from the debate. The reader may have started to speculate, as I have, that perhaps the momentum in the change spiral becomes highly influenced by shifts in the object relationship developing between clients and therapists. We observe that clients relate differently from one stage to the next. Dick, for example, seems far more open to the therapist just before his action move following session 10, than at any previous time in the treatment. Possibly the therapist, and not just the client, also makes different object relations offers as the treatment passes from one motivational stage to the next and as different change processes come into play. Prochaska and colleagues have grasped this point, too, and it's a key one.

The therapist's stance at different stages can be characterized as follows. With patients in precontemplation, often the role is like that of a *nurturing parent* joining with a resistant and defensive youngster who is both drawn to and repelled by the prospects of becoming more independent. With clients in contemplation, the role is akin to a *Socratic* teacher who encourages clients to achieve their own insights into their condition. With clients who are in the preparation stage, the stance is more like that of an *experienced coach* who has been through many crucial matches and can provide a fine game plan or can review the participant's own plan. With clients who are progressing into action and maintenance the psychotherapist becomes more of a *consultant* who is available to provide expert advice and support when action is not progressing as smoothly as expected. (Prochaska & Norcross, 2001, pp. 444–445)

Richard Fitzpatrick, PhD (personal communication), has designed a sophisticated "meta-model" of brief therapy, partially based on Prochaska's work. It's equally applicable to individual or couple therapy. For those in precontemplation, Fitzpatrick increases the client's perception of the risks and drawbacks associated with his or her current behavior. In contemplation, he tries to evoke positive reasons for change. (McCullough's short-term dynamic therapy [1994] follows this same initial step.) Fitzpatrick uses Weiss's control mastery theory (1993) to guide him in strengthening the client's sense of self-efficacy, by analyzing separation or survivor guilt that blocks the client's moves toward constructive shifts in behavior. For those in preparation, he helps to determine the best course of action. He then guides them in devising thought experiments through which they can rehearse attempts at change. Fitzpatrick next coaches clients through the action phase and helps them to develop relapse-prevention strategies. Fitzpatrick is a psychodynamic therapist, so he attends to unconscious guilt, transference, and defensive maneuvers in his complex model.

So both Prochaska and Fitzpatrick have offered us carefully crafted principles to steer the therapists as they gradually alter their stance to clients through each sequence of the stages-of-change model. The therapist evolves into a different object, according to the shifting needs of the clients. However, clients can feel their conditions of security violated at any point in a therapy. Our orientation to the client does need to shift with the introduction of each new stage of change, but it also needs to stay the same. Simultaneously, or sequentially, we need to hold the pair *and* to challenge them. I think this is a substantial charge that represents perhaps the most testing demand on the brief couple therapist.

CONCLUSION: THE NECESSARY AND SUFFICIENT ELEMENTS OF THERAPIST PARTICIPATION

To return to the questions with which we began this chapter, What is our ultimate goal in brief object relations couple therapy? What circumstances must we arrange from the start of the treatment to maximize our chances of attaining that goal? When a couple terminates, we hope that the partners will have undertaken the independent actions required to suspend defenses, which, in turn, will allow them to devise tools to negotiate, rather than to battle through, their fight.

This represents our desired outcome. But to reach it, it now appears that therapists will need to keep effectively switching between three tracks of thinking, relating, and intervening. On the first, and most self-evident, of these planes, we'll investigate, with the couple, the family-of-origin issues and the attendant character problems, the triangles of conflict and of focus, that underlie the fight. On the second track, we'll have to plan, in advance, to monitor the couple's evolving motivational stage and to introduce the change processes appropriate at each phase of the sequence. In particular, we must stand prepared to challenge, at the right time, an individual or a pair toward significant action. On a third dimension, we'll need to devise those relationship offerings that will increase a particular client's or a couple's sense of security and so maximize their chances of daring to lift a primary defense within the triangle of conflict.

Norcross (2001) seems to paint a similar picture of the therapist's required role, marshalling solid empirical support for his position. He points out that technical variation (my Number 1, in figure 6.2) accounts for perhaps only 15% of psychotherapy outcome variance. Norcross (2001) and Strupp (1981) argue that relationship variables (Numbers 2 and 3, in figure 6.2, particularly Number 3) appear to account for much of the remaining 85%. Norcross succinctly paraphrases the Clinton campaign by explaining positive change in psychotherapy with "It's the relationship, stupid" (Norcross, 2001, p. 347). I agree.

If we can integrate this coordinated therapist activity with the tempo of the clients' naturally occurring motivational development within the treatment, it looks as if we'll come as close as possible to satisfying the necessary and sufficient elements of therapist activity within the five-step model or within any other similar system. If we neglect regular attention to any of these three dimensions, we risk undermining our method. We also cannot forget that much of the outcome variance rests with the client. Real life presents the therapist with far more precontemplators than contemplators, and relapse, followed by renewed efforts toward change, remains a more common result of any episode of treatment than does dramatic breakthrough, solidified by maximally effective maintenance.

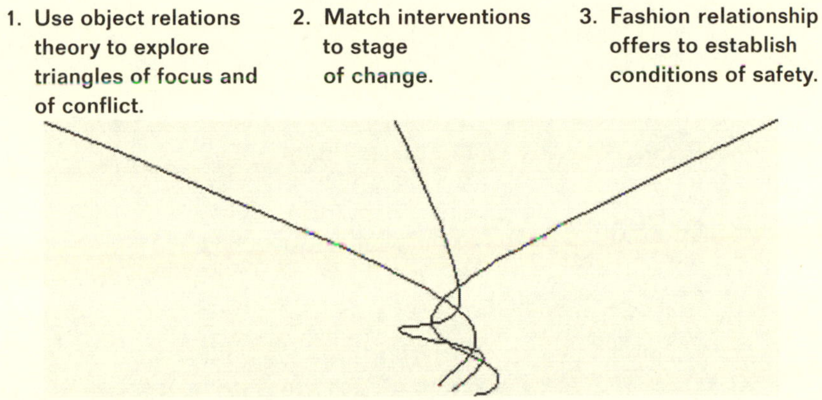

1. Use object relations theory to explore triangles of focus and of conflict.

2. Match interventions to stage of change.

3. Fashion relationship offers to establish conditions of safety.

FIGURE 6.2. Therapist Activity

Prochaska's findings point to a transtechnical and transtheoretical picture of therapy, which then suggests the possibility that perhaps a generic model of change underlies all effective couple treatment and that the five-step approach, for instance, represents just one example of that basic model. At the start of chapter 7, I'll consider whether such a generic couple treatment model exists, and if it does, what significance that holds for us as therapists. I'm attempting to develop as complete a picture as possible of the workings of couple treatment. One or two issues require more pursuit, so I'll close with some final thoughts about how object relations theory can direct us more surely toward the core of the change process in couple treatment.

CHAPTER 7

Completing the Couple Therapy Puzzle

A Hybrid Approach, a Generic Model, and Closing Thoughts on the Mechanisms of Change

I designed this book in an attempt to study couple therapy as it actually occurs in the session-to-session life of the clients and of the clinician, close to the ground and close to the office. For this reason I've quoted verbatim excerpts from solo and group sessions and summarized a number of additional cases, so that no shortage of primary data would hamper our ability to plumb the action of couple therapy. I've also outlined my object relations approach and tried to show why I think that orientation faithfully explains the conscious and preconscious information that flows toward us, as we sit with a troubled couple. Sometimes the couple or the individual moves appear dramatic, sometimes more subtle, but our case reports suggest that constructive actions, by the clients, appear preceded by the object relations investigation and by offers on the part of the therapist to counteract the influence of those original relationships. We've observed that this general approach to couple treatment displays considerable conceptual and technical strength but also has limitations. I'll examine some of the latter now.

A HYBRID MODEL

In fact, my session-to-session behavior often borrows from influential colleagues who do not share the object relations persuasion. As the Scharffs and Dicks have emphasized, it takes time for clients to discover and communicate many of their important feelings and experiences about their inner objects. William, the attorney, realized his problematic identification with his father well into the couple group and publicly acknowledged it only in the very last session. But what should the therapist do to respond to the time pressure? I do not think we must rush importunately forward with our object relations model or demand from our clients, and from ourselves, unrealistic early insights. I have found, though, that we can make appropriate use of additional short-term treatment strategies when they constructively support our work. Put otherwise, although our *theoretical understanding* of cases comes directly from the object relations viewpoint, this does not require that all our *interventions* must proceed exclusively from the same conceptual context.

Borrowing From Wile's Collaborative Tact

When the couple presents as inhibited or tongue-tied, or in silent lockjawed rage, then I usually find the introduction of Dan Wile's (1999) script writing approach helpful, sometimes a godsend. At these times, we can prime the pump of the therapy process by attempting to speak out the partners' basic affects and conflicts for them. First, we need to gather some ideas about the dimensions of the fight, of course, but most couples can readily provide those. Then, like Joan and Brad, they sometimes stop bewildered.

Joan and Brad

> *Joan, a 32-year-old nurse and the mother of daughters aged 4 and 2, complained that she and her husband, 38-year-old Brad, fought when he criticized her failure to perform household and child-rearing tasks to his standard. In our first meeting she then could add little more verbally to her story, but she began to cry. Brad, a computer engineer at a large firm, countered that he thought his requests reasonable and his wife immature. Neither volunteered additional feelings or perspectives. Silently, both looked directly at me. I felt nominated as the referee but also as the mentor for this frustrated and genuinely lost couple. What is your next intervention, therapist?*
>
> *As a first guideline, I try to resist the pressure to speak immediately. I let the clients' affects register on me for a few moments. I attempted to absorb the meaning of Joan's tears and to validate my observations with her. "I think, Joan, that you're crying out of frustration. You're a nurse. Your job teaches you what's clean, and what's*

not. From a professional standpoint, your husband knows much less about these matters than you do. You must feel so accused, and that it's so unfair for him to criticize you in this way. Perhaps you have a memory of a parent yelling at you and not feeling able to fight back?" (In my countertransference, I didn't sense rage or guilt coming from Joan but rather the helplessness of a blamed child.)

This tentative scripting broke the ice. Joan began to talk about her exacting accountant father and his condescending attitude toward her mother's free-form housekeeping. When the last child went to college, her father packed his possessions, left the home, filed for divorce, and soon remarried. (Perhaps Joan has identified with her mother's story and assumes she must toe the line or face abandonment and replacement if she stands up to Brad.)

At this point Brad had barely participated, and his square-jawed, military profile wasn't showing much emotion. I offered, "The situation must seem unfair to you, too, Brad, because you try hard to do things properly, and your wife doesn't seem to appreciate it and even seems to undermine you. Perhaps that reminds you of some situation in your childhood as well?" Brad responded, "Well, my father's a business executive and does boss my mother around quite a bit. My brothers and I consider her scatterbrained and a little irresponsible."

So the inner persons, each of the couple's parents, quickly make their appearance in the treatment, ushered into the office by script writing with an object relations twist. We haven't forsaken the object relations metapsychology, but we have added a general technique, pioneered by Dan Wile, to put motion into the treatment. (The reader can promptly sense the dilemma in formulating the next step of the treatment plan. I didn't know if I needed to explore the influence of repressed objects in more depth. Or if I could acknowledge these presences and coach around them, to help the partners with their day-to-day conflicts, in an attempt at a much less time-intensive therapy. We'll rejoin Joan and Brad later in the chapter to find out the eventual direction of their treatment.)

Adapting From Eron and Lund

When one or both members of the couple suffer from severe personality disorder and the often accompanying trauma history, we can borrow from the narrative solutions method taught by Thomas Eron and Joseph Lund (1998, 1999).

Jeannine and Audrey

Jeannine, age 56, and Audrey, 42, a lesbian couple, sought treatment to calm their dangerous recurrent fight. Both grew up terrorized by violent alcoholic fathers, and Audrey's sister beat her as well. The mothers of both appeared detached from the boiling conflict in their families and apparently rarely made motions to protect their daughters. Jeannine had served in the Gulf War in a technical unit. Not only did she witness daily death and injury, but she was also raped by a commanding officer. Both Jeannine and Audrey experienced humiliating rejection by their families over their homosexuality, and each endured life-threatening chronic illnesses, epilepsy and MS (Muliple Sclerosis), respectively. They both lived on disability income in the house owned by Jeannine.

In their fight, Jeannine became enraged when she perceived any lack of commitment or interest in Audrey's response to her. For example, if she felt that Audrey was not monitoring her own illnesses, which would mean a possible hospitalization and separation, she exploded at her partner. She quickly threatened to eject Audrey and her pets from the home. Audrey, once again with no safe haven, immediately regressed into suicidality and contacted her individual therapist or sometimes rushed to an emergency room. When her anger subsided somewhat, Jeannine sometimes began to feel suicidal as well, and she called her individual therapist. Predictably, the major medical problems of each flared up during the fight. Both women had histories of alcoholism and prescription medication abuse. Because they each had large doses of medical and psychotropic pills on hand and because each had histories of prior suicide attempts, it seemed like a lethal household indeed.

Any couple therapist, no matter how experienced, would draw a deep breath and wonder where to start with two women reporting so many past traumas and present stresses. What intervention holds any possible hope of success? If I fail to cement an alliance, will one of my clients ultimately die? When the initial clinical picture contains great hurt, danger, and abandonment, the risk arises that therapists will allow themselves to become inundated, consciously and unconsciously, with the client's discouragement. When I feel pulled in this downward course, I begin to look for genuine positives in the couple situation, as we'll see in a moment.

With this challenging pair, I decided that I'd start by making ready use of the triangle of focus, a productive strategy with nearly any couple. Everyone has a fight, a family of origin, and problematic character features, the three poles of the triangle of focus. However, the triangle of conflict work in these cases of major personality disorder represents a challenge usually too complicated for any short-term therapy. Both Jeannine and Audrey felt, probably correctly, that their lives had been on the line as children, and Jeannine, a combat veteran, had the additional terrifying memories of death all around her in wartime.

The anxiety pole, for each, introduced so much intensity into their intrapersonal and relationship dynamics that they both seemed forced toward automatic, extreme defenses: to masochistically give in to the other, to sadistically threaten the other, or to regress into suicidal despair. Antidepressant medications kept these dangerous maneuvers under control for both, but only tentative control. The rigid defenses appeared attempts to protect these ladies from overwhelming primary anxiety but also to bring to life an early fantasy. "At last, I'll be protected and cared for, the way I always needed." This represents an understandable wish under the circumstances of their lives, but the rage that exploded when both became disappointed in that longing threatened to destroy their relationship and them, on a weekly basis.

I grasped in the first session that the triangle of conflict for both Audrey and Jeanine contained too much hurt, too much fear, and too much desperation for me to enter it productively for either participant. I think Marsha Linehan (1993) came to a similar conclusion when she devised the DBT (Dialectic Behavior Therapy) approach. Her method teaches her clients to tolerate their feelings of rage and self-hate and to cope with these within the limits of reality, but DBT pointedly does not push the client to relive or to unravel the origin of those affects, with any deep triangle of conflict work.

Instead of pursuing the triangle of conflict, I used the concept of the preferred view of self to position myself to help this couple. (The fact that I quickly liked and respected these two courageous women made this stance easier to assume.) First, I congratulated each on her tenacity and empathized with the disappointments and injuries each had endured. I then speculated that both of them must possess a number of skills and strengths that had carried them through their many perils. Neither had given up on herself or on the other. I encouraged Jeannine and Audrey to view themselves as survivors, bloodied but unbowed. Each then expressed the glimmerings of preferred views of self. No, neither had given up, they agreed. Yes, each of them did demonstrate much personal strength to endure this much trauma and this much illness.

When the partners now start to refight their bitter battle over dependence—who should take care of whom at any given moment?—I remind them of their positive characteristics and their commitment to fairness and growth. I encourage them to bring these values into play. I tell them directly that I think they can find their way out of the conflict of that particular day,

no matter how overwhelming it seems at the time. They have both conquered destructive childhoods and personal addictions, and now both cope
with frightening chronic disease. I suggest to them that when they feel about
to enter the fight, probably one or both senses abandonment approaching,
and they're trying to ward that off by rejecting the partner prophylacti-
cally. I instruct them to attempt to share their feelings of fear and frustration and not to immediately blame the partner, who, after all, has treated
them much better than their previous primary objects.

So far, these ladies seem to enjoy improvement in their relationship
and continue to offer each other realistically limited, but still genuine,
nurturance and support. After 13 meetings spaced intermittently over 16
months, Audrey told me, "We get along much better now. We've never had
a model of how to interact before."

An object relations analysis of their triangles of conflict remains an
important guide to understanding this couple's interaction. In particular,
when Jeannine feels Audrey moving away even slightly, she strikes out at
her with withering criticism, which provokes an angry skirmish and often
an upsurge in the physical symptoms of both partners. I call immediate
attention to the causative patterns in this interaction. Following Eron and
Lund, I ask Jeannine to consider the effects of her behavior and to decide if
she wants to choose this outcome, a standoff in which both feel angry,
guilty, frightened, and medically ill. But I have not as yet challenged her to
begin working through her shattering separation anxiety and her automatic
need to defend against that panic. If I do so in the future, I will start in a
most tentative fashion and back away if Jeannine begins to feel overwhelmed.

As I struggle with this case, I do not forsake object relations theory,
but I borrow a constructive maneuver from my colleagues Eron and Lund:
focus on the preferred view of self. I do this because I think the central
technique suggested by the object relations approach, that is, exploring the
influence of early repressed presences, too destabilizing for this fragile pair.

The direction I've taken with this couple presupposes that, eventually,
the partners will introject the therapist's benign attitude toward them, build
it into their relationship, start to forgive the self and the other, and some-
time terminate. This may prove a parlous hope, however, because the capacity for both ladies to maintain a positive identification seems seriously
blocked by early internalizations of punitive objects. Moreover, their lives
will probably remain punctuated by medical crises; both suffer severe chronic
illness. If they can never reach termination, I'll keep meeting with them, off
and on. With clients such as these, therapists can become anxious that an
end will never arrive and that they'll have to adopt the pair indefinitely. If
we can accept that we're attempting to teach the couple a little more independence in each session and that some of these lessons actually seem

efficacious, then the open-ended format need not feel so frightening for any of the participants.

This treatment plan represents the analogue of Gustafson's (1995) long, intermittent, individual treatments with characterologically vulnerable clients. As Gustafson sometimes does, I've purposefully spaced the sessions far apart with this couple, to control the intimacy of the interplay between the three of us. Object relations theory tells us what has gone missing with Jeannine and Audrey. They lack giving objects in their central egos to support them through emotional upheaval. The therapist has to assume that role for a time, maybe for an extended time. Clearly, we need to vary our methods and our responses according to the capacities and disabilities of our clients. It's much easier to change the therapist and the format of the therapy than to assume naively that the clients will suddenly begin to display strengths that they've never previously possessed.

Learning From Philip Guerin

If I sense a case stuck, I often turn to Philip Guerin (Guerin, Fay, Fogarty, & Kautto, 1999) for help. Remember from chapter 1 that Guerin has taught us that when any couple—a marital pair, a father-son, and so on—fall into an impasse, they frequently try to involve a third party in the struggle in an abortive attempt to resolve the conflict. Like the tar baby, that third person becomes mired in the interchange and then starts to play a hidden, pivotal role. What began as a troubled dyad transforms into a sticky triangle.

For Guerin, these enmeshed triangles always involve a third person. For example, please recall a case of Guerin's cited in chapter 1. An otherwise psychologically healthy young man succumbs to panic attacks at the time of his engagement to an appropriate young woman. Guerin discovers that his identified patient has a major relationship conflict. Although he's strongly drawn to his attractive fiancée, the young man feels paralyzed by guilt over the prospect of marrying and thus deserting his lonely mother. Guerin confronts the triangle and invites the mother into the treatment with the son to work on their separation—a classical Bowenian move.

I find that it often helps to think of the Guerin triangle more broadly, as a model that might include *third factors*, as well as *third persons*. For example, let's rejoin Paul and Maria, again from chapter 1, the 40-year-old academics who fought almost nonstop and never could gain stability in their relationship. Each additional life challenge for Maria—a new condo, infertility, or a job change—brought more blow-ups with Paul and more recriminating threats of divorce hurled toward him. After solo couple treatment, short-term couple group treatment, and individual treatment for Maria with an experienced woman therapist, all to small avail, I concluded this to be a stuck case.

I realized that another husband, another profession, or another child would not console Maria. Despite her liveliness and frequent good humor, underneath she suffered a despair that she could never grasp lasting satisfaction from any important part of her life. The fights took the form of her blaming Paul for this chronic lack. If only he were more flexible, more understanding, the next job would work, and so forth. In fact, ever-conscientious Paul turned his schedule topsy-turvy to cushion Maria from daily pressures, a strategy that predictably rarely sufficed.

I decided that Maria suffered from a third factor, a circumstance well beyond the dyadic interaction with Paul. This factor probably represented PTSD fused with survivor guilt, the residue of her years of savage abuse at the hands of her father and of the traumatic loss of her sister. Maria certainly exhibited the extreme irritability and reactivity to stress that would justify the PTSD diagnosis. I suggested a trial of antidepressant medications. We await the eventual outcome of that intervention.

I'll offer another example of the influence of a third factor from earlier in the book. Please remember Bill and Andrea, also from chapter 1, the 52-year-old consultant and the 52-year-old French teacher, respectively. Bill recurrently turns on Andrea, accusing her of not "being a team player," in discussing the renovations of their city house or their country cabin or the reworking of their professional schedules. Andrea then becomes so defensive and self-justifying that the couple enters an adversarial state, arguing over whether she does, in fact, ignore Bill's needs. They usually don't get to discuss the topic at hand constructively, and then they withdraw from one another in frustration. The adversarial state quickly becomes an alienated one. The utter failure in cooperation that Bill fears, and has helped create, has come true, and he wonders out loud whether he should stay in this 30-year marriage.

On a family camping trip, the couple's 23-year-old son and 22-year-old daughter began a heated argument, which started with the daughter accusing the son, and by extension her parents, of never treating her as an equal to the males in the family. All of a sudden, I reflected that Bill's father dominated his family with his meandering, philosophical discourses and sometimes with harsh punishments, while the mother stood quietly by. I then recalled that Bill's brother's wife suffered from chronic depression and that Bill described his sister as "lifeless." All the women in his extended family, then, seem to live lives of quiet desperation; the men overbear and the women capitulate and get depressed. It is rare that Bill spontaneously mentions his family of origin. When he does, he seems critical of and bemused by his pedantic, self-centered father. I realized that Bill also treated Andrea with some apparent indifference and trivialized many of her concerns. In fact, he made few accommodations to her wishes. I began to hypothesize that although Bill dismissed his father as an unrealistic blunderer, he might also carry an unconscious identification with his father, which would explain, in part, the chronicity of his difficulties with Andrea. They periodically return to the clinic with a recurrent mirror-image complaint of Bill's unavailability and Andrea's lack of cooperation. Perhaps Bill, like his father, has withdrawn into his own world of ideas, will not leave it, and blames Andrea for intruding on him.

If I fail to explore this third factor and continue to overlook Bill's silent identification with a stubbornly demanding father, Bill and Andrea will likely come back to my office every few months, possibly for years to come, mired in the same bitter standoff. But if we focus our object relations exploration by reorienting it in terms of Guerin's search for a third factor, then we may be able to escape from the confusing no man's land of this case, in which the lines spoken by each character never change. I was late in perceiving this theme, however. In our last three meetings I have begun gently to confront Bill's rigidity and insularity. Surprisingly, perhaps, he has acknowledged that he's "project oriented" and more "difficult to live with" than Andrea is. He even praised her flexibility on one occasion. They both report the relationship progressing better, although neither can account for the change.

Looking for the third factor outside the dyad, Guerin's technical gift to us, brings its own complexity because that factor might or might not arrive embodied in an actual person. It could come upon us in the form of an affect—for example, Maria's survivor guilt, or in that of an identification, such as Bill's with his father. The search for these new dimensions requires that therapists offer themselves self-supervision and step back from the work in which they have become so involved, a difficult task indeed, as we'll pursue further in a few moments.

In reviewing my own cases, I've tentatively concluded that I'm prone to two general errors. One occurs when I unwittingly unbalance the treatment and concentrate too enthusiastically on exploring the triangle of conflict in one of the members, usually the more aggressive one, as if to exonerate the other. This strategy causes me to miss the interactional significance of the symptoms and of the fight.

My second category of mistake intrudes when I neglect to search for a third factor in a stalled case. I continue to try to chase down the repressed object relations in the pair, with a hopeful, but unsubstantiated, view that just a little more exploration will crack open the impasse. Probably like most therapists, I find it somewhat wrenching to admit that the case is stuck fast, and that under these conditions my sincere efforts can't start or restart its momentum. Therapists have to remind themselves of Prochaska's findings and reflect that they're probably not responsible for the entropy.

Most of the impetus for change must come from the clients' side. At these times we need to shift the plane of our perspective and search for a third external circumstance, character feature, or person that may prove to play a highly influential role in the couple interaction, but one that we've overlooked thus far.

Further Borrowed Techniques

Up to this point, the adjunctive contributions I've described have taken broad-gauge forms that necessitate a major shift in therapeutic stance—use script writing with tongue-tied clients; introduce the concept of the preferred view of self with traumatized, personality-disordered clients; search for a third, clandestine factor in stuck cases. But other couple therapists suggest smaller-bore, specific techniques that do not turn the particular treatment in a new direction but nevertheless can augment the therapist's armamentarium.

Susan Johnson's (1998, 1999) affective focus, almost always a constructive one, serves as one example. Johnson seems particularly skilled at demonstrating how one affect may mask another and may obscure the deeper, more central feeling. In chapter 3 we saw how Mark's truculent assertiveness covered over his confusion about relationships. In addition, the downcast timidity of his wife, Joanne, concealed her wish for individuation and her need to have her voice heard. Joanne rarely became overtly angry at Mark. She asserted her power by withdrawing from him as a hurt, inconsolable victim, leaving him in sputtering impotence. Joanne's passivity covered her anger. In other words, Johnson teaches us that certain problematic affective responses by one partner can persistently dominate the couple interaction, and we need to consider whether that characteristic rigid emotional stance functions as a defense to obscure more troubling feelings.

Jake and Betty

When 53- and 48-years-old, Jake and Betty, a financial consultant and a homemaker and medical secretary, respectively, arrived at the office, the chief complaint appeared to be Jake's demanding irritability. He impatiently snapped at his two sons, ages 11 and 13, and gave his wife little more leeway. Although she worked hard to manage the home and her career, Jake criticized Betty for spoiling the children and for ignoring him and his wishes. Exhausted, Betty collapsed into bed at 9:30 each evening, leaving Jake alone to read until midnight.

Immediately upon meeting Jake, I found it impossible to ignore a large scar stretching from his knee to his ankle on his right leg, the result of cancer surgery 2 years earlier. Jake suffered debilitating chronic pain but denied concerns about that burden or about the possibility of the disease returning. "That's the way life is. There's no point in complaining or worrying about things you can't control."

Over our next three meetings I praised Jake's courage and stoicism but questioned whether anyone could keep himself from railing at fate and perhaps from displacing fear and anger outward in an attempt to control family members, as substitutes for a disease that he could not influence.

Jake waved away my interpretation, but I persevered in an attempt to connect empathically with his physical pain and his probable terror. "Anyone would feel furious, scared, and lonely in your spot." Over 14 meetings and 21 months, Jake never did consciously acknowledge inner turmoil about the possibility of cancer recurrence, but he did become more cooperative with Betty and less explosive with the children. Both partners reported the counseling helpful. Jake ascribed the positive shift to the fact that he felt his point of view more heeded in the family. I assumed that he had relaxed his triangle of conflict a bit in response to his wife and to me, sympathetically, reacting to his multilevel pain. I never pushed this point with Jake, though. Clients do not need to cognitively and affectively connect all the dots in their conscious minds, evidently, for change to occur.

Mike Nichols and Salvador Minuchin (1998, 1999), experts on appropriately solidifying and softening boundaries *between* persons, teach us much about how to help our couple clients manage divisive adolescent children. These young adults have perceived the rigid boundary separating the parents and, consciously or unconsciously, manipulate this to further split the couple apart, in service of gaining their own short-term ends. I adapt Nichols and Minuchin's technique as a specific maneuver to help couples with their teenagers, particularly when that parent–child relationship represents a major issue of conflict in the marriage.

Ming and Cathy, the Vietnamese contractor and his real estate underwriter wife from chapter 2, could not cooperate on how to parent their 17-year-old son, Jerry, to the point where they could not even agree on a time to sit down to discuss their older son's behavior. A rigid boundary had grown up between Ming and Cathy, rendering it impossible for them to confront any family topic. On the other hand, the boundary between each of them and their son had become so permeable that Jerry felt free to debate, endlessly, any discussion with either parent about his behavior and to direct, or misdirect, his own life in nearly every detail, independent of parental input. Jerry largely refused to study, temporized on requesting college applications, and even moved his girlfriend into the home. Ming and Cathy, otherwise effective professionals, both distressed and angry about their son's conduct, could only wring their hands in separate parts of their house.

Borrowing Nichols and Minuchin's ideas about boundaries, I explained to Ming and to Cathy that parents could effectively require of their children any reasonable behavior, so long as the perimeter around those parents stood sufficiently strong that they could function as a powerful, cooperative unit, the rightful leaders of their family. I told them that to save their son from the potentially unfortunate consequences of his actions, they first had to discuss their guidelines for him with each other, in order to come to genuine agreement about a few simple rules. Next, they had to communicate these to Jerry *together,* and then they had to enumerate the penalties for his ignoring the rules. I forbade them from individually confronting their son about his behavior. Mirabile dictu, when Jerry perceived the parents unified, realistic but authoritative, he managed to pass his high school courses and apply to and gain admission to a local college. He matriculated this fall, carried a B average his first semester, and his girlfriend returned to her parents' home.

At the latest session Cathy summed up the therapy.

> *Nothing has changed from last time. Things are still going well. Something profound is happening. We are reconnecting, like being part of a team, of a partnership. Before, walls or barriers prevented having a connection. Jerry got an A and three Bs. Ming is giving him lots of positive support and is more attentive at home and does not work so many hours. Our younger son is not doing his homework, but we're all getting along really well. It's the best Christmas and New Year's we've had in a long time. Our schedules still don't match, but we get time together in the morning sometimes." Ming said, "When we started these sessions, I realized she was giving some, so I did, too.*

I used the same approach with Jake and Betty to support them to confront their children's bickering and passive-aggressive rebellion. Both children engaged the parents in extended psychological dialogues as rejoinders to any parental request for behavioral change. They also played the parents against one another. The 13-year-old son argued, "I would stop bouncing the basketball in the house, but Dad gets mad at me for everything anyway, so what's the point?" I told Jake and Betty that they needed to function as co-CEOs of their family. They should set the guidelines and not explain or debate every detail of the rules with their children. Predictably, when the children felt the parents united, firm but not unrealistic, much of the destructive carping in the family ended. Jake and Betty felt the home atmosphere had become much more constructive.

Harville Hendrix's use of the "couple's dialogue" offers two specific strategies that are constructive in almost any couple therapy (Luquet & Hendrix, 1998). First, he suggests that when couples discuss emotionally troubling topics, one should speak for 10 to 15 minutes uninterrupted and then the other can take his or her turn. For most pairs, in the past, the fight has erupted well before the 10-minute mark, and each never has gained an emotional understanding of the other's position. Most couples do not know what they're battling about in any meaningful detail. As a second part of the couple dialogue, Hendrix teaches empathic listening and validation. He instructs each member of the pair not to agree with the partner but to respond by articulating, within his or her own perspective, an understanding of why the partner feels a certain way.

I've recently used these techniques with Brad and Joan, the younger couple I introduced earlier. I asked each person to listen carefully to the other's position and to attempt to grasp it, without being under any obligation to accept it as his or her own. Brad and Joan still seem very different in style, and they still experience major disagreements over housekeeping standards and personal schedules, but these have lost much of their bite. The couple reports a more harmonious relationship after a total of only 10 meetings over 15 months. They seem to have agreed to disagree, but they also have cooperated to curtail most of their snapping over their characterologic incompatibilities. They report that understanding each other's viewpoint has helped a lot.

I feel that this couple is probably typical of those we can aid with a brief, straightforward method. They're young, they're committed to each other and to their small children, and they appear readily influenced by an older, kindly, though authoritative, therapist. Also, neither seems crippled by a rigid triangle of conflict, containing many brutal hurts and much unresolved anger from the past, despite the fact that each emerged from a quite dysfunctional family matrix. The surprising psychological health of many individuals and couples born from troubled origins represents a key topic, one to which I'll return at the end of the chapter.

I've offered these remarks about a hybrid model of couple treatment not because I think mine a unique or ideal synthesis, but because I think this discussion helps illustrate how we can mix and match from a spectrum of approaches to accommodate our clients more quickly and more deftly than if we employ one approach exclusively. Most couples do not conform to the textbook prototype for one or another intervention model, which can leave the therapist at a loss for the first move. However, if clinicians can apply different pieces of a number of different systems to the case, they likely can respond constructively to almost any couple. We need to stay ready to change or add to our method to meet our customers and not demand that they bend themselves around to conform to any one doctrinaire approach. It's easier to adjust the therapist and his wares than to transform the client's habitual posture, and it's better to store more than one size of arrow in our quivers. This policy obtains particularly strongly for brief couple or individual treatment, where time pressure lurks, but I think it applies for any therapy. James Gustafson (1984) argues a parallel point when he observes that we require methods from all the schools of psychiatry—psychodynamic, interpersonal descriptive, and so on—to meet the client effectively in brief treatment.

When we illustrate the hybrid alternative with specific cases, we come to realize just how acutely a therapist sometimes requires a Plan B. Adding script writing or the narrative concept of the preferred view of self can represent quite dramatic shifts in direction from an object relations approach, yet I don't see how I could have treated Ming and Cathy, Jeannine and Audrey, or Jake and Betty without this reorientation away from my initial stance. The decision to use a mixed model, though, requires that the therapist have the courage to conclude his or her original strategy to be inadequate and to formulate a new plan for the case—not an inconsiderable demand.

Does "Hybrid" Mean "Integrative" Model?

Almost all clinicians, no matter how experienced, probably practice expertly in only one or two ways (Hans Strupp, 1981). For this reason I think that true integration of psychotherapy schools is usually a practical impossibility. Only in an unusual circumstance can a clinician become equally adept at two markedly different theoretical approaches and then meld them into an integrated treatment model. Wachtel's (1977) psychodynamic-behavioral approach and Eron and Lund's (1998, 1999) narrative-solutions tact stand as exceptions. Certainly, others must exist but not many.

In the future we will probably see clinicians continue to shift away from theoretical and clinical exclusivity and toward hybrid models, but they will usually still use one core theoretical system to direct their approach, not the thorough integration of two disparate orientations. I've discussed integration here because I think it unreasonable for therapists to worry about gathering true mastery in a number of areas. A working familiarity with one or two models seems sufficient, so long as the clinician can flexibly apply, and add to, these formats.

This consideration of hybrid and integrative approaches leads me to wonder if an unspoken generic model of brief couple treatment underlies our work, because diverse methods seem to push a broad group of clinicians in the same common directions within any given phase of treatment—that is, try to build trust early and push for action later.

A GENERIC MODEL OF BRIEF COUPLE TREATMENT

As you recall, Prochaska and his colleagues conducted transtheoretical, transprocedural research, studying nearly the entire spectrum of change methods and target symptoms, from weight loss to smoking cessation to insight-oriented psychotherapy. We'll see in a minute that their findings provide us with a point of departure to begin to identify the outlines of a generic model of short-term couple treatment. If we pursue this project, perhaps we could isolate the required components of any couple treatment model and also glimpse the future by predicting the issues that we, and our colleagues, will next explore, as we all try to address the dimensions of the generic model that are missing or undeveloped at present.

We could start to discover the generic format by reviewing how this approach might conceive of clients at each of Prochaska's stages of change: (1) precontemplation, (2) contemplation, (3) preparation, (4) action, and (5) maintenance.

The Response to Precontemplation in a Generic Model

Let's begin with the first stage of change, precontemplation. Precontemplators, those wondering if they have a problem and making no plans for change in the immediate future, bring with them a particular and important challenge for couple therapists. Precontemplators often arrive in the office at the demand of their spouses, usually, though not always, the wives. Sometimes their primary care doctors or their individual therapists send them. How should couple therapists deal with these precontemplators?

The first pass at this question seems relatively simple. Because precontemplators usually have a treatment career marked by early dropout and poor outcome (Prochaska et al., 1992), offering them an extended therapy contract, such as a 15-session group, represents an obvious error. I have redefined my couple evaluation as, in part, an attempt to identify precontemplators and then, if they cannot alter their stance, to decline any extensive treatment at present.

Irene and John: A Crisis Beyond Our Reach?

My colleague, the distressed individual therapist of the wife, referred Irene and John, a couple in dangerous conflict. Wisp-like 41-year-old Irene suffered from anorexia, her weight falling under 90 pounds. Irene's heavy-set, strident husband, John, age 45, responded to my inquiry about his childhood by conveying that his family, which included a number of alcoholics, had largely abandoned him as an adolescent and a young adult. They discouraged him from going to college, supplied no funds to help with advanced training, and almost ridiculed his ambition. Impoverished and working at marginal jobs, John had to give up his higher education after only 2 years and has struggled occupationally since. John became enraged with Irene, a lawyer, when she departed on trips to attend to her clients and left him at home to care for their two sons, ages 8 and 6. At these times John sometimes drank heavily, overlooked the children's needs, and shouted accusations at Irene when she returned. As the family conflict became more acute, Irene's weight plummeted.

After hearing John's story of his early life, I offered, "I don't know you very well, John, but it appears that you've been abandoned so hurtfully by your original family that you're furious when your wife leaves, too, to look after other people." To my disbelief and not inconsiderable anger, John laughed rudely, "Oh, isn't that neat, you've heard 20 minutes of my story, and you've got it all in a neat pattern explaining everything. Isn't that just great!" Only a few minutes old, the treatment had already reached a critical turning point. I knew that John needed to devalue me, as his parents did him, to maintain his fragile equilibrium, but I felt like retaliating with a confrontation over his self-defeating alcoholism. Most of us can recognize a pointless strategy, if we don't jump for it too quickly. At moments like this, I gather myself and try to say nothing. I then redoubled my efforts to forge a better alliance with John and overcome his resistance in this first meeting, efforts made the more intense by Irene's pressing medical problem. I still felt unable to contact John with any offer that proved workable. The couple left, not to return for some months.

After our visit, because I thought them precontemplators, I did not pursue them, even though Irene's psychotherapist, a valued personal friend, and her internist were nearly frantic about her weight loss. I simply couldn't discern a constructive direction in which to move with these clients. At no point did Irene attempt to intervene with John in our session or voice her concern at their interactional pattern, which had progressed, or regressed, to such serious, even life-threatening levels. This couple defined precontemplation. Neither could suggest, in any productive fashion, the existence of any interactional problem, despite dramatic evidence to the contrary. John assigned the blame to Irene and Irene to John. Danger surrounded this couple, but they seemed affectively to be oblivious to it.

I'm not sure of any one right move in these situations. In this case, not struggling further with this couple proved fruitful. Four months later they returned. John stated that he had resolved to work on his weight and his alcoholism. He felt that he had made headway in these areas with the help of his individual therapist. He now stood ready to deal with the couple issues. I praised his progress, and we've tentatively started out again, although John remains quite paranoid about Irene's intentions toward him. He feels that she purposefully overspends in order to punish him. This time, delaying a second appointment with a precontemplative couple worked out well, but we clearly need to develop a range of interventions for this special group.

For instance, Judith Coché, PhD (personal communication), reports herself in the midst of constructing a new treatment model, in which she first offers incoming couples a series of educational groups regarding marital conflict. Those who feel ready then join a 1-year psychotherapy group. Coché's intervention appears an attempt to begin with a large unselected pool of couples, many of whom inevitably reside in precontemplation and others in contemplation. Then she draws, from this reservoir, contemplative couples who demonstrate the motivation to pursue their issues more deeply, although, of course, she does not use this precise descriptive terminology.

Coché's model fits Prochaska's framework neatly, and we can predict success for it. My guess is that more and more innovators will attempt some form of this general strategy in the future. Coché's referrals, not ready to join an actual therapy group or commit to solo couple treatment, can presumably spiral out of the change cycle for the moment, with the option of reading and talking more on their own and then registering for the class again. Perhaps they can start more intensive couple treatment later, either group or solo.

I find it troubling that most brief couple treatment models do not articulate a method to identify precontemplators and, second, to specify which clients don't fit their system but might fit another one. For instance, Christensen and Jacobson's integrative behavioral approach (Lawrence, Eldridge, Christensen, & Jacobson, 1999) seems to make great demands on prospective clients. They need to cooperate successfully in the trust-building exercises and then in the later behavioral-change training. Christensen and his colleagues explicitly reject pairs with personality disorders or active addiction. However, I think it unlikely that any couple burdened with years of anger and hurt could readily put those affects aside—that is, suspend their triangles of conflict—and begin to mesh quickly and smoothly within the Christensen–Jacobson behavioral exercise model. They work poorly together on other tasks. Why should this new arena prove a striking departure?

The five-step object relations approach likewise appears demanding for incoming clients, although along completely different dimensions from the Christensen–Jacobson method. My couples need to begin to talk about their fight and also about their pasts. Because some people cannot readily contact their internalized objects, we've observed that I often introduce a modified script-writing approach to broaden the access for more rigid pairs like Ming and Cathy. The relationship counter offers also clearly represent one general strategy to deal with precontemplators. Ming might have fallen into this group, for instance, but, luckily, I could help him join the treatment by assuming a specified supportive stance to him, obviating his probable precontemplative state. By altering my initial strategy, I can accommodate most, though certainly not all, couples.

Bart and Susan: No Therapeutic Solution?

Forty-one-year-old Bart and 39-year-old Susan presented with their 5-year marriage in a shambles. Susan reported that Bart interacted with her minimally and expressed almost no affection or romantic interest. From cell phone and computer evidence, she realized that he carried out involved relationships with other women, although she remained unclear whether these included sexual infidelity. Bart treated her family and friends with an aloofness bordering on insolence. He apparently demanded her attention and support but sulked or complained when she requested that he help her or attend to the couple's two young girls.

It turned out that Bart's father had sexually abused him at age 6 or 7 and that his parents, although successful professionally, seemed almost oblivious to their children's basic needs at any age. All four of Bart's siblings lived with a range of personality and marital difficulties. Bart seemingly spent his late teens and early 20s in a haze of drugs, alcohol, and promiscuity, although he had achieved a more stable lifestyle by age 32, when he met Susan.

I tried hard to contact a preferred view of self inside Bart, some wish for a give-and-take relationship, but he seemed unable to suspend his easily pricked narcissism even for a few minutes. If Susan criticized him or asked too much of him, he withdrew to his wounded isolation and to his computer chat rooms. Bart displays the symptoms of major depression, for which he takes medications, but, at a fundamental level, the central problem appears that he can't rally enough hope to contemplate personal change for more than a few hours. Unfortunately, this represents an understandable impairment, given the betrayal he experienced at the hands of his early caregivers. The "bad" internalized objects evidently dominate all later intimate transactions for Bart. I referred Bart for a weekly individual therapy, which he

pursued for some months, but which he has just terminated with few
gains. Susan suffers from survivor guilt. Her parents, aunts, and uncles
all remain in destructive marriages, and it turned out that she uncon-
sciously felt convinced that she should do the same. However, finally
her patience has become exhausted, and she's demanded a divorce.

Hybrid models, here an object relations approach fused with Eron and
Lund's narrative-solutions methods, however energetically applied, sometimes fail to chip through the bastion of precontemplation. Through this
unfortunate case, we can see that personality disorder, in which the client
continually blames some second person for the problem, virtually impris-
ons him or her in the precontemplative state and keeps the client beyond
the reach of any attempt at any form of treatment, however flexibly conceived. This case illustrates an important limitation to the five-step model
(and to most other couple therapy schools as well). To gain from this approach, both members must live somewhere within Klein's depressive position versus the schizoid-paranoid position (Greenberg & Mitchell, 1983,
chap. 5). Bart can experience for only a moment empathy for Susan's pain
and how he has harmed her (depressive position). He then lapses back into
blaming and withdrawal, probably paranoid/schizoid mechanisms.

A generic model of couple treatment, then, must focus on selection
issues and the best fit for particular clients and must also account for the
precontemplative group. It must face the fact that many couples do not
meet the motivational requirements for any intensive intervention at a given
time. In addition, the generic model, following the Coché's innovations,
should specify an alternative disposition for precontemplators, an educational group, or a return meeting in 3 months. We cannot simply send the
precontemplators off from whence they came. Precontemplators do not
represent an inferior group of therapy applicants whom we should avoid as
quickly as possible, but they are clients who present a special requirement
for an intervention pitched to their particular motivational stage.

The Contemplation and Preparation Stages
of a Generic Short-Term Couple Treatment Model

Prochaska's findings suggest that a generic model should devote its early
sessions to an exploration of the contemplation and the preparation issues
of the clients, as explicitly as possible. We can observe that many approaches
do begin by directly taking on these matters. For example, the first two
stages of the five-step model, investigating the fight and the triangle of
focus, attempt to involve the pair in exploring the object relationships, past

and present, that contribute to their recurrent standoff. I can't resist some general coaching toward change in many early solo or group sessions, but, for the most part, I'm asking couples to accompany me on an investigation of how old relationships may shadow the present one. I'm not suggesting any actions yet. Speaking in Prochaska's language, in these early stages we utilize the change process of "consciousness raising," that is, learning more about the self; about others, past and present; and about the problem. We also use the change process of "helping relationships," supporting the client toward more openness with two caring persons, the therapist and the partner. These represent contemplation-stage interventions.

We structure the middle sessions of treatment as the time for preparation. We can see this pattern most clearly in the short-term group format. In chapter 5 we could observe that in meetings 6, 7, 8, and 9, many members struggle with their commitment to the group and therefore to change, and some start to experiment with small behavioral shifts (preparation). Here the change processes of consciousness raising, experiencing and expressing feelings about the problem and about its potential solutions, and dramatic relief, that is, grieving the past and role-playing new possibilities, become all-important.

But we've seen that two traps lurk for the therapist, one on either side of the path. We can push for action too fast, or we can postpone that thrust too long, maybe indefinitely. The strengths of different schools, ironically, may render them particularly vulnerable to one or the other of these characteristic mistaken directions. The strategic approach (Keim, 1999), for example, moves quickly to change the clients' behavior and to involve them in exercises to promote that change. But couples bring resistance with them, particularly resistance borne out of past hurts with the present object-partner and with previous objects. If these go unaddressed, the motivation to move into the contemplation and preparation stages may remain short-circuited.

To my knowledge, strategic and behavioral authors often do not directly address the matter of resistance. What if the couple refuses to engage in the homework tasks or begins to rebel against any of the therapist's suggestions? Any generic model needs to include thorough contemplation and preparation stages and requires the built-in capacity to confront the possibility that the couple's past may introduce issues that freeze the therapy in its tracks. Everyone doesn't have to subscribe to psychoanalysis, but every therapist does need to account for resistance. (When Christensen and Jacobson added their trust-building exercises to the beginning of their model, they tried, I believe, to speak directly to the issue of resistance and to prepare the couple for the behavioral interventions that they subsequently use.)

The Action Step

I think that by now we've become convinced that any generic model must include an explicit action stage. In chapter 6, we observed William, Dick, Tom, Nancy, and Mary taking strong actions that brought about dramatic changes in their marriages. There remains some ambiguity, however, about whether the therapists contributed a great deal to framing those actions or whether the clients embarked on them more or less on their own. Here we encounter the potential weakness of psychodynamic models like mine or Dicks's or the Scharffs'. I often find it difficult to pull myself away from exploring object relationships to suggest concrete behavioral changes for the couple. In Prochaska's terms, I'm less likely to include explicitly the change process of self-liberation—that is, choosing to commit to an act—but Christensen or Hendrix readily embrace this step.

Psychodynamic action might not seem to be a tangible discrete behavior, such as when the therapist emphatically stops the fight and introduces the couple dialogue, as Hendrix might, but psychodynamic therapists can still deal in actions. I could have challenged William, the attorney, to suspend his authoritarian tone and to observe what happened next, but I didn't, probably an error. He took on the role of participant observer at his own initiative. He made the change, evaluated the results, and reported back to us.

In the future I'm predicting that we'll see more dynamically oriented therapists experiment with explicitly adding action steps into their treatments. I know that lately I'm more likely than in the past to confront a client with, "Michael, you've learned a lot about your mother and her effect on you. Now it's time to check out, directly, whether your wife, Mary Ann, really is manipulative like her." Psychodynamic training institutions certainly don't teach their students to push for action in this way, and, overdone, the strategy could easily become intrusive, but dynamic therapists probably need to tolerate their understandable anxiety and take calculated chances like this to learn the limits of their method.

Maintenance

The maintenance stage may represent the step in the generic model about which we know the least. Couples often seem to solidify change out of our sight. The therapist may become an internalized object in that process but not a present object, because the couple has terminated. Mary underwent a remarkable breakthrough in her therapy 8 years ago, when she realized herself a gift to Joe. This once chronically bickering couple clearly found a method to maintain that change over a long time period, but I don't know how the two did it.

Substance-abuse specialists probably comprise the experts among us on relapse prevention, because recidivism poses so great a problem in addiction treatment. The best programs acknowledge this risk and build a long-term group into the therapy format, available to those who have successfully negotiated the acute phases of detox and of attaining initial sobriety. In a similar vein, Virginia Goldner, PhD (personal communication), at the Ackerman Institute in New York, includes a veteran couple from a previous group in each new domestic violence group. This arrangement not only offers neophyte pairs "sponsors" and role models but lends the more-experienced partners the opportunity to continue to review their areas of conflict. Our couple groups often arrange to meet for dinner on a monthly or bimonthly basis after the official termination, an example of a self-initiated maintenance maneuver.

In the future I trust that we'll observe a number of practitioners devising flexible approaches that can accommodate the maintenance needs of many of their clients. For instance, I can imagine a monthly drop-in group, with an updated self-help reading list available, as a support for a large couple practice. Clients could use, or not use, this resource as they saw fit. I have a feeling that some of us already have experimented with similar options but have not reported on them in their literature, because the techniques appear so mundane or haphazard. We need to acknowledge maintenance as a key change stage and share our ideas about this approach more fully. We also need to remain wary about any proposed treatment model that overlooks or dismisses maintenance issues.

Intermittent Couples Treatment

Before leaving the discussion of maintenance, we need to note that short-term couple treatment can begin to look more like intermittent couple therapy, the more we study it. I may see a couple for some solo work, then treat the partners in a couple group, and then follow up with more solo sessions a year later. I imagine that other couple therapists have found that their practices follow similar lines.

I don't think we should consider this intermittent pattern as proof that our treatments don't work. Budman and Gurman (1988) point out that individual clients use their therapies according to the same format. They come and go as they feel the need, and they may contact the same practitioner, or different ones, off and on for decades. Budman and Gurman also tell us that mental health professionals engage in an average of five different therapies through their adult lives, even when one of these comprises a "full" psychoanalysis. A definitive psychotherapy apparently does not exist, in the same way that we cannot conceive of a definitive training program or a definitive vacation trip.

Susan Edbril (1994) and James Gustafson (1995) describe models of planned intermittent treatment that include no initial intensive phase. Edbril treats women with relationship problems in a once-monthly pattern. She helps her clients work on their attachment issues over a year or more within this model. Gustafson offers distant, more vulnerable clients intermittent therapy in the same fashion, because relating intimately seems so difficult for these people. In real life the distinction between brief and long-term therapy seems to blur into a spectrum of different treatment options, constructed to fit the client's personality orientation, life circumstances, and presenting problems. For example, regardless of his original plan, Dicks often seemed to treat his clients in a staggered format over 1 to 2 years, meeting perhaps twice per month, due to logistical interruptions.

The intermittent pattern inevitably taken by many couple treatments speaks directly to the maintenance requirements of a generic model. Any approach needs to provide the opportunity for off-and-on meetings into the indefinite future when needed, but this may not imply that the clients will use a great many visits in a calendar year, or that a definitive termination does not fit the requirements of other couples. Such a position is consistent with object relations theory because the influence of repressed objects waxes and wanes, more dramatically with some couples than with others, but it never entirely disappears.

Utility of a Generic Model

This discussion of a generic model does not represent an exercise in reductionism. I'm not trying to prove that all couple therapists do, or should, pursue the same goals and fundamentally use variants of the same methods introduced in a similar sequence. But the advantages of holding a generic model in mind seem manyfold. For instance, as we've observed, we can use that model as a template against which to evaluate the comprehensiveness of any particular couple approach. If we encounter a treatment system that does not explain how to handle precontemplative couples or does not spell out its action stage, then we should begin to view that strategy with some skepticism.

We can also use the generic model to identify the strengths and weaknesses of our own or any other format. For example, the five-step model's action phase requires altering the triangle of conflict, but if the clients completely founder there, we can't honestly point to a well-defined fall-back position. Or, as another example, many of the strategic and behavioral systems, as I've mentioned, don't explain how to confront resistance in the contemplation and preparation phases. Finally, the generic model can help us to locate our position in any couple treatment, when the therapy begins to stray or slow down. For instance, what if we've met with a pair eight times in 2 months, but the fight still rages? We can ask ourselves some of the following questions: What is the motivational phase of the couple? Why can't the partners prepare for important action? Do they remain in contemplation or even precontemplation? If so, why?

In this chapter so far, I've addressed a series of interrelated topics. First, I described possible hybrid approaches to time-managed object relations couple treatment. Then I presented the outline for a generic couple therapy system and discussed some reasons for the importance of that development. Using the generic format as a starting point, I speculated about future developments in short-term couple treatment. Clearly, I'm guessing that the next innovations in our field will represent refinements of each stage of that generic model.

MAJOR QUESTIONS UNRESOLVED

I'm trying to describe many of the pieces of the brief object relations couple therapy puzzle and show how they fit together. Inevitably, a few get left to the side. I'll try to pick these up now and insert them in their proper places. Many of our observations, up to this point, have come from the somewhat-removed planes of theoretical conceptualization or treatment-planning guidelines. But we haven't yet explored how the participants actually feel when they engage in this kind of therapy. So we can't complete our study until we take on a series of further questions. For instance, we need to know more about the subjective affective demands on the therapists within the treatment and how they learn to cope with these and turn them to positive advantage. On the other side of the office, we must understand more about the clients' complex emotional states, moment to moment, as they engage in the therapy, if we're really going to attempt a more complete grasp of how this treatment works.

The Therapist's Role: Required Skills, Affective Demands

Through the previous chapters, we've watched therapists grapple with a number of cases in detail, which has lent us a general understanding of the skills required of the clinician to work within the five-step model and, to a lesser extent, within other systems. It's clear that this represents a complex job. They have to contend with a gusher of data coursing toward them, make sense of it, choose a path through it, and then return to the clients a new understanding of their recurrent conflict. They have to do this in a style that the clients find helpful and supportive, and they need to respond relatively quickly—all in all, a fairly imposing challenge. I'll enlarge on our understanding of the objective skills required of couple therapists. Then I'll try to capture their inner affective state as they attempt to pursue this multidimensional work.

First, the clinician needs a general theory of couple attraction and, subsequently, of couple conflict, a point emphasized by Susan Johnson (1999) and before her, by the Scharffs (1991) and Henry Dicks (1967). We require a basic understanding of how members of the couple draw together and how that connection becomes disrupted. By now, we can appreciate that those two processes occur closely linked. We need a widely applicable theoretical approach that makes sense of the ebb and flow of the couple interaction, because the partners present us with such a reservoir of material about their individual exchanges that if we can't place these into some system, we'll quickly get overwhelmed and confused. The five-step model rests on object relations theory as its explanatory concept of attraction and subsequent conflict. But Susan Johnson makes use of attachment theory to fulfill the same function, and Nichols and Minuchin introduce the structural view of boundary rigidity and enmeshment in much the same way. Therapists' background, training, and temperament will determine which framework they choose as the centerpiece of their approach, but we all require a general theory to orient the work.

Next, therapists need a plan based on their theory. Brief therapy, in particular, necessitates that the clinicians exercise disciplined selective attention to the data. They can't possibly follow every potential lead, or they risk resembling a confused bloodhound, trying to track every scent on a picnic ground. They must recognize the pieces they seek and, once these are uncovered, have the knowledge to fit them together into the gestalt. If Ken, from chapter 5, has a burdensome hypochondriacal mother, the therapist must pounce on that information and connect it to Ken's dismissal of the complaints of his wife, Beatrice. The therapists need a plan, then, and, as Michael Nichols (1999) tells us, they must stick to that strategy, often in the fact of great resistance, if they hope to shake clients out of their habitual interactional patterns. He observes that this steadfastness marks an important difference between experienced and more neophyte therapists. By keeping their template in sight on the horizon, therapists can track the progress of the therapy and recapture its arc when the focus begins to blur.

However, we can't treat each pair of clients with identical methods, so therapists need to remain prepared to shift their stance when necessary. Brad and Joan's troubled original families greatly influenced their marital conflict, but this couple responded better to concrete coaching than to a historical object relations investigation. Flexibility seems a common virtue to which we all would subscribe, but, in fact, therapists often find that the decision to switch their plan and move in a different direction provokes some anxiety and self-doubt. Maybe their initial approach was incorrect? Maybe they didn't understand this couple as well as they thought? The necessity to retain flexibility places still another emotional demand on the therapist.

We've also noticed that to undertake these complicated tasks, therapists rely on one primary investigative instrument, their own affective reactions, the receptive "negative capability" summarized by Scharff, to which I referred in chapter 2. Mary-Joan Gerson also describes this important open orientation required for family therapists in her 1996 book. Therapists allow their clients' emotional messages to register directly on them so they can grasp the affective content of the clients' conflict and learn, firsthand, how partners sweep the other into their self-created worlds. No experience in therapy seems so real as finding ourselves actually wrapped within the client's affective force field. Then we can sense that person's inner state in an unmistakable way. If I couldn't feel, in myself, Ming's fear and anger toward authority, I would have missed the opportunity to bond with him as a teammate and to coax him toward more open negotiation with Cathy. If I had allowed Mark to lure me into a squabble, I would have lost all hope of alliance with him, and I would have joined his repetition compulsion. But I needed to experience how strongly he tempted me to fight, before I could catch the meaning of his standoff with Joanne.

Certainly, we've all heard previously about the need for a receptive, open, affective, therapeutic stance. I haven't found it that easy a one to assume, though, particularly when I need to worry simultaneously about the treatment plan, the outcome, and the timetable of the therapy. I'm not sure how to teach someone to clear his or her mind, but we all can practice dismissing other thoughts and tracking our affective responses to the clients. You can check back on the treatment plan at the beginning and the end of the session. If therapists find that they cannot follow the clients', and their own, emotional reactions, it's important to speculate about why and how you and the couple have come to collude in shutting down your consciousness. At these times the answer often turns out that one or both members of the couple remain convinced that they, or their partner, cannot change, and they've projected that feeling of confusion and hopelessness onto you. Addressing this discouragement and ambiguity inevitably becomes the next order of business.

The scanning of our affective reactions also provides us with the first clues that we need to formulate the relationship counter-offer. This proposal from therapist to clients supports the latter in suspending their defenses in the triangle of conflict. Sitting with the couple, I often find myself musing, "What counter-measure will it take to help these people relax their guard?" Verbal reassurance plays some effective role here, but I've found that a full relationship offer, with its nuances, body language, and preconscious exchanges, often seems required to assure clients of the conditions of safety.

The relationship proposals that we extend differ from one person to the next, of course. Sometimes therapists must find the nerve to act in a somewhat unconventional fashion in making their offers. In our first session I invited Ming to criticize my approach and to tell me, frankly, if he found me intrusive. This hardly represents the usual way to start a couple therapy. However, I felt it an overture that I had to attempt in order to neutralize Ming's passive-aggressive jujitsu maneuvers toward authority. In the relationship possibilities we offer, we can't present ourselves fraudulently, but we do allow the client's needs to change us for the moment. I can remember feeling exquisitely sensitive to all-powerful authority the first few times I exchanged with Ming. This autoplastic capacity to permit ourselves to become reformed for the moment and then to regain our original shape later can feel somewhat frightening and alien when we first experiment with it. Experienced therapists probably find these transformations more comfortable and may frequently undertake them without realizing their shifts in ego state in any troubling fashion, because this type of self-rearrangement has become part of their daily work. Norcross (2001) also emphasizes the crucial point that experienced therapists can probably offer a wider range of relationship possibilities than can less seasoned practitioners, who must push their learning in that direction.

The clinician's internal experience during the therapy usually seems to oscillate between security and doubt. Because therapists work from a theory and its accompanying model for technique, they can plan their next moves, but nature rarely unfolds with Euclidian precision. Clinicians must keep themselves open and alert to the moment-to-moment peregrinations on which the relationship with the clients may embark. By definition, they cannot know in detail what will come next, because these developments occur under the sway of the preconscious interactions of all three participants. So therapists will have to tolerate confusion about the material and insecurity about the outcome of any series of interventions or about the fate of the treatment as a whole. Clinicians must stay vulnerable to surprise, the unexpected twists that any client couple may introduce at any time. It's much easier to remain receptive to doubt and to the unknown if, in your conscious and unconscious memory, you can refer back to a number of other ambiguous treatments in the past that ultimately progressed constructively. Experienced therapists can hold this open perspective toward uncertainty more readily than can inexperienced clinicians, whom teachers need to support as they begin to nurture this capacity.

The Clients' Subjective State in the Midst of Brief Couple Therapy

Whatever doubt and confusion therapists may experience during the treatment, the emotional burdens for the couple obviously weigh far heavier. Because Prochaska reports on separate cohorts in the different motivational stages, he can't communicate the turmoil and anxiety that clients undergo as they struggle from level to level. Also, since Prochaska's approach remains atheoretical, he can tell us nothing about the drama with internalized objects, which may pulsate through his clients through the sequence of change stages. He can tell us that couples pass from stage to stage, but he doesn't say exactly how and with what degree of inner difficulty. However, given the frequency of relapse, that passage clearly often becomes a harrowing one. I'm afraid I've underemphasized the struggle and fear that clients must tolerate as they traverse the stages of change. I'll address that here. Precontemplative people can feel terrified to acknowledge that their marriage displays major conflicts. Learning more about those problems in the contemplation stage can become even more unsettling. Preparing for and initiating an action often seem too frightening for clients to approach even in fantasy.

Gustafson (1984) conveys the tension that accompanies the change process as well as anyone does. Reading Gustafson, we learn that the short-term individual dynamic therapist must accompany the client on three quests for the treatment to work. First, therapist and client complete a focal inquiry of the problem area. Clear enough, we've learned to investigate the fight and the triangle of focus. But second, the therapist confronts the clients' "constant attitude," read triangle of conflict, their rigid wall of defense, and breaks through into the turbulent, uncontrolled feelings below or beyond that wall. In object relations terms, this means that the client must reencounter negative repressed objects who threaten, sabotage or fail to support the self. Third, the therapist helps the person develop a capacity to manage and integrate these newly uncovered feelings into an increasingly competent self-image. McCullough's message about confronting and restructuring defenses also emphasizes the clients' pain and difficulty in trying to alter their habitual stance (1994). If Gustafson is correct, and his argument in his 1984 paper does appear convincing, then we've missed some of the drama of the piece, as the clients begin to grapple with their triangles of conflict and attempt to manage the very feelings, and the attendant repressed object relations, that have bitterly stymied and demoralized them in the past.

Breaking into the rigid wall of character could move in one of two directions, it seems, but following either, clients might emerge with a fundamentally different experience of themselves and probably of their past objects. In the first possibility, clients might spontaneously discover a new positive sense of self that hitherto they had repressed. Mary's sudden real-ization that she represented a gift, to motherless Joe, of an intact, reliable, loving person, not about to die as his mother did, represents a fine example of this class of breakthrough. Although, to achieve this new experience, Mary probably had to renegotiate unconsciously with her critical internal mother, this transformation seems relatively painless, because Mary quickly started enjoying an optimistic outcome, her realistically enhanced sense of personal power.

For William, the 40-year-old attorney whose father invoked the unfor-gettable "Let's drop it," however, the search for new insight forced him to confront strongly negative aspects of his family and of his own controlling self. These developments took place off camera. William does not describe how difficult and frightening he found the process, but, clearly, he did need to undertake a breakthrough, or he never would have changed. Almost certainly, he found the passage, from contemplation to preparation to ac-tion, arduous at key moments.

Dick tells us a bit more about the pain involved in his growth when he shares how scared he felt before deciding to pursue Peggy. How he realized that his marriage would never change if he didn't say "yes." He was also forced to acknowledge that many of his previous forays toward her now seemed self-defeating and inept. He had to realize that he stood responsible for many of the frustrations in their relationship, not easy knowledge to confront and assimilate in the contemplation and preparation stages. In addition, Dick tells us directly how angry he became at the therapist's con-frontation. "I don't like it when someone pushes me like that."

Mark, too, had to reevaluate the developmental failures of his family, and of himself, before he could move forward. Mark had to accept that now, in his late 50s, he knew almost nothing about how to carry on a relationship. Mark sadly observed that the last 53 years, the time before his insight, now felt like a waste to him. We can conclude that he had to con-tend with much fear and anxiety in order to achieve this transforming in-sight, although he didn't relate any details about any such ordeal.

A new case illustrates why some decisive thrust through the wall of character might represent a necessary change step in many couple or indi-vidual therapies.

Victor and Pamela

Victor, a 48-year-old business executive, and Pamela, his wife of the same age, arrived with two complaints. Their 13-year-old daughter, Samantha, presented them with major behavioral and management problems. Samantha had ADHD, and failed most of her school classes, "forgetting" to complete assignments. She often acted in an insolent way toward her parents as well, flouting their rules and occasionally swearing at or physically threatening her mother. The couple also reported major conflicts over communication. Victor would snap at Pamela, questioning her ability to think and act responsibly—a core issue for Victor, as we'll see in a minute. They disagreed over their approach to their daughter and over whether Victor behaved in a respectful, constructive fashion toward either his wife or Samantha.

Victor, a massive, red-faced man, frequently alluded to his combat experience as a Green Beret and accused Pamela and Samantha of not understanding realistic thinking and responsible follow-through. He directed a large department in a major corporation and often seemed to apply the same management techniques to his wife and child that presumably worked effectively downtown. Pamela, burdened with ADHD herself, had pursued advanced training but had not yet developed a successful career. Pamela, half her husband's size, in earlier years meekly capitulated to Victor's tirades but now began lashing back at him, accusing him of having a controlling and condescending attitude. Samantha's behavior deteriorated as she entered more deeply into adolescence and as her parents continued their adversarial relationship.

Pamela implied that Victor's parents had treated him and his siblings with cold strictness, expecting great achievement but offering little warmth and positive feedback in return. All, including Victor, attained substantial professional success, but, apparently, all seemed overbearing, highly sensitive to criticism, and prone to angry outbursts, and all had serious weight problems. When Victor was 16, his parents threatened to disown him over a behavioral infraction, an event that constituted a major issue for Victor, one to which he and Pamela frequently alluded, but which he refused to specify in detail. During his tirades, of course, Pamela and Samantha could easily imagine that Victor wished to disown them.

It appears clear that Victor and his brothers and sisters carry damaging projective identifications from their parents. The latter projected unwanted parts of themselves, such as passivity and rebelliousness, into their offspring and then excoriated the children for their shortcomings. Apparently, the children strived desperately for achievement to prove themselves innocent of their parents' implicit charges. Victor, however, could not grasp that his parents had projected disobedience into him and that he, in turn, had inserted the same into Samantha. So Victor has evidently repeated with his daughter the cycle that started in his original family.

It appears that to solve his marital problem, Victor will have to confront his fury at his parents, who imported so negative a self-image into him. In order to change, Victor will need to realize, at some level, that he's identified with the aggressor and has come to react to his wife and his daughter as his parents treated him. Now we arrive at an important controversy, centered directly in the client's subjective state in the treatment. Victor represents the extreme case of that issue. He will probably have to experience some kind of breakthrough into new insight about his parents. Initially, we would predict this to include major turbulence, given his bottled-up anger, regret, and sadness. But Victor is a rigidly defended man who rails against the irresponsibility of others with a sometimes-paranoid fervor. If the therapist directly confronts his triangle of conflict, Victor may well bolt the treatment. But if he can't lighten that triangle, how much can we expect his family chaos to subside?

Gustafson seems to contend that the penetration through the defenses must progress in quite dramatic fashion and must be mediated by the therapist, who provides powerfully confrontative interpretations to breach those defenses. This experience seems required in his form of brief individual treatment, in order for it to unfold effectively. I do not know as yet how Victor, Pamela, and Samantha will ultimately fare. Other of our case reports, though, seem to support a more mixed conclusion than Gustafson's. Some of our couples and individuals—for example, Mark—might undergo great turmoil to gain insight and others, like Mary, far less subjective upset. Sometimes the therapist apparently plays a direct catalytic role in this change and other times an almost imperceptible one. The reports do suggest that all the couples who achieved positive outcome had strong emotional involvement in the therapy. Mary could recall her gift speech, almost word for word, 8 years later. It seems that this involvement might or might not include a wrenching breach of defenses.

Couple therapy is not individual therapy. In the former, much of the action takes place around the problematic boundary between the partners, and in the latter, around the barrier between individual client and therapist, a point emphasized by Mary-Joan Gerson (1996). The partners continue to relate and experiment, intimately, in their daily lives outside the therapy sessions. In the couple group, we've also already seen that clients listen to other members and apply their own experiences silently to the reports of their group mates. Therefore, breakthroughs in new understanding for couples may occur in a less shattering, more ambiguous, and less conscious fashion, and certainly more out of the awareness of the therapist, than might obtain in individual treatment, where the central interactions clearly unfold between the intimate pair of therapist and client. The changes Gustafson describes in brief individual treatment often seem quite similar to the ones I've observed in couple therapy, but the physical location in which that change takes place and the cast of characters involved may not be quite the same.

Therapist–Couple Moment-to-Moment Affective Interchange

Prochaska puts forward his format of the stages of change to describe the journey through the treatment from the clients' side of the room. The five-step model, or any similar approach, directs the therapist's plan for the sequence of their interventions, but both systems stand above the therapeutic interaction at some distance. Good and obvious reasons dictate such a perspective. However, we've just observed that neither system captures the minute-to-minute dramatic strain of the treatment.

Like the therapist, the clients, within the session, must attempt to sort through a plethora of complex information, data that activate their most basic defenses, so their confusion will more than match the therapist's, and at many points their anxiety may feel overwhelming as they start to suspend defenses. No wonder the therapy progresses according to a halting and apparently disordered rhythm, with an outcome, a next phase, or even a next sentence that none of the participants can foretell. What prevents this unstructured interaction from going hopelessly astray and becoming a repeat of the marital breakdown? Our case reports and transcripts suggest a number of hints toward possible answers.

I'll try to spell out a little about how the therapist and the couple interact constructively in the moment-to-moment unfolding of the hour. Therapists keep their eye on their explanatory theory and their treatment plan, but I think they focus there mostly at the beginning and the end of the session. When they're deeply involved in the intimate matrix of the meeting, clinicians probably keep two important immediate goals in mind. They hold fast to these at all costs, no matter how overwhelming the momentary ambiguity. First, the therapist supports the partners to restore their morale (Frank, 1974), not to lose heart. Second, the therapist opposes the repetition compulsion and strongly intervenes to keep the couple from initiating the same self-defeating cycle all over again. Even with their inevitably inadequate minute-to-minute grasp of the meaning of each exchange, therapists push for understanding, for memories, for associations, for delay in impulsive actions, and for new possibilities. Let's return to Victor and the trap in which he finds himself.

Victor really does behave rigidly outside the therapy session and within it. He yells at Pamela, during and outside of therapy hours, and he has dismissed, sometimes in a fury, some of my gentle suggestions that Samantha will not rein in her behavior until she perceives her parents as a cooperative unit. Pretty clearly, business as usual will not work for Victor. He can boom out his disagreements with me and with his wife, meeting after meeting, but nothing will change. Victor will need to gain access to a different, more conciliatory affective state for a shift in this marriage to take place. Mary-Joan Gerson has studied these crucial moments in couple and family therapy.

She introduces the concept of "liminal moments," in which time stands still, structure decreases, and the client can entertain a new look and a new experience.

At some point soon, Victor will need to allow himself the subjective realization that his anger represents some significant part of the problem, not part of the solution. This change may or may not take place suddenly, but whatever the timing of its arrival, Victor will have to gain access to a new part of himself, as he interchanges with Pamela and Samantha, separately and together. He will have to realize that he needs to try out different offers to them, if he hopes to renegotiate the boundary between the three of them that has become so problematic. Our case studies suggest that this key alteration in boundaries may appear in the therapy hour or may take place mostly outside of it, but the seeds for the change are probably sown in the treatment session. Even though Mary's remarkable insight, "the gift," occurred on the drive home, the inklings of it, for her, began while sitting in the couple group that evening.

If the therapist can maintain this stance long enough, maintaining morale, opposing the repetition compulsion, and promoting liminal moments, we've seen ample evidence that a remarkable process can then occur within one or both members of the couple. This development represents the last and, in some ways, the most mysterious puzzle piece. I'll close with a deeper examination of this phenomenon, in which the couple seems to take hold of the treatment and to decisively move forward toward self-cure.

THE ROLE OF "HIDDEN FEELING"

I, and probably all of us, stand struck, often dumbstruck, with the realization that something inside Mark, inside William, inside Dick, inside Mary, and inside many of our clients clearly fosters change. On the other hand, Bart and Irene and John, from this chapter, seem to founder in the therapy. Yet we use the same spectrum of techniques with each pair. Evidently, some clients bring crucial capacities with them that facilitate change. Others do not. We obviously need to learn more about these inner resources.

Each of these people who experience constructive change must have connected with some positive sense of self, some sustaining identification that lent them the courage and the strength to prepare for, and to embark on, their determined actions. Surprisingly, a happy early life does not appear to be prerequisite. William described a solid family as a child, but Mark seemed almost set adrift by his parents and lost his father at age 16. Brad and Joan gained quickly from minimal treatment, but both their parents' marriages appeared problematic at best. Joan's parents divorced, and Brad's father routinely devalued and mocked his mother. *Disaster* seems the only fitting word to describe Dick's family—his father, gone apparently without a trace; his mother, cold and scheming; his sister, depressed and suicidal; and his brother, wildly destructive and disorganized. How could Dick, or anyone, emerge from this swamp of fear and disappointment with any sense of trust intact? But emerge, he did.

Earlier, I hypothesized that from somewhere within, Dick drew on a positive identification that he could then connect with me to generate enough hope to reach out for Peggy. I admitted that I could not readily identify those positive relationships, although Dick did appear to have a strong reciprocal bond with his sister, despite her crippling illnesses. In the group Dick always sat next to me and seemed to hang on my words. In the countertransference, I felt him leaning toward me, or on me, and I found it natural to offer him a warm shoulder of respect and encouragement. Our connection, no doubt, activated his optimism and helped him move forward.

How Mark managed his about-face seems even more curious. Somehow Mark, too, found positive identifications upon which he based his shocking change in outlook, but from where? I liked Mark, but, in the countertransference, I didn't feel him moving toward me with any particular warmth. On the contrary, he seemed to keep his distance from me, the co-therapist, and the rest of the group. Mark hinted that sometimes his father stood up for him and told his mother, "Don't make him into a sissy." He mentioned, in passing, a close relationship with a male cousin. After these potential sources of positive bonding, we have to shrug our shoulders about the sources of Mark's strength.

Here we encounter a frustrating irony of our work. Through our training and experience, we therapists have learned a lot about trauma and disappointment, about the compulsion to repeat damaging relationships, and about an array of other resistances to change, but our grasp of the underpinnings for *positive choices* toward constructive growth appears sorely lacking. From our studies here, we can conclude that a productive alliance with the therapist and his or her helpful interpretation, apt coaching, and patient confrontation probably account for some, but for only a part, of this process. Much of the mystery still alludes us.

Let's return to the triangle of conflict (figure 7.1) to search for more clues.

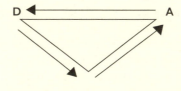

HF

FIGURE 7.1. The Triangle of Conflict

We understand a lot about the A → D connection and can quickly sketch in the specifics for any of the clients we've met in this book. This exercise represents the purebred psychodynamic ego psychology reasoning about which Malan and Osimo (1992) and Leigh McCullough-Vaillant (1994) have taught us. William's anxiety over loss of control impels him toward his authoritarian stance to Barbara, with his father's phrase "Let's drop it" ringing in his unconscious. Mark's provocativeness represents a defense against his ignorance over how relationships operate in the first place, and so on, from client to client. Therapists work well with the A → D section of the triangle. In many ways it represents our stock and trade. But when we move around to the HF pole, matters become more vague. The HF material seems so bound up with the change process that we must further explore this area, however murky it may now seem.

Other writers can illuminate some of the shadows that play across the HF area. Eron and Lund probably enter hidden feeling territory when they focus on the preferred view of self. William *prefers* genuine negotiation with Barbara. He *does not* prefer the breakdown in relating that his argumentative behavior precipitates. He dislikes the "effects" of his behavior, in Eron and Lund terminology. He feels loss and disappointment when Barbara throws up her hands and walks away from him, as she has so often in the past. Somewhere, among his hidden feelings, William holds an image of a cooperating self, which he prefers to his condescending self. He gains useful access to this self when the group helps him to resolve his ambivalence over control, originally based on a regressive identification with his father.

I don't wish to blur meaningful distinctions between these concepts, but the positive hidden feeling and the preferred view of self may refer to similar general psychological phenomena. We've already seen that these entities have caught the strong attention of at least two widely differing schools of psychotherapy. Malan, McCullough, and their psychodynamic colleagues have termed it *hidden feeling*, and Eron and Lund give preferred view of self a central place in their narrative-solutions approach. From our review of cases so far, we can quickly conclude that our understanding of the HF pole remains incomplete, although wisps of evidence have already begun to suggest that this area plays a necessary role in couple change. For example, Jeannine and Audrey, despite very real personality deficits and major stressors, appeared to alter their behavior markedly in response to the activation of their positive views of self. HF evidently represents the positive goal to which the individual members of our couples unsurely stumble, as they grope with us toward productive shifts in their outlook. Luckily, as we study the clinical vignettes, more and more features of hidden feeling emerge.

Hidden feeling apparently does not imply positive infantile fantasy. William and virtually everyone entering couple treatment wish for a happier marriage. They wish that their partners would suddenly change their attitude and become loving and accepting of their motives, without William, or any of us as protagonists, needing to change much or even to explain ourselves more extensively. This fantasy, common to all of us at one time or another, probably starts within the early, undifferentiated level of object relations. "A warm person will envelope me in his or her love, regardless of my behavior and of that person's own present needs." Such language seems to refer back to the primary mother–baby bond. But hidden feeling, for our clients, represents an entirely different class of relatedness. For instance, it seems to imply a proactive stance by the self. "I, William, can behave more cooperatively toward Barbara and alter my tone of voice." "I, Dick, can offer Peggy some real interest and ask for affection from her." Intimate outcomes do happen, but only after the self initiates positive actions toward the other person.

Hidden feeling also seems to imply that the main character has assumed some personal responsibility and has genuinely, affectively relinquished the impulse to blame the partner. Mark's, William's, Dick's, or Mary's accounts of their change clearly do not accuse the other person. For example, none mention the possibility that they might have changed much more readily had the partner previously shown greater receptivity. Interestingly, the protagonists do not idealize the partner, either, or express profound guilt over having harmed them. Hidden feeling apparently does not belong deep within the depressive position, in which the self has injured the object and must hasten to make reparation. Rather, the message of hidden feeling seems to be "He or she is a good-enough partner. This is not about my partner. It's about me and the concrete offers I can make to my partner and to myself." Dick, in the previous chapter, directly stated this proposition.

A third characteristic of hidden feeling appears its emphasis on realistic hope. The self does not seem to grasp desperately for love or succorance from the partner but seems quietly convinced of the possibilities of a positive interaction. The self, at the breakthrough moments, expresses little anxiety about rejection or failure in the anticipated interaction. I carefully reviewed Mark's revelation at the end of his couple group. Nowhere did he refer to the fear that Joanne might dismiss his new insights and subsequent behavioral change. He seemed to assume support and positive response but not to depend on it. William apparently did not wonder if his wife, Barbara, would accurately perceive his shift in attitude and follow his lead toward more constructive interaction. When Mary suspended her defense and suddenly realized her role as a "gift" to Joe, her motherless husband, anxious, underconfident Mary did not appear to doubt or to worry very much about Joe's response.

I'll add some final words about hidden feeling that may clarify, somewhat, one of the conundra we've wrestled with for several chapters: why change often appears to take place at a distance from the therapist's influence. I'll start with a personal story. I noticed that our son, at age 12, would usually refuse my requests that he perform simple household chores and then, shortly, he would take on the job and complete it effectively. I questioned, "You know, Brian, I was thinking. When I ask you to do something, you usually say no and then 10 minutes later you do a really good job on it. What's going on?" His memorable answer, "That's the game, Dad." Here, our son captured the adolescent dilemma, how to remain free and still respond to the reasonable wishes of a parent.

The emergence of hidden feeling often surprises us because the clients freely decide on their own to go forward. They don't just comply with our suggestions but jump into the task voluntarily. We've observed Dick saying "yes" and Mary realizing she's a "gift," as well as Mark buying the book mentioned on the radio, not because they should or just because the therapist or their partners pushed them toward the action, but because they exercised their free will and wanted to try the leap. The "hidden feeling," then, represents an example of mature object relations in almost pure state. The self freely decides to reach toward another in a warm and constructive fashion, does not denigrate the other or fear his or her coldness, but feels reasonable hope for a positive, mutually satisfying encounter. We can tentatively hypothesize that many, maybe most, of our clients directly draw upon this hidden feeling, object-relatedness resource, when they suspend their investment in the automatic anxiety-defense reflex action, which so frequently becomes the harbinger of the fight.

Now we face a central paradox of our work. Clearly, the volitional move into more mature object relations represents the goal of the therapy, but because this goal seems embedded in the client's free will, to influence him or her toward it appears to be a philosophical, as well as a pragmatic, contradiction. Maybe yes, maybe no. We can begin by introducing the issue early on in the treatment. If affirming hidden feelings stands as the end state we seek, we need to begin preparing for it from the start. Most therapists regularly ask their clients, "What do you really want?"—clearly a step in the right direction. I think we can do more.

We need to search for positive identifications, as well as for libidinal and anti-libidinal ones in the history, and to call attention to these. We also might underscore instances of mature relatedness within the couple and inquire how the partners reached this closeness, a standard solution-focused move. During the contemplation stage, once we explore resistances and help couples prepare for change, we can begin to investigate their free choice about actions that will move them closer to their partners and about identifications that would support this shift. In other words, couples and individuals naturally connect to hidden feeling as the defense lifts, but we can facilitate this development, from our side, by bringing the HF dynamic

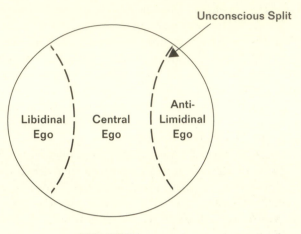

FIGURE 7.2

into play at opportune moments. Then we need to stay out of the way, as the couple decides on how to experiment with these positive possibilities.

To summarize and deepen the discussion, let's return to the Fairbairn object relations diagram of the self (figure 7.2), which I first introduced in chapter 2.

Please first recall that the libidinal and anti-libidinal egos represent the problematic *unconscious* object relations experienced in the family of origin, which return to play so influential a role in the present couple fight. The former includes disappointed bids for love and the latter hateful angry conflict with intimate objects. The central ego refers to the *conscious,* more adult object relations that the partners bring to the marriage, Subsystem 2 in Dicks's thinking, summarized in chapter 2. We now can see two possible corrections that we might propose to this classic model.

The first alteration in the diagram represents a somewhat minor one. I've replaced the solid with a dotted line to indicate that the split between conscious and unconscious never remains complete. Mark stood partly aware that his parents had failed him, but when he participated in the group and read the book mentioned on the radio, his repression dramatically lifted. The line became much more dotted than solid. He then knew, for a fact, that his parents had abandoned him, and he also knew that that this trauma still played an unmistakable role in his adult marital and general interpersonal difficulties.

However, you may have noticed a second, more significant element missing as well. The diagram, in its original form, cannot account for hidden feeling, the preferred view of self. This important entity carries the opposite valence of the libidinal and anti-libidinal objects, so it cannot possibly reside within those regions. However, HF remains unconscious, preconscious, or both, so it can't represent some specialized corner of the central ego either, but by this point in the discussion, we have to conclude that it's too real, and too crucial, to leave out of our metapsychology.

We can amend Fairbairn:

Here we can picture the HF as an unconscious or preconscious area (or

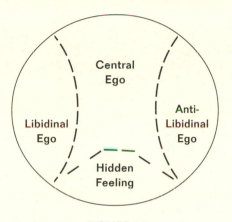

FIGURE 7.3

both) of the central ego. Growth-promoting, as well as conflict-laden, object relations can become split off. Modifying the diagram in this fashion will remind us not to forget to search for hidden productive identifications, as well as for repressed problematic object relations, as we pursue the therapeutic dialogue or trialogue with our clients. Greenberg and Mitchell (1983) also point out that Fairbairn's original model does not spell out in much detail the origins of positive object relationship capacities, nearly to the extent that he pursues psychopathological development. Scharff and Scharff (1998) draw attention to the same issue, to some extent, when they clearly include an "ideal or good-enough" object within the central ego region (pp. 49–50).

Reading Fairbairn (1952) in the original can quickly become a confusing exercise, partly because of his highly theoretical and dense writing style and partly because he considered his papers a conceptual work in progress. He admitted that he never intended to return to edit his earlier propositions to render them consistent with his later thought. Fairbairn does posit an "accepted object" (pp. 178–179) or an "ideal object" within the central ego around which maturation appears to take place. He does not describe this as a repressed object and says little more specifically about its role in positive growth. This concept requires further explanation.

Fairbairn apparently treated mostly quite ill, paranoid, schizoid, and depressed patients and understandably he appeared most concerned with studying and explicating their dynamic conflicts. For example, consider Bart, from earlier in this chapter, the man sexually abused in childhood. Fairbairn's formulations, help us a lot in understanding how Bart's repressed "bad objects" compel him to spoil all later intimate interactions. However, the data from the majority of the people in the book, particularly those who struggle toward a positive outcome, seem to suggest a central role played by repressed "good objects," so I have tentatively proposed a modification, or re-emphasis, within Fairbairn's basic theory, along these lines. Fairbairn appears the first to suggesst that maturational development occurs when we begin to differentiate from problematic primary identifications with original family objects (Fairbairn, 1952, p. 163). Here his ideas aid us immeasurably in our grasp of the constructive shifts that we've observed in a number of our clients. Consider, William, the attorney, separating from his father's controlling style, and pugnacious Mark, no longer having to provoke all new acquaintances, as if they stood for his inert parents.

Matters metapsychological usually remain well out of the reach of any objective proof. However, we could perhaps test our contention that the HF sector lies in the unconscious or, more accurately in the preconscious, by a thought experiment. If we interviewed Mark, William, or Dick, pursuing *why* or *how* they had changed, they would probably find themselves unable to explain their important shifts. They might mention something like the HF, a wish to become a better person or closer to their wife, but I doubt they could describe the change process in much further detail, even though it occurred entirely within them and held such crucial importance. This would represent prima facie evidence of its mostly unconscious nature, as well as a strong indication that HF does not belong within the libidinal or anti-libidinal ego because these pertain to elements that block and do not support intimacy. HF evidently refers to a special area related to, and strongly influencing, the orientation of the central ego.

Why has the HF sector undergone repression? I think for many of the same reasons that the libidinal and anti-libidinal ego exist behind the repressive barrier. From what I can gather from our case vignettes, from my own psychoanalysis, and from additional self-analysis, the HF represents our most important strivings and wishes to give and receive love. I think we feel embarrassment about these feelings, although personal therapy and analysis can relieve some, though not all, of this pressure. Shame over vulnerability leads us to repress the hidden feelings and often repress them quite deeply. In my experience, after a thorough analysis, many of us gain greater comfort with our aggressive feelings than with our needs to give and receive intimacy. When I dictated a draft of this paragraph about the wishes for closeness embedded in HF, my wife came into the room, and I stopped speaking out loud, evidently still reluctant to talk too much about this tender area of human longing.

From this viewpoint, I think we can understand change in most therapies as a shift inside the person in which the influence of libidinal and anti-libidinal objects diminishes, the repetition compulsion embedded in the anxiety → defense connection becomes less automatic, and the day-to-day power of HF becomes greater. Our clients shift away from destructive relationship attachments to earlier objects. Let's take a case from Nichols and Minuchin (1999) as an example. Boundaries in a family do not get enmeshed for no reason or for some haphazard cause. In the family that Nichols and Minuchin described in this 1999 chapter, the mother, Janet, had become overly involved with her adolescent son, Jeffrey, as a libidinal object, presumably because she had identified with him as a frightened, somewhat passive teenager and because he offered her more gratification than did her angry, judgmental husband. The husband stood as a punishing, frustrating object. The young man clung to his mother for parallel reasons. Becoming more responsible and more adult felt frightening to him. His mother seemed like a warm, approving presence who, alienated from her husband, also appeared in need of his companionship.

Yet for this therapy to succeed, Janet needed to individuate from her son and to step closer to her husband, and Jeff had to move away from his mother and toward his peers and their age-appropriate activities. But why would either of the parties willingly surrender readily available libidinal pleasure and psychological safety? The most convincing answer now appears to be because of the preferred view of self or hidden feeling. If Janet prefers to seek intimacy with her husband, Keith, and if Jeff prefers to see himself not as a "teddy bear" for his mom but as an increasingly independent young man, both will start off in more mature directions. Change in any system of therapy may depend on the activation of hidden feeling, described in whatever terminology the therapist chooses.

The content of HF intrigues us still further, though. How do we develop genuine hope for intimacy and cooperation? A few pages ago I hypothesized that Dick and Mark reached back to earlier positive identifications upon which to build their picture of change in the present. Essentially, I argued that they aspired toward what they already knew but held in their preconscious. Partial positive identifications with loving aspects of parents or siblings, no doubt, account for a significant proportion of the HF content. I couldn't actually specify these identifications, though, and even I didn't feel simply postulating their existence entirely satisfying.

It seems equally likely to me that we possess some inborn capacity to relate and that this inner resource empowers the hidden feelings as well. Repressed early positive experiences can easily meld with innate motivations to lend the hidden feeling deeper affective life. I have rarely seen constructive change in partners who have proved unable to suspend their triangles of conflict, slow their automatic anxiety-defense reflex, move away from early negative relationship transactions, and gain more access to hidden feeling. Some contact with the HF regions apparently represents a necessary condition for change.

BRIEF COUPLE THERAPY OUTCOME: WORDS IN CLOSING

Because development continues through life, therapists cannot expect their couples to depart "cured." At the least, we should strive to support a couple to move toward the next stage of change—for precontemplators to begin to consider, seriously, the meaning of their marital fight; for contemplators to learn more about their conflict and to start preparation for change; and so on. At the most, we can hope that couples will leave our offices with a greater psychological grasp of their recurrent difficulty and with a few methods or tools, tested by action, that work to unravel the fight pretty well, not perfectly. Younger therapists, in particular, need to study Prochaska's findings that teach us that change does not take place in inexorable, linear progression. Over our careers, we'll see many more partially failed attempts at alterations in behavior than we will decisive transformations. Couples and therapists must learn that to summon the courage to try again, after a relapse, may signify a more important therapeutic event than striving to resolve the issues in any complete fashion. Fairbairn's ideas explain why this must be so. The regressive influence of early, repressed, problematic objects will never disappear entirely or at one moment in time.

Cardiac valve repair and orthopedic knee or hip replacements represent once-and-for-all interventions, after which the patient's life almost always shows permanent improvement. Couple therapy has not developed any such magic bullet techniques, and it never will. Human relationships carry with them such complexity and such ambivalence that permanent resolutions of core marital conflicts will always remain an impossibility. But small changes, beginning to suspend one's triangle of conflict and speaking from a shared relationship platform usually, though not always, represent tangible, significant progress in intimate connection.

Let's return to the image of hidden feeling a final time. These affects, and the object relationship pictures they convey, vary from person to person and couple to couple. This means that positive outcome for clients follows their template and not necessarily the therapist's. Mary realized herself a gift to motherless Joe, and 8 years later she still operates in terms of that original insight, but in our most recent return visit, Joe continued to struggle to reciprocate his wife's warmth. He had to keep wrestling, apparently often not successfully, with his defensive need to control through criticism. To me, Joe remained distant from Mary, and she still seemed to contribute disproportionately to the marriage with her insight and her patience. But she might not have agreed with my assessment, and perhaps Joe offered all the intimacy this guilty, unconfident woman could tolerate. The marriage appeared genuinely satisfactory to both, but Mary could not use her constructive work in her family as a counterweight to depression and low self-esteem. She had contacted the clinic for individual psychotherapy and a psychopharmacological referral.

Joanne, Mark's wife, yearned to continue her professional training as a lawyer and to create a work life separate from Mark's frustrating business, but she's still burdened with low self-confidence and passivity. In her late 50s, she probably won't strike out on any individuated job course, although I might wish this for her. Bill and Andrea have made recent strides in their intimacy. Bill can acknowledge some, but only some, of the rigidity in his triangle of conflict. Andrea stands up for herself more readily and now rarely collapses into hopelessness and self-blame when he withdraws. Bill, however, still gets lost in his work and his home-renovation schemes; when Andrea complains, he often criticizes her as his first impulse. Couple therapy can lead toward specific, though delimited, interactional change, but the individual psychologies of the pair, apart from the dyad, may continue much as before.

"Mostly happier ever after" appears more accurate than "happily ever after," even for those couples we've come to know, who have struggled for and clearly have enjoyed positive treatment outcome. Couple therapists find themselves in the business of gains, not cures. If pressed, probably all of us would endorse this statement, but we need to acknowledge our unconscious inflated expectations for our clients, lest we subtly criticize them and ourselves for less-than-optimal progress. Relapse and, I hope, trying again remain a more likely scenario than transfiguration into an entirely new level of object relatedness.

Tolstoy begins *Anna Karenina* with "Happy families are all alike; every unhappy family is unhappy in its own way." As we leave the couples we've met here, some of whom we've come to know well as they lurch toward becoming different, I'm struck with how those that have earned a measure of change do sound the same. As pairs enter treatment, each looks different, one from the next. Each fight carries its own destructive features. Each family history includes any number of unique details. However, when some of our couples have achieved a meaningful shift during treatment, they still suffer personal trials, and they continue to struggle in conflict with each other, but they all can *talk constructively* with their partners about these issues. One hundred and twenty-five years later, Tolstoy appears to be correct. "Happy" couples do all seem alike.

Wile, in his 1999 chapter (p. 219), offers us examples of exchanges that might take place between partners who have achieved, sometimes, the ability to collaborate. He quotes members of a couple who have gained the capacity, in his words, to build a "shared platform" from which to view their relationship or, in mine, who have learned to work through their fight. "Do we really want to be doing this [participating in the fight]?" "What I'm saying is coming out a lot harsher than I wanted it to." "I'm doing what I vowed never to do. Act like my father." "I guess I'm being a little defensive here." "You're probably right, but I'm too angry at the moment to want to admit it." "Should we stop now or go on and ruin Sunday also?" "This is the moment in the fight that I usually storm out or refuse to talk for the rest of the afternoon. But I don't feel up to it today."

These phrases at first sound so ordinary and so obvious. Of course, the fight turns on the participants acting out identifications from the past; becoming angrily defensive; withdrawing in wounded, accusatory fashion; or refusing to acknowledge the valid aspects of the partner's position. But the capability to initiate these collaborative conversations that Wile's couple has just demonstrated means that both members of the pair have faced their triangles of conflict and their constant attitude and, to some extent, have dared to tolerate the rush of uncontrolled feelings that was previously restrained behind that wall. They admit to their characterologic defensive behavior. They confess to their anxiety. We can also hear them acknowledge their regressive identifications inherited from their families of origin, their triangle of focus. The partners appear veterans of the five-step model, but, of course, they aren't. Wile treated them with a completely different approach. To return to the idea of a general dynamic psychology (Pine, 1990) for a final pass, we can see from the previous illustrations that the speakers have developed in their object relatedness but also in their ego functioning and self-awareness. They can take perspective, delay action, question the self, and work toward higher-level, more complex goals than they did previously.

The couples we've encountered in this book who have used their treatment constructively not only sound like each other, they sound very similar to Wile's clients, as well, and probably to the successful changers treated by Susan Johnson, Harville Hendrix, and Mike Nichols. Collaboration sounds the same and works the same, no matter what model you employ to foster it. It may matter less what system the therapists use, so long as they utilize it confidently and flexibly.

In these chapters I've illustrated one model and taken you through it step by step, but I've tried to include enough descriptions of alternative approaches to suggest their efficacy and sophistication as well. As my primary objective, I've tried to demonstrate the great benefit to the therapist, and to his or her clients, of experimenting with any, or many, of these systems to observe which fits a particular practitioner and a specific client most aptly. We've seen that couple work makes a paradoxical and powerful demand on the therapist. Simultaneously, we need to connect with the pair affectively but also to keep one eye on the overall treatment plan. Under these conditions, only a strong model can help us stay on track and guide us out of the many cul-de-sacs into which we'll inevitably stumble. If we can stop and ask ourselves: What past repressed object is operating now for one or both members of this couple? Which third factor might function to impede this treatment at this time? In what stage of change do these partners find themselves at present? This will mean that we're working from a model, and we will have gained crucial technical leverage.

"Send not to ask for whom the bell tolls." It tolls for us. The stakes for us to improve our methods loom large because the cost of divorce burns so painfully, not only for the couple but for their children, who will, all too often, find their way to the offices of other therapists years from now. It behooves us to examine our work, and that of others, carefully and to have the courage to experiment with the new departures that this study inevitably suggests.

References

Balint, M. (1968). *The basic fault: Therapeutic aspects of regression*. London: Tavistock.

Balint, M., Ornstein, P. H., & Balint, E. (1972). *Focal psychotherapy*. London: Tavistock.

Berkowitz, D. A. (1999). Guilt in couple therapy. *Psychotherapy Forum, 6*(1), 559–583.

Bollas, C. (1987). *The shadow of the object*. New York: Columbia University Press.

Budman, S. H., & Gurman, A. S. (1988). *Theory and practice of brief therapy*. New York: Guilford.

Budman, S. H., Simeone, P. G., Reilly, R., & Demby, A. (1994). Progress in short-term and time limited group psychotherapy: Evidence and implications. In A. Fuhriman & G. M. Burlingame (Eds.), *Handbook of group psychotherapy: An empirical and clinical synthesis*. New York: Wiley.

Burlingame, G. M., Fuhriman, A., & Johnson, J. E. (2001). Cohesion in group psychotherapy. *Psychotherapy, 38,* 373-379.

Coché, J., & Coché, E. (1990). *Couple group psychotherapy*. New York: Brunner-Mazel.

Dattilio, F. M. (1998). *Case studies in couple and family therapy*. New York: Guilford.

Dattilio, F. M. (1998). Cognitive-behavioral family therapy. In F. M. Dattilio (Ed.), *Case studies in couple and family therapy* (pp. 62–84). New York: Guilford.

Davanloo, H. (1978). *Basic principles and techniques in short-term dynamic psychotherapy*. New York: Spectrum.

Dicks, H. V. (1967) *Marital tensions: Clinical studies toward a psychoanalytic theory of interaction*. London: Routledge and Kegan Paul.

Donovan, J. M. (1986). An etiologic model of alcoholism. *American Journal of Psychiatry, 143*(1), 1–11.

Donovan, J. M. (1987). Brief dynamic psychotherapy: Toward a more comprehensive model. *Psychiatry, 50,* 167–183.

Donovan, J. M. (1989). Characterologic intervention and the physical position of the patient. *Psychiatry, 52,* 446–461.

Donovan, J. M. (1995). Short-term couples group psychotherapy: A tale of four fights. *Psychotherapy, 32,* 608–617.

Donovan, J. M. (1998). Brief couples therapy: Lessons from the history of brief individual treatment. *Psychotherapy, 35,* 116–129.

Donovan, J. M. (Ed.). (1999). *Short-term couple therapy.* New York: Guilford.

Donovan, J. M., Steinberg, S. M., & Sabin, J. E. (1991). A successful fellowship program in an HMO setting. *Hospital and Community Psychiatry, 42,* 952–953.

Donovan, J. M., Steinberg, S. M., & Sabin, J. E. (1994). Managed mental health care: An academic seminar. *Psychotherapy, 31,* 201–206.

Edbril, S. D. (1994). Gender bias in short-term therapy: Toward a new model for working with women patients in managed care settings. *Psychotherapy, 31,* 601–609.

Eron, J. P., & Lund, T. W. (1998). Narrative solutions couple therapy. In F. M. Dattilio (Ed.), *Case studies in couple and family therapy* (pp. 371–400). New York: Guilford.

Eron, J. P., & Lund, T.W. (1999). Narrative solutions in brief couple therapy. In J. M. Donovan (Ed.), *Short-term couple therapy* (pp. 291–324). New York: Guilford.

Fairbairn, W. R. D. (1952). *Psychoanalytic studies of the personality.* London: Routlege and Kegan Paul.

Feld, B. G. (1998). Initiating a couples group. *Group, 22,* 245–259.

Framo, J. L. (1973). Marriage therapy in a couple's group. In D. A. Block (Ed.), *Techniques of family psychotherapy: A primer* (pp. 87–97). New York: Grune & Stratton.

Frank, J. D. (1974). Psychotherapy: The restoration of morale. *American Journal of Psychiatry, 131,* 271–273.

Friedman, S., & Lipchick, E. (1999). A time-effective solution-focused approach to couples therapy. In. J. M. Donovan (Ed.), *Short-term couple therapy* (pp. 325–359). New York: Guilford.

Gerson, M. J. (1996). *The embedded self.* Hillsdale, NJ: The Analytic Press.

Gottman, J. (1994). *Why marriages succeed or fail.* New York: Simon and Schuster.

Greenberg, J. R., & Mitchell, S. A. (1983). *Object relations in psychoanalytic theory.* Cambridge, MA: Harvard University Press.

Greenson, R. R. (1967). *The technique and practice of psychoanalysis.* New York: International Universities Press.

Guerin, P. J., Fay, L. F., Fogarty, T. F., & Kautto, J. G. (1999). Brief marital therapy: The story of the triangles. In J. M. Donovan (Ed.), *Short-term couple therapy* (pp. 103–123). New York: Guilford.

Gurman, A. S. (1992). Integrative marital therapy. In S. H. Budman, M. F. Hoyt, & S. Friedman (Eds.), *The first session in brief therapy* (pp. 186–203). New York: Guilford.

Gustafson, J. P. (1981). The complex secret of brief psychotherapy. In S. H. Budman (Ed.), *Forms of brief therapy* (pp. 83–128). New York: Guilford.

Gustafson, J. P. (1984). An integration of brief dynamic psychotherapy. *American Journal of Psychiatry, 141,* 935–944.

Gustafson, J. P. (1995). *Brief vs. long psychotherapy.* Northvale, NJ: Jason Aronson.

Hoyt, M. F. (1993). Group psychotherapy in an HMO. *HMO Practice, 7,* 127–132.

Johnson, S. M. (1998). Emotionally focused couple therapy. In F. M. Dattilio (Ed.), *Case studies in couple and family therapy* (pp. 450–472). New York: Guilford.

Johnson, S. M. (1999). Emotionally focused couple therapy: Straight to the heart. In J. M. Donovan (Ed.), *Short-term couple therapy* (pp. 13–42). New York: Guilford.

Keim, J. (1999). Brief strategic marital therapy. In J. M. Donovan (Ed.), *Short-term couple therapy* . (pp. 265–290). New York: Guilford.

Kempler, H. L. (1985). Couple therapy in a health maintenance organization. *Psychotherapy, 22,* 219–223.

Lawrence, E., Eldridge, K., Christensen, A., & Jacobson, N. S. (1999). Integrative couple therapy: The dyadic relationship of acceptance and change. In J. M. Donovan (Ed.), *Short-term couple therapy* (pp. 226–261). New York: Guilford.

Linehan, M. M. (1993). *Cognitive behavioral treatment of borderline personality disorder.* New York: Guilford.

Luquet, W., & Hendrix, H. (1998). Imago relationship therapy. In F. M. Dattilio (Ed.), *Case studies in couple and family therapy* (pp. 401–426). New York: Guilford.

Malan, D. H. (1976). *The frontier of brief psychotherapy.* New York: Plenum.

Malan, D. H. (1979). *Individual psychotherapy and the science of psychodynamics.* London: Butterworth.

Malan, D. H., & Osimo, F. (1992). *Psychodynamics, training and outcome in brief therapy.* Oxford, UK: Butterworth-Heinemann.

MacKenzie, K. R. (1990). *Introduction to time limited group psychotherapy.* Washington, DC: American Psychiatric Press.

McCullough-Vaillant, L. (1994). The next step in short-term dynamic psychotherapy: A clarification of objectives and techniques in an anxiety-regulating model. *Psychotherapy, 31,* 642–654.

McCullough-Vaillant, L. (1997). *Changing character.* New York: Basic Books.

Minuchin, S., & Nichols, M. P. (1998). Structural family therapy. In F. M. Dattilio (Ed.), *Case studies in couple and family therapy* (pp. 108–131). New York: Guilford.

Mitchell, S. A. (1988). *Relational concepts in psycho-analysis: An integration.* Cambridge, MA: Harvard University Press.

Nichols, M. P., & Minuchin, S. (1999). Short-term, structural family therapy with couples. In J. M. Donovan (Ed.), *Short-term couple therapy* (pp. 124–143). New York: Guilford.

Nichols, M. P., & Schwartz, R. C. (1998). *Family therapy: concepts and methods* (4th ed.). Boston, MA: Allyn & Bacon.

Norcross, J. C. (2001). Purposes, processes and products of the task force on empirically supported therapy relationships. *Psychotherapy, 38,* 345–356.

Ogden, T. H. (1982). *Projective identification and psychotherapeutic technique.* Northvale, NJ: Jason Aronson.

Pine, F. (1985). *Developmental theory and clinical process.* New Haven, CT: Yale University Press.

Pine, F. (1990). *Drive, ego, object, self.* New York: Basic Books.

Prochaska, J. O., DiClemente, C. C., & Norcross, J. C. (1992). In search of how people change: Application to addictive behaviors. *American Psychologist, 47,* 1102–1114.

Prochaska, J. O., & Norcross, J. . (2001). Stages of change, *Psychotherapy, 38,* 443–448.

Rako, S., & Mazer, H. (Eds.). (1980). *Semrad: The heart of a therapist.* New York: Jason Aronson.

Rutan, J. S., & Smith, J. W. (1985). Building therapeutic relationships with couples. *Psychotherapy, 22,* 194–200.

Sander, F. N. (1998). Psychoanalytic couple therapy. In F. M. Dattilio (Ed.), *Case studies in couple and family therapy* (pp. 427–449). New York: Guilford.

Scharff, J. S. (Ed.). (1989). *Foundations of object relations family therapy.* Northvale, NJ: Jason Aronson.

Scharff, D. E., & Scharff, J. S. (1991). *Object relations couple therapy.* Northvale, NJ: Jason Aronson.

Scharff, J. S., & Scharff, D. E. (1998). *Object relations individual therapy.* Northvale, NJ: Jason Aronson.

Slipp, S. (1984). *Object relations: A dynamic bridge between individual and family treatment.* New York: Jason Aronson.

Stadter, M. (1996). *Object relations brief therapy: The therapeutic relationship in short-term work.* Northvale, NJ: Jason Aronson.

Strupp, H. H. (1981). Toward the refinement of time-limited dynamic psychotherapy. In S. H. Budman (Ed.), *Forms of brief therapy* (pp. 219–242). New York: Guilford.

Vaillant, G. E. (1983). *The natural history of alcoholism.* Cambridge, MA: Harvard University Press.

Wachtel, P. L. (1977). *Psychoanalysis and behavior therapy: Toward an integration.* New York: Basic Books.

Weiss, J. (1993). *How psychotherapy works.* New York: Guilford.

Wile, D. B. (1981). *Couples therapy: A nontraditional approach.* New York: Wiley.

Wile, D. B. (1999). Collaborative couple therapy. In J. M. Donovan (Ed.), *Short-term couple therapy.* (pp. 201–225). New York: Guilford.

Yalom, I. D. (1994). *The theory and practice of group psychotherapy* (4th ed.). New York: Basic Books.

Index